Rafael Capurro | Michael Eldred | Daniel Nagel

Digital Whoness

Identity, Privacy and Freedom in the Cyberworld

Rafael Capurro, Michael Eldred, Daniel Nagel
Digital Whoness
Identity, Privacy and Freedom in the Cyberworld

Rafael Capurro | Michael Eldred | Daniel Nagel

Digital Whoness

Identity, Privacy and Freedom in the Cyberworld

ontos
verlag
Frankfurt | Paris | Lancaster | New Brunswick

Bibliographic information published by Deutsche Nationalbibliothek
The Deutsche Nationalbibliothek lists this publication in the Deutsche Nationalbibliographie;
detailed bibliographic data is available in the Internet at http://dnb.ddb.de

Cover painting by José María Guijarro *Sin título* water-colour
69 x 98 cm 1997
Photo by Theo Roos

North and South America by
Transaction Books
Rutgers University
Piscataway, NJ 08854-8042
trans@transactionpub.com

United Kingdom, Ireland, Iceland, Norway, Turkey, Malta,
Spain, Portugal by
Gazelle Books Services Limited
White Cross Mills
Hightown
LANCASTER, LA1 4XS
sales@gazellebooks.co.uk

Livraison pour la France et la Belgique:
Librairie Philosophique J.Vrin
6, place de la Sorbonne ; F-75005 PARIS
Tel. +33 (0)1 43 54 03 47 ; Fax +33 (0)1 43 54 48 18
www.vrin.fr

P.O. Box 15 41, D-63133 Heusenstamm
www.ontosverlag.com
ISBN 978-3-86838-176-4

2013

Version 1.0 2011-2013

Printed on acid-free paper
ISO-Norm 970-6
FSC-certified (Forest Stewardship Council)
This hardcover binding meets the International Library standard

Printed in Germany
by CPI buch bücher.de

The authors

Rafael Capurro is Prof. emeritus, founder of the International Center for Information Ethics, Karlsruhe and editor-in-chief of the *International Review of Information Ethics*. His work has concentrated on a phenomenological approach to information ethics in which he has numerous publications in many languages. Books include: *Information: Ein Beitrag zur etymologischen und ideengeschichtlichen Begründung des Informationsbegriffs* 1978, *Hermeneutik der Fachinformation* 1986, *Leben im Informationszeitalter* 1995 and *Messages and Messengers. Angeletics as an Approach to the Phenomenology of Communication* 2011 (co-edited with John Holgate).

Michael Eldred trained as a mathematician at Sydney University and then gained a doctorate in philosophy, where he has numerous publications in several languages in the areas of phenomenology and political philosophy. Currently he is engaged as phenomenological ethicist in the project, A Culture of Privacy and Trust for the Internet of acatech, the National Academy of Science and Engineering, Berlin. Books include *Critique of Competitive Freedom and the Bourgeois-Democratic State: Outline of a Form-Analytic Extension of Marx's Uncompleted System* 1984, *Phänomenologie der Männlichkeit* 1999, *Social Ontology: Recasting Political Philosophy Through a Phenomenology of Whoness* 2008 and *The Digital Cast of Being: Metaphysics, Mathematics, Cartesianism, Cybernetics, Capitalism, Communication* 2009.

Daniel Nagel is a solicitor in Stuttgart whose work focuses on legal issues around the internet and digital technologies. He is a member of the Jean Monnet European Centre of Excellence, University of Leeds and studied law at the University of Heidelberg, the University of Innsbruck and at Leeds University. Recent publications include 'Beware of the Virtual Doll: ISPs and the Protection of Personal Data of Minors' 2011 and 'IPv 6 and Data Protection: Personalized Surfing with its Dangers for the Private Sphere' 2011 (in German).

Table of contents

Acknowledgement

This study arose in the context of the project *A Culture of Privacy and Trust for the Internet* of acatech, the National Academy of Science and Engineering, Berlin in 2011-2013, of which the authors were a part. An abridged version was published: Rafael Capurro, Michael Eldred & Daniel Nagel 'IT and Privacy from an Ethical Perspective — Digital Whoness: Identity, Privacy and Freedom in the Cyberworld' in Buchmann, Johannes (ed.) *Internet Privacy - Eine multidisziplinäre Bestandsaufnahme/A Multidisciplinary Analysis* Berlin: Springer 2012 pp. 63-141.

Sola autem nos philosophia excitabit,
sola somnum excutiet gravem.
But only philosophy will wake us up,
only it will shake off the heavy sleep.

Seneca
Epistulae ad Lucilium Ep. LIII

0 Introduction

On Wednesday, when the sky is blue,
And I have nothing else to do,
I sometimes wonder if it's true
That who is what and what is who.
A. A. Milne *Winnie-the-Pooh*

The concept of privacy cannot be adequately determined without its counterpart, publicness. Privacy and publicness are not properties of things, data or persons, but rather ascriptions dependent upon the specific social and cultural context. These ascriptions relate to what a person or a self (it may also be several selves) divulges about him- or herself. A self, in turn, is not a worldless, isolated subject, but a human being who is and understands herself as always already interconnected with others in a shared world. The possibility of hiding, of displaying or showing oneself off as who one is, no matter in what way and context and to what purpose, is in this sense, as far as we know, peculiar to human beings, but precisely not as the property of a subject, but rather as a form of the interplay of a human being's life as shared with others.

This, in turn, implies that the possibility of revealing and concealing who one is always already concretely shaped within the rules of interplay of a concrete culture within a shared world. We understand by culture the totality of values, customs and principles on which a society is explicitly and implicitly based. Accordingly, the very meaning of private and public varies depending on the culture, which does not imply that these meanings and practices are equivocal or incommensurable, for they occur in a shared world-openness constituted by a network of referential interconnections of signification. This network of interrelated signification is today marked deeply by digital information technologies.

World-openness is not only always already concretely structured semantically and pragmatically in the sense of a culture, but also subjected to an historical process of forming and shaping over time. What constitutes a world can change as a consequence of diverse, unpredictable events. When a culture changes, and not merely the situation, values and customs within a culture, then the sense of the difference between private and public also changes. Jürgen Habermas has shown this in relation to the structural transformation of the public sphere,[1] but only in presenting, so to speak, largely one half of the story. A structural transformation of the public sphere (or rather: publicness as a mode of social being) implies also a structural transformation of the private sphere (privateness as a mode of social being), and both can be reflected upon. The latter is the task of information ethics when it is a matter of problematizing given values, customary life-practices and principles of action, that is, an ethos, in connection with digital technologies and the cyberworld to which they have today given rise.

If today we proceed from the fact that on the basis of these technologies and, in particular, the internet, a structural transformation of publicness is taking place, then this holds true equally for privacy. Information technologies do not hover in empty space but are embedded in the cultural life of societies. The distinction public/private in connection with the cyberworld is a socially and culturally dependent difference. Cultural dependency means that differences in the understanding of information technologies must be discussed if an encapsulation of societies and cultures is to be avoided, through which a potential ground for *reciprocal* trust would be forfeited. It is plain from what has been said that such a ground is always provisional. Trust is essentially also a mood that is counterposed to the moods of unsureness, fear, anxiety, and even Angst and dread. If Angst reveals the groundlessness of human freedom, trust signifies something like the experience of the formation of a tentative ground on which we can depend on each other, no matter in what fragile forms and within which limits. Hence trust does not signify, at least not primarily, putting oneself into the hands of another in line with the sentiment, 'Trust me, I'll look after you'. That is a particular form of (paternalistic) trust that is fostered, for instance, between parents and their children. In contrast to this (and there are many intermediate shades and variants of trust),

1 Habermas 1962/1990.

reciprocal trust means that a self lets itself in for an interplay with other selves in certain situations and contexts, for which then customs, norms and values, including ethical and moral and legal usages and norms, are required to give this interplay a certain consistency and constancy, that is, some sort of ground. In this ongoing interplay, trust is engendered, won, put at risk, lost, regained, etc. but never produced like a thing.

To foster trust in a globalized world and with respect to the artificial dimension of the cyberworld is certainly no easy task. The objective of the ethics strand within the present overall project[2] consists in providing the foundations for a phenomenological explication of privacy and publicness in the context of the cyberworld enabled by digital information technologies. This will allow options for shaping life-worlds to be uncovered that are both shared and also culturally differentiated with regard to valued, customary living practices. Accordingly, everything will depend upon whether privacy and publicness and their respective socio-ontological foundations can be attuned and brought into play with each other so that differing, but nevertheless mutually permeable, casts of good living in the world can be outlined. From what has been said it is plain that the phenomenon of the self as well as that of a shared digitized world, the cyberworld, are given special weight and significance. The distinction between self and thing or, more precisely, between *who* and *what*, is an eminently ethical difference from which the difference private/public can be thought. Therefore we take pains, on an extended detour, to spell out what whoness means.

0.1 The significance of a phenomenology of whoness as the starting-point for discussing the question concerning privacy and freedom in the internet

The difference between self and thing, or who and what, already points to the necessity of working out and presenting a phenomenology of whoness in a turn away from the modern subjectivity of a worldless subject vis-à-vis an objective world, an ontology which is tacitly

---

2 This study arose as part of the acatech project, *A Culture of Privacy and Trust for the Internet* 2011-2013; cf. Acknowledgement above.

presupposed and taken for granted as the self-evident framework for reflecting upon privacy, identity and freedom in the internet age. In contrast to this, the who is always already cast into the world and has an identity, whose phenomenological concept has to be explicitly unfolded whereas, strictly speaking, the worldless subject cannot have an identity, a point that will be made clear, especially by engaging critically with selected authors. Identity is only possible where a who finds itself mirrored back from the world, and chooses, casts and takes on its self from this shining-back from the world. This is an essential hallmark of *freedom*, since the who fashions its self from the mirrored-back options including, above all, the world of others.

Our approach is characterized by the endeavour to open our eyes for the phenomena we encounter in today's world that shape and determine who we can be. These phenomena are very familiar to everybody, but nevertheless stir discomfort that not least of all gives occasion to penetratingly and explicitly ask the question, 'Who are we in the internet age?' or 'What historical options are open to us to cast ourselves *as* free selves in the context of the cyberworld?' The question concerning whoness is hence a foundational and also an essentially historical question in the sense that we change who we are in the world through thinking and acting, and bear a special responsibility for fathoming these changes in their ramifications. Such a thinking (which is in itself already a kind of acting) can serve as a kind of orientation for action in its quotidian concreteness, where this linking of thinking and action that is peculiar to ethical reflection should never be misconceived in the sense of recipes or unchangeable laws or norms, but rather as a question concerning good, enhancing life-practices treasured and cultivated by specific cultures — and their opposites. The fragility of whoness in all its historical and cultural diversity repeatedly provokes thinking to engage in ethical reflection and also in practical action in caring for the lived 'goodness' of a shared world that is understood differently in different times and places.

Today this world is becoming increasingly occupied and permeated by digital, cybernetic technologies of multifarious kinds. The care that is directed toward the whole often dons the garb of an elevated universalism which only makes sense when its values and principles are thought through and lived through over and over again in the concreteness of an historical constellation. This, in turn, happens on the basis of differing cultural stamps and contextual preferences. It is precisely the diversity of self-interpretations of human being which always gives rise to a thoughtful, albeit provisional, reassuring of our selves in the question concerning whoness. In the openness vis-à-vis our specific identities we experience freedom in and as an interplay that today is being played out in, with and through the cyberworld.

0.2 A provisional stocktaking of the discussion in information ethics on privacy and freedom in the internet age

The discussion in information ethics on the concept of privacy has changed and intensified over the past fifteen years due to the broad commercial and social use of the internet. This discussion sometimes assumes an ideological flavour when privacy in the internet age is declared to be obsolete or, conversely, defended in its traditional sense, frequently without having understood the unique, new, existential possibilities and even new, valuable, systematic, social formations that are emerging. Often cultural differences and specificities are left out of consideration in favour of considering human beings simply as apparently autonomous subjects in the Western sense. Analyses in information ethics show, for instance, that conceptions of privacy in Buddhist cultures are the complete opposite to those in Western cultures, but that nevertheless reasons can be given for why privacy in Buddhist cultures still can be regarded as worthy of protection in an ethical and legal sense. Such a discussion is still in its nascent stages, for instance, with regard to Latin American and African cultures.

To what extent and in what form can universalist approaches such as the Declaration of Principles made by the World Summit on the Information Society, or the Internet Rights & Principles Coalition pay regard to the particularities and singularities of differing cultures, as well as to concrete 'good practices', if both global and local cultures of trust and privacy in the internet are to be engendered? Who are we when we are in the cyberworld? What does it mean to have a digital identity? And how can one's identity wander off into the cyberworld? In the debate in information ethics on privacy in the cyberworld, this question is understood mostly in the sense of '*What* are we when we are in the internet?'. It then concerns digital data on individual persons that are to be protected technically, legally and ethically. Implicitly, however, this question includes also the question concerning *who* in the sense of the person to whom the data relate, revealing and concealing *who* this person is. How are we to play the who-game in the cyberworld? When the question concerning who crops up in the discussion in information ethics, it does so usually in the guise of implicit, and therefore unclarified, preconceptions of what 'whoness' and 'personhood' mean.[3]

The debate over privacy thus presupposes and skips over the philosophical interpretation of what whoness means in the digital age. It begs the question. The question cannot be answered through a digital reduction that equates whoness simply with digital information about a person, or even declares personhood itself to be (ontologically) an informational data bundle, for such a reductionism leaves open the question concerning how 'person' is to be understood, what the specifically digital dimension is in a conceptually clarified sense, and what the interconnection is among these phenomena. The philosophical-ethical foundations are either missing entirely — as in the current discussion on privacy and the internet, where the protection of privacy is simply presupposed as a 'value' without any phenomenological-conceptual clarification —, or the foundations are borrowed unquestioningly from subjectivist metaphysics, that is caught in its subject/object split, or else the digital itself as a mode of being, i.e. of how beings come to presence and present themselves, is not laid out at all or only cursorily.

With few exceptions,[4] a phenomenological approach to identity, privacy and freedom in the cyberworld has received scant attention. The

---

3 Tavani 2008, Van den Hoven 2008. Cf. esp. Chap. 3.

4 Introna 2005, Eldred 2008/2011, Capurro & Holgate 2011.

debate in information ethics, however, needs a philosophical and especially a phenomenological grounding with the simple phenomena themselves in view if it is not to rely on unexamined preconceptions. On the ground floor this task includes interpreting what has already been thought throughout the philosophical tradition (albeit mostly at a tangent and without clarifying the distinction between what and who) on the question concerning the whoness of human beings. This question is closely related to that of freedom. And ultimately, we are interested in the options for freedom in the cyberworld.

Our investigation therefore takes on these decisive questions underpinning the debate in information ethics on privacy and publicness in the internet by undertaking a detailed, stepwise phenomenological analysis of whoness in the cyberworld.

0.3 Course of the investigation

The question concerning whoness is only at a first, unquestioning glance one relating to an isolated individual subject. From the outset, our approach is characterized by a recognition of the *plurality* inherent in human togetherness in the world. Who I am in each instance always depends on reciprocal interchanges of estimation and recognition in a world shared with others. Hence, the question concerning whoness is simultaneously an ontological and ethical question. The ontological aspect refers to the mode in which human beings come to presence and present themselves in the world to each other. In the age of the internet the question concerning whoness is posed anew because the ways of being in time and in space that characterize human being, along with togetherness in the digital medium of the cyberworld, are going through hitherto scarcely imaginable reshaping and recasting.

The philosophical tradition offers an almost inexhaustible quarry of interpretations of the whoness of human being, but invariably without ever employing the term 'whoness'. In the first chapter *1 Phenomenology of whoness: identity, privacy, trust and freedom* we go into these matters and engage with the interpretation of whoness, whose rich beginnings are to be found already in Greek antiquity. The analysis of whoness, in turn, will be put into relation to phenomena such as freedom, private property and autonomy in an engagement with classical authors such as Locke, Smith, Ricardo, Marx and Kant. A treatment of private property with regard to the socio-ontological structure of capitalist market economy is indispensable for distinguishing personal privacy from the privacy of private property, a task sorely neglected elsewhere, thus seeding endless confusion. Our presentation considers exemplary approaches that contribute to clarifying the question concerning the phenomenon of whoness with respect to the dimensions of identity, privacy and freedom. Our analyses are initially restricted to the Western tradition of thinking. However, in the fourth chapter we delve into exemplary discussions of cultures in the Far East, Latin America and Africa. We also engage in particular with Hannah Arendt's treatment of whoness, which not only works up many insights into the sharing of world by a plurality of human beings, but also takes on many of the principal themes of the Western tradition with regard to privacy and publicness. Arendt's interpretation of whoness thus represents an implicit extension of Martin Heidegger's phenomenology in the direction of political and social togetherness and world-sharing, since Heidegger's 1920 lectures, some of which Arendt heard, provide a rich treasure-house for reflecting upon whoness. In this study, however, we do not provide an interpretation of Heidegger's thinking, but rather attempt, in a new theoretical approach, to make use of Heidegger's ontological insights into the phenomenality of whoness, its privacy and freedom, as well as today's digital cast of the world.

The second chapter *2 Digital ontology* engages with the interpretation of the digital ontological cast of the world that underlies and overlays the interplay between privacy and publicness. That today we are confronted with a fast-moving embrace by digital technologies of the most diverse kinds is not merely the result of a history of stepwise (and also abrupt, leaping) developments in the natural sciences and technologies, but of paths of access to the world as a totality in philosophical thought that have been pre-cast and fore-cast by thinkers such as Plato, Aristotle, Descartes and Leibniz. Already with the Greeks, a certain logico-mathematical dissolution (ana-lysis) of the world is under way. This beginning casts a long historical shadow right up to today's increasingly digitized world. A brief sketch of the main stations along the way of the grand unfolding in the history of thoughtful spirit hence makes our contemporary situation clearer. This chapter thus provides the precondition for taking on whoness in a digitized world — the *cyberworld*. In this cyberworld the concern is growing about the protection of what constitutes our whoness in different cultures. Whoness grounds the non-self-evident sense of privacy.

Privacy itself has many shades that can all be understood in the sense of a *privatio* either in a negative or positive sense. Not only a spatial, but also a temporal meaning of privation is here in play. Hence it is conducive to preface the analysis of digital whoness with a discussion of space and time in relation to the cyberworld. What is the adequate phenomenological concept of the cyberworld? The basic phenomenon of personal privacy, however, is not-showing-oneself as a *privatio* of showing-oneself-off in public life, which initially has nothing at all to do with the digital dimension. The sketch provided of an explicitly *digital* ontology serves not only to reflect upon the privacy of the who in a world pervaded by digital technologies, but also to conceptually grasp in a well-founded way the space where the who, so to speak, spends its time in a peculiar artificial, digitized world. The cyberworld that was enabled historically not only by technologies of the twentieth century but, more deeply, has only opened up through the tacitly presupposed digital cast of the world made possible through the mathematico-scientific access to the world, is the automated materialization of our own world-understanding which, in turn, is a granting from an inexhaustible source of historical eventuation. What do cyberworld, cyberspace, cybertime mean, and how does the who sojourn and live in such a cyberworld thus technologically enabled? Only on the basis of such a phenomenological clarification can the question be posed regarding what it means for a who to enjoy privacy in the cyberworld, or how privacy can be protected in this cyberworld.

The third chapter *3 Digital whoness in connection with privacy, publicness and freedom* delves into the phenomenon of whoness against the horizon of the digital and explicates initially the specifically *digital* identity of somewho. Privacy and publicness, too, increasingly assume peculiar features in connection with the cyberworld in whose medium and through whose interfaces today we spend more and more life-time today. Here the 'cyber' aspect of the cyberworld comes forcefully to the fore, for every movement in it is automatically given a digital trace that throws up completely new questions with respect to the protection of freedom. The question as to *whose* freedom is enabled by the cyberworld raises doubts about whether the cyberworld is truly subject to 'our' control. Who are 'we' as such controllers? Is the freedom empowered by the cyberworld simply the freedom of individuals to communicate in and through the digital medium? To mark off and highlight our approach, the second part of the chapter is devoted to the critical appraisal of the current debate in information ethics on the digitized world and privacy (Tavani, Floridi, Ess, Beavers) and, in particular, engages with the thoughts on privacy offered by Helen Nissenbaum.

In the fourth chapter *4 Intercultural aspects of digitally mediated whoness, privacy and freedom*, the foundations laid in the preceding chapters are concretized in an intercultural dialogue with approaches to the phenomena from the Far East (Japan, Thailand, China), Latin America and Africa.

The fifth chapter *5 Cyberworld, privacy and the EU* is another concretization to situate important EU conventions, covenants, resolutions, guidelines and directives that impinge on personal freedom and privacy.

The concluding chapter *6 Brave new cyberworld* briefly indicates why it is worthwhile laying a theoretical foundation through a phenomenology of digital whoness by showing how the topic of e-commerce can be approached.

1 Phenomenology of whoness: identity, privacy, trust and freedom

Michael Eldred[5]

In this chapter, the phenomenon of *whoness* will be illuminated in its various facets with respect to privacy, publicness and freedom. A phenomenology of whoness thus serves as a foundation for approaching *privacy*. The subsequent chapter will then present a sketch of *digital ontology* as a basis paving the way to the succeeding chapter, which investigates whoness and privacy specifically in a *digitally* mediated world.

1.1 The trace of whoness starts with the Greeks

> And now I ask, 'Who am I?' I have been talking of Bernard, Neville, Jinny, Susan, Rhoda and Louis. Am I all of them? Am I one and distinct? I do not know. ... [T]hose old half-articulate ghosts ... clutch at me as I try to escape — shadows of people one might have been: unborn selves.
> Virginia Woolf *The Waves* p. 775.

Humans beings share a world together. They are always already a *plurality*. Whoness is the phenomenon of a plurality of human beings who show themselves to each other in a shared world. A phenomenon is a showing, a disclosing, a revealing which, in its broadest sense, encompasses also the privative or negative modes of disclosing: concealing and revealing only distortedly. Because whoness is the

5 All sections of this chapter are the final authorial responsibility of Michael Eldred, apart from the sections 1.9 and 1.10 by Rafael Capurro.

phenomenon of human beings ('men' in older discourse) showing themselves *to each other*, it cannot be located in a single human being like a 'what', as in: 'What's that?' 'A stone.' There is also a reciprocity in human beings showing themselves *to each other*.[6] This observation is key for approaching the phenomenon of whoness as distinct from that of whatness, which has a rich tradition in metaphysics starting with Plato and Aristotle. Whatness has been thought in this tradition as οὐσία, substance, essence, quidditas, etc. whereas whoness has tended to be subsumed under the metaphysical determinations of whatness. The distinction between what and who, quid and quis has not attracted the sharp focus of philosophical thinking, as evidenced by the very absence of the apt words 'whoness' and 'quissity' in English. Thus, for example, what a human being is has been determined metaphysically as an animal with a soul and intellect. The trace of whoness, however, is by no means

---

6 William James, for instance, captures this "to each other" with his notion of the Social Self: "A man's Social Self is the recognition which he gets from his mates. We are not only gregarious animals, liking to be in sight of our fellows, but we have an innate propensity to get ourselves noticed, and noticed favorably, by our kind." (James 1890/1950 p. 293) This he contrasts with the Empirical Self: "The Empirical Self of each of us is all that he is tempted to call by the name of *me*. But it is clear that between what a man calls *me* and what he simply calls *mine* is difficult to draw. We feel and act about certain things that are ours very much as we feel and act about ourselves. Our fame, our children, the work of our hands, may be as dear to us as our bodies are, and arouse the same feelings and the same acts of reprisal if attacked. And our bodies themselves, are they simply ours, or are they *us*? (...) In its widest possible sense, however, a man's Self is the sum total of all that he CAN call his, not only his body, and his psychic powers, but his clothes and his house, his wife and children, his ancestors and friends, his reputation and works, his lands and horses, and yacht and bank-account. All these things give him the same emotions. If they wax and prosper, he feels triumphant; if they dwindle and die away, he feels cast down,- not necessarily in the same degree for each thing, but in much the same way for all." (p. 291-292). Whereas James emphasizes the self as what a man "CAN call his", i.e. a notion of ownership, in the present study, as outlined below, the self's identity consists of the assemblage of masks that are nothing other than adopted existential possibilities of who somewho 'CAN be' in the world.

entirely absent from the Western philosophical tradition but, instead of being treated in its own right as a mode of being, and thus as an ontological question, it has been relegated to the realm of ethics and politics, again starting with Plato and Aristotle. Whoness leaves its trace throughout Western thinking in phenomena and terms such as ἀνδρεία, φιλοτιμία (manliness/courage, love of esteem/honour/value, Plato), τιμή (esteem/honour/value, Aristotle),[7] virtù (Machiavelli), vainglory (Hobbes), amour-propre (Rousseau), Anerkennung (Hegel) and so on, and only starts to come into its own with the originally German tradition of dialogical philosophy[8] and Heidegger, who focuses on casting human existence itself explicitly and ontologically under the heading of whoness (Wersein, Werheit).

Human beings showing themselves to each other can be regarded as their *showing off* to each other, their *self-display*, even to the point of hiding from each other exemplified in phenomena such as diffidence.[9] Human beings present themselves to each other in the open space of presence and, in doing so, show themselves off *as* who they are, including deceptively. Such showing-off may be simply 'as a man' or 'as a woman', and the showing-off to each other implies *acknowledging* each other's presence, even in the privative mode of ignoring each other's presence, say, when travelling in a crowded underground train. A nod or a wave or a salute or some other slight bodily gesture already

---

7 James addresses the phenomenon of honour as follows: "A man's *fame*, good or bad, and his *honor* or *dishonor*, are names for one of his social selves." (James 1890/1950 p. 294), thus continuing a venerable tradition.

8 Starting with Ludwig Feuerbach and on through authors such as Martin Buber, Eugen Rosenstock-Huessy, Ferdinand Ebner, Eberhard Grisebach, Karl Heim, Gabriel Marcel, Friedrich Gogarten, Helmut Plessner, Adolf Reinach, Dietrich von Hildebrand, Wilhelm Schapp, Alfred Schütz, Ludwig Binswanger, Karl Löwith, Hermann Levin Goldschmidt, Emmanuel Lévinas and Hans-Georg Gadamer. Cf. Michael Theunissen *Der Andere: Studien zur Sozialontologie der Gegenwart* 2nd ed. W. de Gruyter, Berlin/New York 1977 for a comprehensive overview of most of these authors.

9 Cf. Eldred 2008/2011 Chaps. 2 and 3 for more detail of a phenomenology of whoness. Cf. also the critical appraisal of Arendt further on in the present chapter.

suffices to acknowledge each other's presence in which they show themselves off *as* some who or other. So, from the very start, there is an *interchange* or *interplay*, be it ever so minimal, among human beings in showing themselves off to each other in the presence of a shared world. For the moment, the focus is restricted to presence, leaving aside the two temporal modes of absence.

1.2 Selfhood as an identification with reflections from the world

> 'Here's Bernhard!' How differently different people say that! There are many rooms — many Bernhards. There was the charming, but weak; the strong, but supercilious; the brilliant, but remorseless; the very good fellow, but, I make no doubt, the awful bore; the sympathetic, but cold; the shabby, but — go into the next room — the foppish, worldly, and too well dressed.
>
> Virginia Woolf *The Waves* p. 761.

It is important for showing-off to have oneself acknowledged by others *as* who one shows oneself to be. One chooses, or neglects to choose, one's masks for self-display in adopting this or that behaviour, wearing certain clothes rather than others,[10] etc. in order to be seen *as* who one presents oneself. The interplay with each other is always a reciprocal *estimating* of each other's self-presentations. Willy-nilly one presents oneself as some who or other, thus making a certain *impression* on others. Who one *is* is always a matter of having adopted certain *masks of identity* reflected from the world as offers of who one could be in the world. Each human being is an *origin* of his or her own self-

---

10 "It [men's dress] not only covers nakedness, gratifies vanity, and creates pleasure for the eye, but it serves to advertise the social, profession or intellectual standing of the wearer." Virginia Woolf *Three Guineas* 1938/2007 p. 797.

movement and has an *effect* on the surroundings, changing them this way or that, intentionally or unintentionally. Moving ably and skilfully in the shared world in some sense and some fashion or other is bound up with adopting the masks of identity through which one understands oneself and also presents oneself to the world. Being estimated in a positive sense in presenting oneself to others is the phenomenon of *esteem*. Such esteeming estimation of one's self-presentation depends also on presenting, or at least seeming to present, oneself as a *capable* who in some sense or other, which will be estimated variously in different circles and situations. A brain surgeon presenting himself at a medical congress will make a big splash, whereas at a football game, his who-mask *as* a brain surgeon is of no import and makes no special impression. In the negative sense, estimation amounts to not having one's self-presentation appreciated, but rather depreciated.

The core mask of identity borne by a who (Gr. τὶς, L. quis) is one's own *proper name*, around which other masks cluster. Above all, it is a matter of adopting masks of *ability* reflected by the world, thus developing one's own potential abilities to developed personal *powers* of whatever kind. Each who ends up in some vocation, profession, job, social role or other, thus becoming who she or he is in living that role, and this is the mask of identity that somewho (L. quisquam), for the most part, presents to the world *as who* he or she is, being estimated and esteemed by the others in the interplay. Since human beings are estimated and esteemed above all on the basis of their personal *powers and abilities* as who they are, and because the exercise of such powers also effects some change or other in the world, the interplay of mutual estimation is always also a *power play*, especially in the sense of mutually estimating each other's who-standing. At first and for the most part, one wishes to have one's developed powers and abilities, whatever they may be, esteemed by the others in the power play. One may *fail* in doing so. In sharing the world, human beings are constantly estimating and assessing each other's performances in presenting themselves *as* somewho or other through their powers and abilities, i.e. their *merit* as that which deserves esteem. Those of a similar who-standing are therefore, for the most part, in a *competitive rivalry* with one another.

The interplay of mutual self-presentation as who one is also can be interpreted as the *sending of messages* to each other. Each player's who-standing is a message to the others, as are his modes of comportment that display his individual powers. In particular, what each player *says* in the interplay is, of course, a message sent out (perhaps to nobody in particular) that is understood in some way or other by others. In the back-and-forth of messages, the players show themselves (off) to each other as who they are, estimating, esteeming and appreciating each other's presence and presentations. The phenomenology of messaging is called *angeletics*.[11] In contrast to rhetoric as an intended productive technique imbued with a will to power to win others over finally to the speaker's point of view, angeletics lets itself in for the end-less interplay of messages back and forth through which something in between, unintended by any single player, may come into view through the groundless interplay of individual powers of insight.

The introduction of individual powers and abilities that have been adopted as masks of identity forces a widening of focus from the temporal mode of presence because such powers refer both to who one has become and also to who one may become in future. The estimation of one's abilities by the others gives rise to one's *reputation* as who one is, and reputation refers to how one has presented oneself to the world in the past, which is never past, because one has inevitably always already established or ruined one's reputation as who in some circle or other. Conversely, who one will become depends crucially also on one's potential being estimated by those who are in a position (especially parents and teachers) to foster the development of that potential to powers and abilities that an individual *actually has* at its disposal. Furthermore there is the *futural* aspect of whoness in the *ambition* that someone has to become such-and-such, usually by honing his or her abilities of whatever kind. Such ambition is always also linked to *as* who one wants to be regarded in the world and is thus tied intimately to the power play of mutual estimation. Ambition is the striving to leave one's mark on the world, even to the point of establishing one's *fame* as

---

11 Capurro & Holgate 2011.

someone about whom the 'world' speaks. Leaving one's mark on the world is a way of making an impression on the shared world, namely, a *lasting* impression, which again refers to the temporal dimension of the past or beenness.

Wanting to make any impression at all on the world, let alone, wanting to have an impact or to leave one's mark on the world, are all manifestations of the *will to power to be who*. To be somewho in the world amounts to having one's self-presentation to the world estimated, esteemed and reflected by the world, to *come to stand* in shared presence as a who with some standing. In the realm of politics, for example, a who may come to stand by being appointed or elected to a recognized political office, which thereby becomes a mask of identity for this particular individual who thus enjoys the *honour* of holding public office for as long as the specifically political power play accords the office in question to the individual in question. Such *standing presence*, however, is very fragile, not just in politics, but in the power play of togetherness in general, for it depends on the mirror game of mutual self-presentation in which having a stand as who depends on the reflections of estimation received back from the others. "To be myself (I note) I need the illumination of other people's eyes, and therefore cannot be entirely sure what is my self."[12] Appreciative reflections of esteem from the others may be very fickle, easily replaced by depreciative, even downright derogatory, reflections. This contrasts with traditional metaphysical determinations of whatness which is a standing presence either in the sense of possessing an enduring, well-defined essence, or in the sense of possessing an underlying, enduring substance that persists in presence. Whoness as a mode of presencing is the way in which human beings share a world with each other, i.e. the mode of mutually mirroring togetherness in the time-space of the world. Such presencing as somewho in an ongoing power play of mutual estimation is insubstantial, that is, lacking an underlying substrate or ὑποκείμενον and is thus *groundless*.

---

[12] Woolf 1931/2007 p. 692.

Hence, crucially, the power play of whoness breaks the ontological cast of the productive power of whatness, i.e. the power play among whos has to be distinguished from productive power *over* somewhat or somewho conceived *as* a what. In the Western tradition, the ontology of power has only even been thought as *productive* power within a metaphysics of whatness, and, to the present day, the phenomena of the power play among somewhos has been misconceived from within the metaphysical cast of productive power.

Furthermore, selfhood conceived as a shining-back from the world in a plural power play of whoness is far removed from any conception of the modern metaphysical subject, first cast by Descartes as the res cogitans. It is instructive, by way of contrast, to note, with the barest of hints, Locke's version of selfhood, which he shares, with modifications, with all representatives of subjectivist metaphysics. In his *An Essay Concerning Human Understanding* from 1690 we read in Chapter XXVII on 'Of Identity and Diversity': "...we must consider what person stands for; — which, I think, is a thinking intelligent being, that has reason and reflection, and can consider itself as itself, the same thinking thing, in different times and places; which it does only by that consciousness which is inseparable from thinking, and, as it seems to me, essential to it: it being impossible for any one to perceive without perceiving that he does perceive." Thus, for Locke, the self is *self-consciousness*, which is a connected consciousness in time through which a self identifies itself with its consciousness at previous instants of time. The constitution of self is thus a retrospective, inward reflection of consciousness on itself, independent of any other individual consciousness. Later, in his *Critique of Pure Reason* from 1781/87, Kant will call this "pure apperception" and extend it to the temporal horizon also of the future. For Kant, the "transcendental ego" will even *constitute within itself* the temporal horizon of past, present and future through its three a priori, synthetic capacities of apprehending, reproducing and reconnoitring, respectively.[13] Later, we will return to this encapsulated subject of consciousness (cf. *3.8 Floridi's metaphysics*

13 Kant 1781 pp. 98-110.

of the threefold-encapsulated subject in a world conceived as infosphere).

1.3 Values, ethos, ethics

In mores fortuna jus non habet.
Fortune has no right in ethics.
Seneca
Epistulae ad Lucilium Ep. XXXVI

The question concerning values[14] has a close relationship with the phenomenon of esteem, which amounts to valuing someone *as* somewho. But values extend beyond whos to all sorts of things, including useful things (use-values), exchangeable things (exchange-values, money) and even intangible values such as local traditional customs, freedom of speech, freedom of religion, etc. etc. A value is what is valued, i.e. estimated highly, by a plurality of human beings living together in some way, whether on a small (community) or large (social) scale, contributing in some sense to living well in the context of everyday, customary life-practices, i.e. a people's mores. All societies cultivate usages through which they value and esteem each other in an interplay of mutual estimation, which gives a connection to the phenomenon of whoness that is foundational for the present study.

Furthermore, things that are *good for living* have worth and value in all societies. The value of (commodity) goods is estimated through market exchange. Such valuation interplay is a reified (from *res* for 'thing') form of estimating and esteeming, as signalled already by the Greek τιμή which, apart from meaning the esteem or honour in which a person is held as somewho, signifies also the value or price of goods as somewhats. The valuing that goes on in social interplay is a component part of all historical peoples' ways of living and therefore *abstract* relative to the more *concrete* customs and traditions valued by particular peoples. As we shall see, this more abstract level of values and

---

[14] Cf. Eldred 2010.

estimation is at the heart of liberal values (see below *1.5 The private individual, liberty, private property (Locke)*).

Since the usages within which human beings live together are historical in the sense of belonging to a particular time and a particular region, they vary, and therefore what is valued as being part of a customary way of life is also historically variable. Furthermore, any plurality of human beings living together will not be unanimous about what, in particular, is to be valued in customary life practices, so that there is always also tension, conflict and even struggle and war over the values according to which a plurality is to customarily live together. Even an absolutist regime, despite appeals even to sacred texts or traditions or divine empowerment, for instance, cannot dictate the values according to which a plurality of people is to live; there will always be dissent, whether covert or overt. Which values, in the sense of valued and esteemed customary practices, are upheld by a way of life is always a matter of the ongoing interplay among people in an historical time-space (cf. *4 Intercultural aspects of digitally mediated whoness, privacy and freedom*). Hence, like the striving to be esteemed as who, values themselves, especially the basic ones on which a shared way of living is founded, are exposed to an ongoing historical power play in which much depends upon disclosing what precisely is being valued and esteemed. Esteem, estimation, values, social power are always and essentially found together since they are socio-ontologically interlinked. This is invariably overlooked when values are simply posited to be such, or proclaimed to be 'fundamental', as if they had fallen from heaven or had arisen in a 'state of nature'.

Because values in the sense of valued and esteemed customary practices make up a way of life, taken together they form an ethos. *Ethics* pertains to how to live well within the ethos (L. mores) of an historical way of life shared by a people, i.e. within its complex of values in the sense of what is held dearly in the context of that way of life. Ethics has to be distinguished from *morality* and normativity, which are focused on the question of the actions an *individual ought* to do or refrain from doing, either generally or in a particular situation, hence bringing into play also matters of *conscience* and *compliance* to norms.

Morality is rooted in mores, not vice versa. Unfortunately, ethics is often understood only in a moral sense, as when so-called ethics committees composed of professionals coming from different disciplines, including ethics, have the task of sorting out the moral dilemma of individual, concrete, moral situations. A broader understanding encompasses also the reflection on ethical options, for instance, when a government is considering how to formulate legislation touching upon and regulating what life-practices are to be allowed, which must be based on what practices and customs are valued in a given historical way of life. This task of reflection can be subverted when an ethics committee making recommendations to a government or a government body, instead of bringing the difficult ethical issues to light, merely takes an official or conservative morality of how things ought to be for granted. In this study, morals are considered only from the viewpoint of *mores*, i.e. of ethos, and thus ethically.

The task of ethics, first and foremost, is the phenomenological endeavour of *learning to see* the socio-ontological structures within which we human beings live. Only when we are able to see the issues clearly are we in a position to assess also which practices and customs are to be valued and which are to be kept out of a cultural way of life. Such assessment, of course, amounts to carrying on a controversy to which ethicists can contribute by shedding light. Such a critical intervention goes against the Stoic stance of a Seneca, who writes, "Non conturbabit sapiens publicos mores nec populum in se vitae novitate convertet".[15]

A phenomenological socio-ontological approach also goes against the grain of what is expected of ethicists when confronted in the present context with issues related to digital technologies. Introna (2012) notes, "one tends to find the debate centered on questions of policy that is intended to regulate or justify conduct vis-à-vis the negative impact produced by certain uses or implementations of IT. These policies are seen, and presented as ways to regulate or balance competing rights or

---

15 "The wise man will not upset public mores, nor turn people's attention to himself through the innovation of his life." Seneca 1974 Ep. XIV.xiv.

competing values in the context of the impact of IT. ... Furthermore, these debates are most often directed at an institutional level of discourse, i.e. with the intention to justify the policies or conduct for governments, organizations and individuals. In these debates on the impact of technology, ethicists are primarily conceived as presenting arguments for justifying a particular balance of values or rights over against other possibilities within the context of specific uses or implementations of IT". This is not the approach taken in the present study. Why? Because learning to see socio-ontological structures comes *prior* to any consideration of consequences in so-called 'consequentialist' ethics.

Nor is a constructivist approach adopted here: "For the constructivist it is the particular way in which interests become built into the technology and practices within which it is embedded that is ethically significant. ... Of particular concern is the way information technology 'hides' these values and interests in the logic of software algorithms and hardware circuits (Introna & Nissenbaum 2000)." (Introna 2011) Learning to see the phenomena at stake is not exhausted by exposing political interests in-built in the very technology. Elementary phenomena are "hard to see" (Aristotle).

Finally, Introna raises the issue of the "virtualization of society", a loaded term which here would rather be called the digitization of the world as cyberworld (cf. *2.5 The parallel cyberworld that fits like a glove*). He suggests a phenomenological approach to this virtual society against the foil of "something more primary — i.e., the conditions that render such acts as the presentation of the self, ongoing communication and sharing meaningful and significant in the first instance", that is, "an already presumed sense of community" in which "social interaction, community and identity (as we know it) are phenomena that are local, situated and embodied, which is characterized by mutual involvement, concern and commitment (Dreyfus 2001, Borgmann 1999, Ihde 2002, Introna 1997, Coyne 1995, Heim 1993)". The debate then focuses on whether virtual reality is "thin" vis-à-vis a "thicker", embodied community, with proponents on both sides.[16] As hopefully will become apparent to the reader in later chapters, this phenomenological approach, too, still skips over more elementary phenomena and thus begs questions concerning the digital cast of being.

1.4 The question concerning rights: personal privacy, trust and intimacy

Absconde te in otio; sed et ipsum otium absconde
Hide yourself in leisure; but also hide this leisure itself
Seneca *Epistulae ad Lucilium* Ep. LXVIII

Whenever the question concerning values crops up, the question concerning rights is never far behind, for what is estimated to be valuable for a way of life is held to be also indispensable for it and hence as making a claim to be protected, guaranteed, secured. Rights invariably pertain to individual human beings in their life movements and, by extension, to groups and communities of individuals. A *right* is a *claim* to a *guaranteed freedom of life-movement* in one sense or another (cf. *5 Cyberworld, privacy and the EU*). Despite the fortunate or unfortunate predicament into which any individual human being may be cast, over which it has no control, starting with the parents who progenerated it in a specific place in specific circumstances in an historical time, any individual is always also a spontaneous, groundless origin of its own life-movements in the broadest sense and hence inalienably *free*, even and especially when it *subjugates* itself to another. Because of this ineradicable nature of human freedom as ultimately *individual*, rights, too, are also essentially always also ultimately *individual* rights, pertaining as they do to free life-movements of individuals.

Because there is always a plurality of individual human beings sharing a world together, their individual free movements are a living maze of winding and intercommunicating movements criss-crossing in bewildering complexity. A 'we' can arise out of this maze transiently or

---

[16] Feenberg (1999), for instance, opposes a critique of virtuality as 'thin' (cf. my critique of Feenberg in Eldred 2009a).

even relatively permanently (say, in institutions or cult rituals), but the many individual sources of free movement always remain the starting-point. Hence, prior to any identification of a 'we' living in some kind uniform, shared life-movement, there are individual rights proclaiming freedom of life-movement of some kind or other, whether it be, say, a right of free speech or a right to enter freely into contracts. Where a uniform, shared life-movement of some kind of 'we' comes about, this is invariably a matter of *duty* and *obligation*, not of right. The individual then has a duty vis-à-vis something 'larger' than itself. Even in the simplest case of two individuals exercising their individual rights to enter into an exchange-contract with one another, this freedom of exercise results in a duty to fulfil the obligation freely entered into that cannot be conceived as residing in either of the two contractual partners, i.e. a contract is already a kind of 'we' constituting an *obligation* on both parties, the obligation to keep a mutually given word. In sharing the world with one another, our free individual life-movements always intertwine us in such a way that we *bind* ourselves to each other and become *obliged* both to each other and to a form of interplay. Even in adhering to customs in intercourse with one another, each individual moves freely whilst simultaneously binding itself to certain valued social conventions.

One kind of individual free life-movement is that of withdrawing into *privacy*, which is always a *privatio* in the sense of a withdrawal from (public) disclosure into concealment. Being able to withdraw or to reveal only those aspects of who one is and one's own life-world is valued in diverse cultural ways of living, albeit that the social interplay of such concealment and disclosure takes diverse phenomenal forms and is protected by diverse customs. Because each individual is somewho, this means showing oneself off in the shared world *as* who one is. This *hermeneutic as* signifies the masks with which each who identifies in pretending to be who he or she is. Such pretence is not to be contrasted with a 'genuine' who who would appear, as it were, naked, without mask, but rather, pretence itself is inevitable to be a who at all, and the question is only whether the identity adopted by a self is fitting or not. 'Masks' here cover all the ways in which somewho can present him- or herself to the world and to him- or herself; they are the identities adopted in a shining-back from the world, as explicated in previous sections. Self-showing in the world is hence a presentation that is also a matter of the self freely casting *as* who it shows itself off to the world. This may be choosing clothes to wear, or it may be writing a book or a letter to the editor of a newspaper, or adopting a certain vocation or profession, etc. etc. In each case a *persona* is presented to the world. Withdrawing from the shared world means leaving this persona aside in favour of more intimate and idiosyncratic masks of comportment presented only within the small circle of intimacy that was traditionally the family. The private person is still a who, but this private person shows itself only within a small circle of friends and family on a basis of familiarity and *trust* that such who-presentation does not become the common currency of mere gossip in the world.

Personal privacy is therefore never the privacy of an individual, encapsulated, autonomous subject, "being let alone" in splendid isolation or brooding introspection, but the hiddenness of a private life-world shared with certain others to whom one is close and from which most are excluded. This private life-world is not a (physically)[17]

[17] Altman's (Altman 1975) approach to the phenomenon of privacy manifests itself in the orientation toward the "relationship between human behavior and the physical environment" (p. 1) with a "focus on the inter-relationships of privacy, personal space, territoriality, and crowding" (p. 3) as already indicated by the book's subtitle. This leads 'naturally' to a *physical* determination of "personal space" as "the area immediately surrounding the body,".(p. 2) (cf. also p. 6: "Personal space refers to the 'invisible bubble',-the area immediately around the body; intrusion into this space by others leads to discomfort or anxiety".). Likewise, "territory" is a physical determination applicable equally to human beings and animals: "The concept of territory has been studied extensively by ethologists interested in animal social behavior and, recently, has been investigated by sociologists and psychologists." (p. 2) The fourth aspect of Altman's approach, "crowding and overpopulation" (p. 2), is likewise understood physically. Privacy is then determined as "a central regulatory process by which a person (or group) makes himself more or less accessible and open to others and that the concepts of personal space and territorial behavior are mechanisms that are set in motion to achieve desired levels of privacy."

separate sphere but includes also as who one presents oneself in public in certain masks whilst simultaneously keeping other masks of self-presentation private. The key to understanding personal privacy is the play of *disclosure and concealment of a personal world*. Others are only admitted to a personal world on a basis of trust and friendship. Within a circle of private intimacy, the individual whos present themselves *as* who they are, but this *as* deviates from the persona presented to the outer world. Such personal privacy is *valued* as one of the goods of living; it is a *privatio* to having to have one's self exposed to general public view.

To gain one's own self requires not only adopting certain chosen possibilities of identification shone back from the world, but also withdrawing from common opinions about who one is or ought to be in order to decide freely which masks of identity are one's very own. One's very own self is what the Greeks called ἴδιος (one's own, 'idiotic', idiosyncratic) in contradistinction to what is κοινόν (common, public, L.

(p. 3) These physical determinations of privacy, personal space, territory and crowding are inadequate. Why? Because personal space as such is not physical, nor can privacy per se be determined as a kind of physical accessibility and openness. E.g. your personal closeness and accessibility to someone has to do only contingently with physical closeness and accessibility. Your personal closeness to someone depends on how openly you show yourself to them, how many facets of yourself you reveal, and vice versa. Living in Darmstadt, say, you can have an intimate relationship with someone in Sydney, to whom you are closer than almost anyone whom you know in Europe (important when considering the technologically enabled cyberworld; cf. Chap. 3). Relationships of personal intimacy take place between you-and-me, i.e. in the first-and-second person, which is a different kind of presencing than that of first-and-third person relationships, in which the other presences (not necessarily physically for the senses) at one remove, like a thing. The distinction between 'with-whom' and 'about-which' is important in distinguishing between the dimensions of whoness and whatness, and it seems to me that Altman cannot cope with the distinction between second and third person, nor with the phenomenon of personal closeness between whos. In his approach, everything ends up in the third person. This itself is rooted in the ancient, venerable, metaphysical predilection for the third person, whose categories and concepts 'self-evidently' proceed from the third person (as in the so-called modern, so-called 'objective', scientific standpoint) and blur the distinction from the second person.

res publica). The pejorative sense of 'idiocy' (which in truth is a synonym for individual singularity) derives originally from the Greek experience that a free man was only free through participating in the common, public affairs outside the 'idiotic' household which was the hidden realm of women and slaves (cf. *1.11 Arendt on whoness in the world*). Individuals in the modern world claim a *right* to enjoy this good of living, and thus a right, in particular, to withdraw from the public gaze to enjoy a private world with family and friends in which the game of whoness is played otherwise than the dance, rivalry and struggle among personae in the outer, public world. The modern sphere of intimacy differs from, say, the Roman family, but both are characterized by a privatio of disclosure to the outside world and both allow the members of that private world to present themselves *as* who they are in ways different from the rules of play in the public world.[18] As already noted, however, the phenomenon of privacy is not exhausted by that of a private sphere.

There are also *many* personal private lives; who I am comes about with each you I encounter, and each time anew. With you I show myself as..., and with you I show myself as...; and conversely for you: your masks of self-presentation change according to whom you are encountering, in a specific situation and at different times. Thus you, too, play a game of revealing and concealing who you are, both publicly and privately. The enjoyment of private life resides largely in the multiple games of who-presentation played within it. In public life, too, the who-presentations are multiple, depending upon situation; the personae vary according to occasion, and differ from the who-presentations in the shelteredness of private life, where a who may risk other disclosures to an intimate. Who you and I are in an intimate sexual relationship, for instance, has its own special, unique flavour. Friends esteem each other by appreciating each other's company and messages.

Privacy also cannot be localized in a particular place, although the *home* has special importance as a sheltered place, sheltered above all

---

[18] Cf. for historical detail Ariès & Duby 1985/1989. Cf. also the first footnote in *4.3 Latin America* below.

from the gaze and hence idle talk and the abuse of private information by others. The private world can 'be' a conversation carried on with a friend in a pub or a restaurant or on a bus, each of which is a public-private place. The intermingling of privacy and publicness, which happens 'physically' all the time, will be treated further in *3.7 An appraisal of Nissenbaum's Privacy in Context*.

The phenomenon discussed so far is that of *personal privacy*, which has dominated discussions of privacy in connection with the internet. However, this discussion is truncated insofar as privacy extends to shared worlds that are not characterized by familiarity or intimacy, but are nevertheless germane to any phenomenology of privacy in today's world. In particular, the question concerning justice in relation to privacy should be postponed until the phenomenology of privacy has been widened to take in also private property and its manifold consequences. What is the privacy of private property? Let us approach this question slowly.

1.5 The private individual, liberty, private property (Locke)

In this section featuring Locke as the father of liberalism, one could well imagine that we have arrived at the heart of a liberal worldview highly specific to the West. Indeed, Locke's famous formula of "Life, Liberty and Estate" as a fundamental, individualized right is at the core of liberalism. It was translated by the founding fathers of the U.S. into "life, liberty and the pursuit of happiness", as formulated in the United States Declaration of Independence, thus providing a deeply rooted value for the way of living in the world's quintessential capitalist country. The Virginia Declaration of Rights adopted unanimously by the Virginia Convention of Delegates on 12 June 1776 and written by George Mason, proclaims "That all men are by nature equally free and independent, and have certain inherent rights, of which, when they enter into a state of society, they cannot, by any compact, deprive or divest their posterity; namely, the enjoyment of life and liberty, with the means of acquiring and possessing property, and pursuing and obtaining happiness and safety", thus adhering more closely to Locke's formula than the Declaration of Independence. It should be noted that the "pursuit of happiness" and the "acquiring" of property name the *potential* of life-movements and not what is *actually* securely had if a state of happiness is achieved or property is *actually* possessed. This tension between potentiality and actuality of living well will become essential below (*1.8 Justice and state protection of privacy*) for understanding the tension between liberal and social-democratic values, the latter being focused on materially securing a way of life by means of redistribution.

Taken as an inalienable, fundamental right of the individual, Locke's formula serves as a bulwark against all kinds of government interference, and that most pronouncedly so in Anglo-Saxon countries. Already in other parts of the West, such as Germany, this liberal value has not taken nearly so strong a root in the customary practices of living, even though a country such as Germany is still counted among the 'Western liberal democracies'. So liberalism itself has many, finely graduated hues in various countries, and one could wonder why a country like Germany is regarded as liberal and free at all. Western liberal values are also said to have been exported to the rest of the world, imposed upon other cultures (historical ways of living) by the West, or welcomed as influences voicing a critique or and promising liberation from customs and ways of governing felt already within those cultures to be oppressive and stifling.

Western liberal values of "Life, Liberty and Estate" have a meaning and make living sense in many different cultures, even when they are strongly diluted and relativized, or interpreted differently, by other valued customs and ideas within which an historical people lives. This is so because there is a deep, incontrovertible phenomenological grounding at least of individual life and liberty insofar as each individual human being is ineluctably and irrevocably a free source of its own life-movements of all kinds, even and especially when it subjugates itself to a superior other, no matter what that other might be (a ruler, a state, a customary ethical order, a religion, etc. demanding submission). Rather than being regarded as 'inherent', 'natural' rights of individuals, life and liberty are *abstract values* arising from human being itself irrevocably individualized in origins of free self-movement. This does not have to do with any 'original' 'state of nature' but rather with the 'nature' of human being itself on an abstract level, where abstractness refers to the simplicity of few determinations. At no time and nowhere has slavery ever enjoyed the status of an ethical value with those enslaved, even among those resigned to slavery. Likewise for serfdom. Slavery and serfdom have only even been *justified* by those *others enjoying* the fruits of slave- and serf-ownership, or an elite, and never in the name of freedom.

Moreover, as we shall see in more detail below (*1.6 The private individual and private property as a mode of reified sociation: the gainful game (classical political economy, Marx)*), the three primary liberal values go hand in hand with the essential, socio-ontological value-form structure of a capitalist economy, which is an *abstract, reified mode of sociation*, as will be sketched in the next section. The abstract reification of value and its movement as capital are abstract in a way that enables a separate economic sphere as well as the modern individual, enjoying/suffering many degrees of freedom in its life-movements. One may want to object that there are many different kinds of capitalist society, which is empirically and historically correct, but all of them have at their (abstract) core the four basic reified value-forms of income and income-source within which the competitive economic game is played out. This holds true even when the Western liberal forms of private property are curtailed by the state. The abstractness of capitalism also allows it to be concretized into and thus made compatible with very different historical ways of life, i.e. cultures, a topic that will be taken up again and deepened in the chapter on intercultural ethics (Chap. *4 Intercultural aspects of digitally mediated whoness, privacy and freedom*).

Locke's "state of nature" is an imagined pre-social situation of a heap of atomistic individuals who are "naturally" free and value their lives, and who then agree to enter into civil society, whilst retaining those natural, inalienable rights. Life, liberty (and perhaps less so private property) have the status of an axiom posited as a non-negotiable precondition for "men" agreeing to enter into an instituted civil society with one another, thus imposing restraints upon the form of government such free individuals are willing to accept. The liberal government's raison d'être is above all to protect the life, liberty and property of its citizens. An axiom is a highly valued positing, from the Greek ἀξίωμα for 'worth, value, honour, rank, reputation'. The liberal axiom is akin to the Cartesian axiom of *cogito ergo sum* that, likewise in the seventeenth century, posited the conscious individual as the underlying subject, the fundamentum inconcussum, of all knowledge of the world. Life and liberty are valued by individuals above all else and are axiomatic also in the sense of being self-evidently valued; to live means the freedom to engage in life's movements and changes of all kinds as a spontaneous origin of one's own life-movements (including choice of where to live, with whom to live including sexual orientation and freedom to found a family, choice of occupation, of creed, etc. etc.).

Since any individual is always already cast into the world and into specific situations, its autonomy can never be absolute, but its freedom of movement is nevertheless given in the *future*-oriented movement of casting itself and its self by grasping the possibilities on offer, thus realizing its ownmost potentials freely without being restrained by an external agent, but only by one's own understanding, convictions and freely chosen obligations. Such an understanding and positing of the value of life and liberty has attraction as values beyond the Western liberal context, so that it is no wonder that Western liberal political philosophy has found a reception in other cultures and that life and liberty have been elevated to the status of universal rights of humankind. Of course, the test is not whether these values have been realized all over the world and, in truth, they constantly have to be fought for everywhere in countless issues ranging from grave to relatively minor.

Unlike life and liberty, private property cannot make such universal claims as a value of living, although each individual's and each individual family's goods and chattels, whatever they may be, and their enjoyment, are everywhere prized and valued. Even the most paltry goods and chattels are private property, at least in the meagre sense of excluding others from their use, and such privacy of the use of things is valued even when it is not protected as a right. Article 17 of the

Universal Declaration of Human Rights proclaims generally a right to property. Collective property tends to be either lived on a small, community scale, or as state-imposed, without eliminating the irradicable individual striving to gain material benefits and own what has been acquired. That is, of course, far removed from Locke's proclamation of private property as a fundamental individual right which first comes to the fore as a lived value and right only in modern bourgeois societies in which the status of bourgeois has been progressively widened over time to today's democratic, middle-class citizen who is 'everybody'. In view of the global capitalism today at play, which is unthinkable without private property and rights of private property and without free individual property owners who are masters of themselves, it could be said that a certain minimal penetration of capitalist-liberal values has been achieved globally on the everyday economic level in which almost everybody today has a stake. Curtailments of the so-called 'rule of law' — which generally amounts to the rights of life, liberty and property, including especially contractual intercourse — in some parts of the world means precisely the *curtailment* of rules of play according to which a market economy 'naturally' operates.

Locke attempts to ground private property by arguing from an imagined state of nature in which things are simply there for the taking. Such a natural thing which a man "hath by this *labour* something annexed to it, that excludes the common right of other Men"[19] thereby becomes his private property. This grounding is spurious, but it does at least point to the justified or unjustified striving of individuals to gain useful things from whose use and enjoyment other men are excluded. The most basic appropriation of things of nature is *land* itself, whose history is full of violent exclusion of other peoples and persons from the land in order to secure it as the land of a sovereign power and as private property owned by a landowner, who well may have been some kind of

---

19 John Locke *Second Treatise of Government* in Locke *Two Treatises of Government* with an introduction by Peter Laslett, Mentor Books, New York 1965 § 27; italics in the original.

prince whose rights of ownership then became hereditary, justified by custom, blue blood, and the like. Today, established private property rights in land are secured by titles that can be bought and sold.

The privatio of private landed property consists above all in excluding from access to the piece of land and allowing access only on terms laid down by the landowner, in particular, in a lease with a tenant. Such a privatio of access to a thing, of course, is very different from personal privacy which signifies a hiddenness of somewho in their whoness, but the restriction of access to the somewhat of a piece of landed property is an important aspect of somewho's keeping his or her private life private, and insofar has to do with privatio in the sense of a privation of disclosure of how somewho lives and enjoys life. As will be seen further on, there is a constant tendency, including in debates over privacy and the internet, to confuse private property with personal privacy.

Locke's reference to "Estate", rather than simply to property, implies in a sense a reference to private landed property in the grander sense connected with the standing, and hence whoness, of the English and Scottish landed gentry which historically *identified* with their estates. An external thing, the land they owned, formed a facet of their identity in the sense of how they understood themselves through a reflection from the world. Today, with the weakening of landed property as a social class, what one owns by way of property of all kinds continues to play a part in how anyone understands who he or she is him/herself in the world, and in how others estimate the standing of such individuals (and families) in their who-status. Thus, although external, private property is incorporated into how a who identifies with the world because what one owns affects also the masks of self-presentation that a who can adopt and display.

To deepen insight into the privateness of private property, the kinds of private property must be extended and the understanding thereof deepened in the sense of private property's being the basis for an entire economic way of life known as *capitalism*.

1.6 The private individual and private property as a mode of reified sociation: the gainful game (classical political economy, Marx)

> Clapping my hat on my head, I strode into a world inhabited by vast numbers of men who had also clapped their hats on their heads, and as we jostled and encountered in trains and tubes we exchanged the knowing wink of competitors and comrades braced with a thousand snares and dodges to achieve the same end — to earn our livings.
>
> Virginia Woolf *The Waves* p. 762

Although Locke proceeds from a heap of atomistically independent individuals with inalienable natural rights, in truth, the existence of the modern individual is itself the consequence of the establishment of a form of sociation through private property, whose ownership frees individuals from other kinds of social and political bonds, thus allowing them socio-ontologically to *be* individuals in the first place in a certain historical world that is still open today. To put it more sharply: the autonomous individual of modernity has always been an illusion, unbudgingly upheld to the present day in all 'bourgeois' discourses, resulting from wilful blindness to the socio-ontological condition of possibility of the free individual, namely, sociation through reified value.[20] Locke's political philosophy, a grounding of liberalism of

---

[20] George Sand on individuality "Toutes les existences sont solidaires les unes des autres, et tout être humain qui présenterait la sienne isolément, sans la rattacher à celle de ses semblables, n'offrirait qu'une énigme à débrouiller. Cette individualité n'a par elle seule ni signification ni importance aucune. Elle ne prend un sens quelconque qu'en devenant une parcelle de la vie générale, en se fondant avec l'individualité de chacun de mes semblables, et c'est par là qu'elle devient de l'histoire." *Histoire de ma Vie* George Sand pp. 240f.

world-historical significance, ushers in also the moral-philosophical discussions of political economy in the eighteenth century and the emergence of the first proper social science, viz. economics. Hence Adam Smith becomes the father of economics, still revered today.

Classical political economy deals with the phenomenality of the emerging capitalist economy in the eighteenth century, attempting to grasp it theoretically. Three revenue-sources and three social classes play a central role in the first attempts to grasp the essence of economic value-creation and wealth, whereby even the triad indicates already a certain ambiguity. In his main work, for instance, Ricardo speaks of three classes associated with "the proprietor of the land, the owner of the stock or capital necessary for its cultivation and the labourers by whose industry it is cultivated".[21] Beneath "stock or capital" are hidden in truth two capitalist classes, the active entrepreneurial class and the class of financiers who lend money-capital for investment in stock, i.e. means of production. Through the emergence of political economy with its various Scottish, English and French schools, the concept of private property itself becomes more differentiated.

Karl Marx's various writings on the *Critique of Political Economy* clarify many of the antinomies in classical political economy, and work out that there are fundamentally *four* sorts of revenue, *four* revenue-sources and *four* social classes in a capitalist economy: *leased land* being the source of *ground-rent*, *invested capital* in an enterprise being the source of *profit* (of enterprise), *loaned money-capital* the source of

English: "All lives are supportive of each other, and every human being who would present his own isolation, without connecting to that of his fellows, would offer a riddle to unravel. This individuality in itself has no meaning or no importance. It takes some direction by becoming a piece of the general life, based with the individuality of each of my peers, and this is where it becomes history."
So, although it seems that in the modern world we are dissociated from each other, each locked in an isolated individuality, in truth we are always already associated with each other, and our individual freedom is only given rein by how we associate within customs and practices of social interplay which include also those mediated by value-things.

21 Ricardo 1821/1996 p. 13.

interest, and *hired labour-power* of labourers the source of *wages*. Despite all the myriad changes that capitalism has gone through since the eighteenth century, so that today's capitalism is hardly recognizable in the mirror of older capitalist societies, the four fundamental categories of revenues and revenue-sources remain the same, although adopting many different deceptive guises in endless configurations and superpositions. This foursome of the "troika formula"[22] must be taken as giving the fundamental socio-ontological structure of capitalism, a very simple structure of forms of private property as income-source and income (to employ an alternative term to 'revenue') that can adopt infinitely many different configurations in the course of historical time and in different parts of the world.

In a capitalist economy, all the players are engaged in earning income by deploying their income-sources in the competitive play. The linchpin that holds together and mediates a capitalist economy is money(-capital), the crystalline, pure, reified form of *value* that can adopt also other forms, viz. commodity, wages, profit of enterprise, interest and ground-rent. The income type, profit of enterprise, can be capitalized as the price of an enterprise and ground-rent capitalized as the price of land. The labourer himself, however, can only hire out his labour power and cannot be capitalized as the price of a labourer, for that would violate the labourer's inalienable liberty. 'Labourer' itself is a misleading term because in this general context it comprises all those employed by a capitalist enterprise, including the managers and even the executives. Here is not the place to discuss details.[23]

Marx's great discovery and achievement, occluded by the historical course of Marxism, was to work out the essential socio-ontological structure of capitalism as an (augmentative) *movement of value through its various value-forms*, something that is not appreciated even today. Value is the medium of sociation (Vergesellschaftung) in capitalism. It is not a substance but a fleeting reflection that comes about on the various kinds of markets through the valuation interplay among buyers

---

22 Eldred 1984/1910 § 7.

23 Cf. Eldred 1984/2010.

and sellers, lenders and borrowers, lessors and lessees, employers and employees. Because value is reified, however, it *seems* to have a substance. To move as capital, value has to strip off its monetary form and *risk* a movement through the circuit of capital in which it assumes other value-forms before returning as the principal advanced plus profit (which could turn out to be negative). *Capitalism is an historical form of economic life that moves by virtue of an ongoing, constantly fluctuating, estimating interplay among people and things.* The economic competition for income by deploying income-sources is the play of a capitalist economy itself which I therefore call the *gainful game.* However, nota bene: "In this broad sense of gainful game as an historical constellation *as* which the world shapes up, the winner can just as well be a loser."[24] Value thus assumes various thingly forms in the course of its movement, exercising its *social power* to transform itself.

Hence capitalism, or the gainful game, is a *reified* form of sociation differing from other historical worlds based on personal social power relations of direct subjugation. This elaborated socio-ontological structure implies already that it is very naïve and inadequate to speak simply of private property,[25] especially when trying to throw light upon

---

24 Eldred 2000/2010.

25 Marxist discussions of privacy invariably conflate, with critical intent, personal privacy (usually branded as bourgeois, competitive, possessive individualism) with the privacy of private property. Consequently, personal privacy itself becomes a right of ownership of, control over and exclusion of others from personal information and data. Cf. e.g. Sevignani 2012 who, on the one hand, in an extension of Marx's insight into the practical societal basis of equality and freedom in commodity exchange (see footnote after next), argues that "individualistic privacy notions" (p. 614) arise from the same basis. On the other hand, Sevignani makes a plea for "an alternative vision of privacy" (ibid.) arising from "accepting and consciously shaping sociality" (ibid.), hence a social construct achieved by a collective social subject in "comprehensive democratic structures" (ibid.). Accordingly, privacy with a socialist face becomes "a collective task on how best to satisfy individual privacy needs, such as a home, being alone, silence, reflection, recreation, freedom of expression and decision-making, personal and intimate relations, trust and respect, secrecy, and protection from harm" (ibid.). Here privacy is conceived as a need,

the privacy of private property, in particular in contradistinction to *personal* privacy, which is the dominant notion of privacy operative in current discussions of privacy and the internet.[26] Private property in its fourfold income-source structure enables in the first place the gainful game of individual and joint players in that competitive game. Only because value itself, in its various value-form guises, has become *the* medium of sociation in the capitalist world, does such a thing as an *individual* exist at all historically. This is by no means an accepted insight today. Rather, for instance, in liberalism and subjectivist political

alongside others, of needy human beings fulfilling their needs through social practices. Such neediness itself is taken as given; only its *satisfaction* is to be socially constructed. Whence comes this casting of human being itself as needy? And how is privacy itself conceived such that it belongs to a panoply of needs? Need is being confused here with usage; cf. Eldred 2008/2011 § 4 v).

26 With his Marxist approach, Fuchs 2011, whilst underscoring their connection, does not conflate personal privacy with private property, and indeed announces in the title of his paper an "Alternative Concept of Privacy". He discusses the *functions* of privacy, both beneficial and (especially) socially detrimental, mainly in the context of capitalist society, without ever laying out what the phenomenon of personal privacy *is* as a mode of social being, viz. *as* the social interplay of showing off and/or concealing *who* one is. A phenomenology of whoness also eludes Fuchs' "typology of privacy theories" as either "Subjectivism", "Objectivism" or "Subject/object dialectic" (p. 224). Fuchs champions an underdog conception of a right to privacy — the rich exploiters should be surveilled, whereas the privacy of the relatively poor and capitalistically exploited should be protected (pp. 231f). Fuchs' alternative "socialist privacy concept conceives privacy as collective right of dominated and exploited groups that need to be protected from corporate domination that aims at gathering information about workers and consumers for accumulating capital, disciplining workers and consumers, and for increasing the productivity of capitalist production and advertising" (p. 232). Such a concept, based as it is on a notion of class exploitation, stands or falls, depending upon the tenability of the orthodox Marxist embodied-labour theory of value which, in turn, grounds the indispensable theory of surplus-value that is the heart of Marx's concept of class exploitation (cf. however Eldred 1984/2010 App. §§ 1-9). At least Fuchs allows for certain situations in which there is an equal right to privacy: "Many humans would both in a capitalist and a socialist society feel embarrassed having to defecate next to others" (p. 233).

philosophy in general (including in this case even Hegel's *Rechtsphilosophie*[27]) this insight is turned on its head, and the individual is taken as the source of private property by positing its will in things.[28] Rather, the private individual today is an outgrowth of private property which, in turn, signifies more deeply the coming to hidden hegemony of the gainful game through which value keeps moving, thus mobilizing the totality of beings.

For a long time, capitalism and the individualism it enables have been branded as morally repugnant, as a ruthless gainful game driven by greed and egoism in which there are also many losers against whom the economic cards are stacked. Left-wing histories of capitalism are replete with moving descriptions of hard lives under capitalism. A reading of Marx's various mature writings on the *Critique of Political Economy* oriented toward its socio-ontological underpinnings, however, will take due note of the critique's attempt to undo the fetishism of reified social relations, i.e. *to see through the reified gainful game, and thus to open our eyes for another 'reading' of capitalism.* This 'other reading' sees that at its dereified core, the phenomenon of value, through which the very possibility of capitalism is historically constituted, is a mutual estimating and esteeming of each other's fluid, living powers and abilities on a basis of mutual benefit. If the veil of reification that covers and disguises the gainful game is rent, this opens up the historical possibility of a capitalism based on mutually caring for each other.[29] Such a move is visible today in endeavours in the area of social enterprise.

---

27 Hegel RPh 1970.

28 Cf. Marx 1974 "Equality and freedom are thus not only respected in exchange based on exchange-values, but exchange of exchange-values is also the productive, real basis of all *equality* and *freedom*." (Gleichheit und Freiheit sind also nicht nur respektiert im Austausch, der auf Tauschwerten beruht, sondern der Austausch von Tauschwerten ist die produktive, reale Basis aller *Gleichheit* und *Freiheit*. S. 156).

29 Eldred 2008/2011 Chap. 9 vi) 'The set-up and the endless cycle of self-augmentation of reified value (Marx, Heidegger) – The historical possibility of the side-step into endless mutual caring-for'.

1.7 Trust as the gainful game's element and the privacy of private property

The gainful game is played by players striving above all to earn income of the four basic kinds, or countless hybrids of these, by deploying their income-sources in the competitive economic interplay. The outcome of this striving is by no means certain; the movement of the gainful game is risky. The players meet each other on various kinds of markets, mutually estimating and evaluating each other with regard to what they have to offer, whether it be personal powers and abilities (labour power) or a thingly productive power, be it produced goods, land, means of production or loan-capital, each of which has a price that fluctuates constantly according to the way the market-valuation interplay plays out. The players come to exchange agreements within the framework of *contract*, which is the appropriate form of intercourse for the economic gainful game. In addition, the players have to estimate each other's *credibility*, *trustworthiness* and especially *credit-worthiness*, since the gainful game can only be played if the players *keep their word* and fulfil their contracts properly. "That men performe their Covenants made"[30] is at the heart of Hobbes' conception of justice which is thus one of *commutative* justice (cf. *1.8 Justice and state protection of privacy*). Since the markets are subject to constant fluctuations in valuation, the players' credit-worthiness is also all-important to ensure that payments are made even if economic circumstances worsen.

Credit-worthiness is an *estimation* of *who* the potential contractual partner *is*, i.e. his or her *reputation* based on others' opinions of the person's *reliability* and an assessment of how the person lives, i.e. which existential options he or she has realized, especially with regard to assets or debts accumulated. Clearing up doubts about credit-worthiness removes the healthy mistrust that is part of playing the gainful game, paving the way for a transaction. When credibility and *trust* among the players evaporate, or when the momentary prospects for making a gain

---

30 Hobbes 1651/1997 p. 71.

worsen, valuations on the market deflate or even collapse, and the gainful game slows or seizes up.

> In all practical interchanges oriented toward future action, whether commercial exchange or united action (as in political deliberative situations), the word given by each of the parties must bridge the gap between the present and the future. This word is a *promise*, the sending-forth (L. pro-mittere) of a word that announces and gives hope to the other or others of the performance of a future action. [...] In coming to an agreement in which a future interaction or concerted action is resolved we must have mutual trust and faith that promises will be kept. Keeping one's word in a defined future is where human reliability lies. The mutual giving of promises is thus a significant part of social interchange, and such promises are embedded in the dimension of trust and faith that opens up a bridge of enablement between free human beings who each has the power (δύναμις) to freely act one way or another, but nevertheless find they also have to act in concert in any common project, or reciprocally in commercial and economic exchange.[31]

Giving promises and trusting each other play a significant role, whether it be in public business, in politics or in the private life-world shared with friends and family. In the last of these, trust assumes the hue of intimacy (cf. *1.4 The question concerning rights: personal privacy*) in the sense that to be intimate with someone is to reveal oneself 'warts and all', which is only possible if one can trust one's intimate that the privacy, i.e. concealment, of the intimately shared life-world is respected and preserved. Promises and trust in a shared, intimate life-world carry greater existential weight than keeping promises made contractually in the gainful game, which can be seen in the phenomenon that the breaking of trust with an intimate can shatter a personal life-world and even shake a person's self-understanding itself, provoking a recasting of the self. The shattering of trust in the gainful game happens more at a distance to one's core self, i.e. the masks with which one identifies most closely, and may be taken as a blow from which one can recover or simply as an annoyance. The breaking of a contract, including contractual fraud, is a breach of trust, but this may be regarded as one of the risks of earning a living that even may be remediable in a court of law.

---

31 Eldred 2008/2011 Chap. 5 vi) b).

What can be said specifically of the *privacy* of private property in contrast to personal privacy? First of all there are the things that an individual (or individual's family) owns, enjoying them in personal life. Income acquired in the gainful game is spent on goods that are privately used, excluding others from their use and enjoyment. Privacy here means not so much *concealment* but *exclusion* of use by others. This applies also to privately owned land and to personal bank accounts; the individual decides who has access to his or her home and decides freely over how to exercise the power of acquired money when spending it. Such free disposal of income is an essential feature of liberal freedom that ties liberty to private property. Since reified value is the medium of sociation in a capitalist economy, in all its reifications, either as money or as saleable property of whatever kind, it is a *social power* to acquire through exchange which is fundamental to such a money-mediated way of life. Likewise, the striving for income depends crucially upon the estimated and validated value of what is offered on the market for valuation, including human labour power (abilities of all kinds), consumption goods, investment goods, land for lease, money-capital for loan. Hence all the various incomes and income-sources are themselves pieces in the *power play* to earn and spend income, thus exercising money's power to effect a change, i.e. an ex-change. The value power play is always a power play of estimation played out on diverse markets, and has diverse phenomenal forms. Accordingly, the privacy of the various kinds of property has very different phenomenal forms, e.g. the privacy of a piece of land looks very different from the privacy of a bank account or the privacy of an enterprise's premises or facilities, but all are characterized by a privation of access and disposal.

Privation of access, use and disposal is the hallmark of the *privacy of private property* rather than the concealment of who one is in one's personal life-world, which is the hallmark of personal privacy. Hence the privacy of private property can go hand in hand with its public display, the very opposite of concealment. Such public display lives from the tension that others have no access to the private property displayed in a game to enhance one's own who-standing. Look but don't touch. Here it is more than plain that being a who is itself a power play of presenting oneself in public in order to have an *impact* of some sort (i.e. to make a difference), to be esteemed in one way or another, perhaps in a game for validating one's own self-importance. The *public* display of *private* property for the sake of who-standing is contradictory in the sense of relying on two different, contradictory kinds of privation, perhaps to incite envy. The drive to *be* a who means the striving to display oneself for the sake of being esteemed and validated in some way. Personal privacy often amounts to withdrawing temporarily from such who-display in favour of enjoying a private world with family and friends.

The privacy of private property in the gainful game itself amounts to the individuation of each player in the game, either as an individual person or as an individual enterprise (ultimately a joint venture of individual private property owners). An individual may hire out his or her labour power, of whatever kind and quality, in exchange for wages. He thereby becomes employed by another who, through hiring, now has the power to direct the exercise of his labour power in the running of some sort of capitalist enterprise, small or large. The employee has access to the enterprise's private property and has temporarily renounced the free exercise of his own powers and abilities in favour of the employing entrepreneur, who may be a single individual or a company. One hires out one's abilities in exchange for income, which itself is a social power play; one does not sell oneself lock, stock and barrel, for that would be indentured labour, a kind of slavery. The individual's life and liberty are preserved in labouring for wages insofar as the individual employee is only temporarily subjected to another's will and can also freely compete on the labour-power markets for employment. The employee is part of the employer's workforce, with certain duties, privileges and authorizations within the private realm of the enterprise, which is not open to the public. The privacy of the enterprise as private property hence has a different character from other kinds. Employees are required to be discreet about their enterprise's activities, which is a kind of privatio as concealment. Revealing/concealing details of a company, however, which is a collective, has a different flavour from revealing/concealing details of an individual, who is a person. Companies themselves are obliged to conceal details about the employees they employ to preserve their personal privacy. Divulging details of a private company's operations may have considerable negative consequences for its strategy in the gainful game, but does not have the intimate character of violating personal privacy and thus an individual's dignity. However, divulging details about an individual's private property would not seem to violate personal privacy so much as revealing intimate details of his personal life.

A private company is itself also public insofar as it is active on markets with the aim of selling its products, whatever they may be (goods or services). It must publicize and advertise details of its products and operations to do business, and it must allow the public's access to its physical premises whilst maintaining other parts of the premises as private. Any company, big or small, has an interface with the public through which it does business. This interface selects which aspects of the company are disclosed and which are concealed and which parts of the company's property have open access to the public and which not.

The privacy of land consists above all in the privation of others' having access to it, its use and its natural products. The landowner is free to enjoy and use the land as he will, that is, subject to restrictions placed upon him or her not by other individuals, but by government in the name of the common good. The government zones the use of land between residential, commercial, industrial, agricultural, etc., and stipulates building codes for what structures can be erected on specific plots of land. Within this restricted framework, the land remains private, however.

The privacy of money-capital is an exclusion of disposal over this crystalline, reified, social power at the heart of the gainful game. It also has an aspect of personal privacy as concealment insofar as an individual's personal net wealth is not open to public scrutiny, whereas in the case of a *public joint-stock company*, which is nevertheless a *private* company, many financial details must be published for the sake of the public shareholders who want to know about their company's operations to assess its success and valuation. Hence the apparent paradox of a public company that is nonetheless private property.

Ironically, the greatest incursions into the freedom of private property in financial assets come from the government itself, one of whose core tasks and raison d'être is precisely the protection of private property. Through this protection the gainful game itself is upheld, with the government laying down rules of play for the game without having any insight into its essential nature as the movement of reified value. The government itself requires revenue, which it raises by way of *taxation*. To this end it must invade the privacy surrounding an individual's or a company's assets in the double sense of the legally enforced *disclosure* of financial details and legally enforced *appropriation* of private financial assets through various kinds of taxes and levies. It is significant that the major part of Ricardo's main work from 1821, *Principles of Political Economy and Taxation*, is devoted precisely to taxation and thus to the question as to how the government can best raise revenue from its private citizens whilst paying regard to the tax-bearing capacity of and the effects upon different kinds of productive resources (land, labour, means of production, finance capital) deployed in a capitalist economy and the incomes they generate. When taxation is complemented by the state's paying out welfare benefits, such benefits are 'paid' for by the citizen with a further erosion of privacy in the double sense of having to reveal more of his or her private life and having to accept restrictions on and oversight over personal finances, including restrictions on how much he or she may earn. The state thus both protects and curtails the gainful game. More on this in the next section.

1.8 Justice and state protection of privacy

Post-war Anglophone philosophy of justice, starting from and dominated by Rawls,[32] is fixated on distributive justice, even to the extent that commutative justice is no longer even mentioned.[33] The

---

[32] Rawls 1971.

[33] Cf. Eldred, Michael 'Anglophone Justice Theory, the Gainful Game and the Political Power Play' www.arte-fact.org 2009 and Eldred 2008/2011 Chap. 6 'Justice'. Cf. also Höffe, Ottfried 'Rechtsordnung als gerechter Tausch' in

distinction between distributive and commutative justice goes back to Aristotle's *Nicomachean Ethics*, the ineluctable wellspring of all Western philosophy of justice where they are termed, respectively justice ἐν ταῖς διανομαῖς[34] and justice ἐν τοῖς συναλλάγμασι.[35] Commutative justice, however, is the appropriate conception of justice for interchanges (i.e. συναλλάγματα) among people sharing a world, esteeming and valuing each other and each other's goods. The concept of distributive justice that has dominated the Anglophone discussion for so long is a direct consequence of the rise of the post-war social welfare state, so that it necessarily implies a superior political instance capable of redistributing the (primarily material) goods of living in a purportedly 'socially just' way which, in turn, acts by legislating *positive* law to this end. Distributive 'social' justice is, strictly speaking, redistributive justice that redistributes value generated in the gainful game through interplays of commutative value-estimation. Hence commutative justice is the deeper phenomenon. The legislating of positive law in the name of redistributive justice, in turn, is strongly influenced by the democratic power struggles in which governments are elected, with the result that the concept of (re)distributive (social) justice becomes increasingly unclear as the merely accidental, transient outcome of political struggles through which 'the people' get what they want, and preferably more and more, with the inevitable tendency to pay for welfare benefits by going into debt that is passed on to unborn generations. Furthermore, the notion of distributive justice is concerned with what people actually *have* by way of goods, and not with the *fairness* of (risky) interplay among people, which is a matter of *potential* life-movements that do not guarantee any final outcome when striving for income in the gainful game or for personal happiness in their private lives.

Recent Anglophone philosophy of justice is therefore ill-equipped to approach the issues of *personal privacy* and the *privacy of property*

Universitas 1/ 1989 pp. 11-17 and Höffe, Ottfried, entry on Gerechtigkeit in *Lexikon der Ethik* Beck, Munich 1997.

34 Aristotle *Eth. Nic.* 1130b31.

35 Ibid. 1131a1.

which are, in the first place, a matter of how the life-worlds of individuals are able to maintain and enjoy an appropriate balance between concealment and public exposure, and also how private property, and thereby the gainful game itself, is to be protected by the state. Both are, in the first place, issues pertaining to the interchanges or commutations among people in civil society. Next to guaranteeing life and liberty, the protection of private property is one of the core tasks of the liberal state and as such has been treated thoroughly by classical political philosophy. The protection of private property amounts to preserving the forms of intercourse essential for the interchanges in civil society, which is the society dominated by the movement of striving for income that keeps the gainful game itself in motion, albeit 'behind the backs' of the players. To this end, possession of private property must be secured against *theft, robbery, trespassing on land, poaching,* etc. etc. and the form of intercourse in civil society, the *contract*, which may be infringed in many ways, including *fraud* and *non-fulfilment*, must be enforced by the state. Such enforcement is at the heart of civil justice, which steps in when trust fails, where justice is not merely what is posited by the state through legislation and the administration of justice in the courts of law but, more deeply, the preservation of the *free* possession, enjoyment, use of and contractual intercourse with private property. (Civil) justice remains incomprehensible without a conception of freedom and fair interplay.

The protection of personal privacy is an aspect of the protection of an individual's private *life*. Incursions by others into a person's private life may amount to revealing publicly details about that private life-world. Personal privacy must be thought of not as the privacy of an individual subject encapsulated within itself, but as the non-disclosure of a personal, individual life-*world*. Other aspects of the protection of an individual's private life include the protection of an individual's public persona, i.e. of the mask *as who* this individual presents him- or herself in public, thus revealing and showing off who he or she is. An important aspect of this public persona, in turn, is an individual's *reputation*, which is *who* this individual is taken and *estimated* to be by others, which is not simply a matter of who the individual presents himself to be in the present, but extends especially to the temporal dimension of the *memory* of how the individual's persona is publicly assessed (cf. *3.7 An appraisal of Nissenbaum's Privacy in Context*).

Damage to reputation is at the heart of an injury to an individual's life, even though it is not a physical injury. There is a link between injuries to a person's reputation through libel and slander, on the one hand, and, on the other, prying into the private details of an individual's life-world in order then to publicly disclose, with malicious intent, reputationally damaging facts about the individual concerned. There is also a link between invasions of personal privacy and monetary gain when media publish private details in gossip-mongering fashion. The converse of protection against such invasions of personal privacy is the right of *freedom of speech* which is an essential feature of individual liberty with respect to both what can be said and revealed about the members of civil society and what can be said and revealed about the government and the state. Freedom of expression is an aspect of the freedom to show oneself *as who* one is, because the opinions, writings, art works, etc. which an individual places in the public realm are all who-masks with which that individual *identifies* (cf. *1.2 Selfhood as an identification with reflections from the world*).

What about the collection of facts about an individual's life that are in some sense already public, such as an individual's personal spending behaviour? Such data are collected automatically when an individual uses a credit or debit card to pay for consumer purchases which can be used to construct a profile of that individual's consumer preferences which, when combined with masses of similar profiles of other consumers, will give a profile of spending behaviour in a given region or a given market segment, etc. that, in turn, can be used to design advertising campaigns. Individual consumer profiles can be used to individually target an individual with specific advertising. Here there is no malicious intent to damage anyone's reputation, but rather the aim of making a monetary gain out of it. Such profiling has only become feasible with the advent of digital technologies. Hence treatment thereof as an issue of infringement of personal privacy will be deferred to later (cf. *3.2 Digital privacy: personal freedom to reveal and conceal*).

The other major aspect of the protection of personal privacy and private property concerns not the interplay within civil society, but the incursions of the state itself into privacy in the name of a higher good, viz., the well-being of the state and society as a whole. Such incursions are made for the sake of both commutative and (re)distributive justice. In the former case, privacy is invaded to fight crime, an important aspect of the protection of both private property, and individual life and liberty. Both the liberal and the welfare aspects of the state motivate it to curtail personal privacy and also private property for the sake of *raising taxes*, as already mentioned in the previous section. In particular, the state itself invades the private life-worlds of its tax-payers, and keeps tabs on their activities, to ensure the collection of taxation. The greater the tax burden in a country, the greater the state's perceived 'need' to surveil and 'stick its nose' into its private taxpayers' income-earning activities of all kinds. Taxation is not a matter of commutative justice but of the state's self-interest in its own existence, which is additionally justified by its role as the instance redistributing social wealth in the name of welfare to those not so well off. Taxation is the appropriation of private property and therefore has no inherent yardstick as it has in the interchanges of civil society, where the *fairness* of interplay serves as a measure for justice. Rather, the raising of taxes is *posited* by the state in line what it deems necessary to finance (a certain, constantly changing, always politically controversial, conception of) the universal good. Taxation should cover the state's budget as differentiated into its many tasks. If not, taxation is supplemented by sovereign debt-raising. What is regarded as 'just taxation' is a matter of habit and custom, and there is a tendency for taxes to rise and especially for the government to invent ever new taxes that, as stealthily as possible, encroach upon its citizens' income and property if citizens are not vigilant and prepared to resist. There is also a mass egoism from below that clamours for more and more welfare benefits in the name of a spurious social justice. The level and kinds of taxation are also an issue in the perennial political struggle within democracies between the liberal and welfare aspects of the state's role as represented by the different political parties. Hence there is an inherent arbitrariness in taxation and thus also in the extent of incursions into privacy and private property for the sake of enforcing the raising of taxes.

The *constitution* of a state is supposed to afford some protection against the government's invasions of privacy and incursions into private property, thus ameliorating also the arbitrariness of government taxation policy and its enforcement.

The gainful game is played today also beyond the boundaries of the modern nation state, in a globalized economy and indeed, the striving for gain was *the* major motor for globalization since the 15th century. Since national sovereignty is limited, other supranational political powers need to be instituted in order, in the first place, to provide internationally valid rules of play which amount to the international protection of life, liberty and private property and legal rules for the intercourse with private property that conform with rights to life and liberty (e.g. child labour) and promote the movement of the gainful game (e.g. bilateral and multilateral trade agreements). The Universal Declaration of Human Rights proclaimed by the United Nations is perhaps the most general expression of an international will to uphold life, liberty (Article 3) and property (Article 17). The ramifications of these supranational political tasks are endless and ongoing. However, it is important to keep in mind that the rights of life, liberty and property *exist* already *as* firmly rooted, prized values of a globalized humankind providing the *motive power* for myriad kinds of political struggle everywhere. A further aspect of supranational political tasks are the (still nascent) efforts to harmonize taxation between states (e.g. customs duties, corporate taxes) or even collect taxes on an international level (e.g. proposals for an international financial transaction tax).

Quite another aspect of privacy as *privatio* comes to light when one considers the (public) servants, agents, functionaries of the state and other holders of any sort of public office, namely, that they are subject to raison d'état of some kind (political or diplomatic considerations, obligation to carry out one's official duties without questioning, etc.) which restricts the freedom of life-movement in the sense especially of being free to say what one likes. With regard to what they think, they are obliged *not* to disclose *who* they are, rather than being free to withdraw from public, which amounts to a kind of *forced personal privacy* in the sense developed in this chapter. This phenomenon is taken up in the next section.

1.9 Kant's free autonomous subject and *privatio* in the use of reason[36]

Who are we humans? The core message of Kant's thinking on this question is that we are not just something or a "what" belonging to the sensory world that is governed by the (Newtonian) laws of physics but that we have a second nature beyond the "phenomenal" one that he calls "noumenal".[37] Noumenal beings ("Vernunftwesen", "vernünftige Wesen überhaupt"), of which, according to Kant, there might be others apart from ourselves, humans, are free and autonomous. Kant's interpretation of human freedom as a "causality of freedom" is metaphysical, in contrast to a phenomenological perspective as addressed above in *1.5 The private individual, liberty, private property (Locke)*. Humans as noumenal beings are persons having "dignity" and not a "price".[38] As free and autonomous beings humans are subject to the moral law that compels them categorically to act according to universalizable maxims. Although the moral law makes evident the social nature of humans, its call does not originate from the encounter with another person but comes from within and beyond the subject due to its dual inner nature as encapsulated subject divorced from the world. The "true self" commands us to respect humanity in our being as persons.[39]

Kantian thinking is dual. We are autonomous and heteronomous beings at the same time, but while our heteronomy with regard to natural laws is unavoidable, we are free to follow or refuse the moral call. There is a gap between our will and the moral law that is specific to the human being as "noumenal" or "intelligible", this not being the case with other

---

36 This section is the final authorial responsibility of Rafael Capurro.

37 Kant 1977 A 65 p. 550, A 2 p. 508.

38 Kant 1974 B 78 p. 68.

39 Kant 1974 BA 118 p. 95.

"intelligible beings".[40] This Kantian dualism of the human self corresponds to the dualism between the sensory and the supersensuous or "noumenal" world, a view that Kant inherits from both Greek metaphysics and Christianity.

This conception of the free autonomous subject is contrasted by Kant with the constraints imposed on human reason by any kind of official duty that restricts the subject from using it freely and universally. In contrast to today's common use of the words 'public' and 'private' according to which an official duty is regarded as 'public', Kant stresses in 'An Answer to the Question: What is Enlightenment?' that the public use of reason as an office-holder is, in fact, 'private' ("Privatgebrauch") since it is not fully free and autonomous. This contrasts to the case where an individual — and Kant mentions explicitly the scholar ("Gelehrter") — employs its reason free of such constraints ("öffentlicher Gebrauch"), addressing "the whole public of the world of readers".[41] The ideal of the free autonomous subject using its reason without external constraints of office is thus something crucial for Kant and other thinkers of the Enlightenment, since it enables the subject to communicate his thoughts — Kant uses the masculine — without being subjected to censorship. It is Kant's intention to protect the free autonomous subject from official constraints by opening him to a potentially universal public through the use of printing technology ("die Schriften") as a medium. Kant's plea for protecting the "public use" of reason is, in today's terminology, a plea for freedom of speech of a free, autonomous subject.

It is important to note that for Kant this individual thinking and acting does not take place in isolation and is inseparable from the freedom to communicate using various media, particularly printing technology. For Kant, orality is a medium for the "private use" of reason, as in the case of religious, political or military leaders. It addresses a group of persons that is always limited or "domestic" ("häuslich").[42] Kant reverses, once

40 Kant 1974 BA 40 p. 43.

41 Kant 1975 A 485 p. 55.

42 Kant 1975 A 488 p. 57.

again, not only today's common linguistic usage but, more importantly, the ethical values related to the concepts of "public" and "private". The public use of reason, which amounts to the individual's freedom of speech or expression in today's usage, is that specific to a free, autonomous individual scholar addressing the whole world of readers ("Leserwelt") which is at the same time the "society of world citizens" "(Weltbürgergesellschaft").[43] The scholar offers his thoughts "freely and publicly" "for critical examination" ("frei und öffentlich der Welt zur Prüfung darlegen").[44] This has a higher ethical value than the so-called 'public' or official use of reason as office-holders which for Kant is 'private' in the sense that it is a privation of its autonomous and free use.

Hence, Kant's notion of privacy is opposite to the determination of personal privacy in the present study as a concealment of *who* one is, in the sense that a public office holder is *obliged* to subject the free use of his or her reason to an alien raison, which may be raison d'état or that of an association, a political party, an institution, a company, etc. *The right to personal privacy is inverted into an obligation to personal privacy.* This notion of an obligatory or forced privacy in showing off *who* one *is* through expressing what one thinks still has relevance today, sometimes in subtle ways. A public servant, for instance, may be prohibited from giving interviews to the media, which is an enforced privacy, but a politician also does not freely express what he thinks and in this sense restricts the free use of his reason, thus concealing *who* he 'truly' is, for political, tactical reasons relating to what he wants his electorate to hear. Something similar holds true *mutatis mutandis* for diplomats, heads of companies or organizations such as universities, etc. They are not free to choose the masks of who-presentation that truly fit.

Kant's insistence on this freedom of expression with regard to scholars is, in fact, arguably a pusillanimous compromise with political, religious and military powers. If scholarly freedom of expression, at least, is allowed, then, Kant gingerly suggests, there might be some hope

---

43 Kant 1975 A 486 p. 56.

44 Kant 1975 A 292 p. 60.

that things might change for the better, since freedom of scholarly thought might induce "little by little" ("nach und nach") the general public to act more freely and live more in accordance with human dignity, humans being more than "mere machines".[45] This is what Kant calls the "true reform of the way of thinking" ("wahre Reform der Denkungsart").[46] This conception of the freedom of scholarly thinking presupposes that the scholars do, indeed, think freely and are not restricted by their 'office' as scholars, which includes that the scholars find in the reflection of their colleagues a confirmation of *who* they are *as* free-thinking. This condition, however, makes the scholar dependent upon what is accepted by the times in which he lives as 'reasonable thought', as determined by the community of scholars, his so-called peers. In 'What Does it Mean to Orient Oneself in Thinking?' Kant stresses the importance of respecting not only the individual's freedom to communicate — having in mind, once again, the scholarly public space — but the freedom to use media for *communication* ("die Freiheit, seine Gedanken öffentlich *mitzuteilen*").[47] The freedom for an individual to think is essentially related to the freedom to communicate his thoughts to others and, in turn, to receive their thoughts. There is no freedom of thinking without freedom to use media to communicate one's thoughts.

Although Kant strictly distinguishes persons from sensory objects, or who from what, this dualism does not mean that humans live in two separate worlds as 'noumenal' and sensory beings, respectively. We are persons in the world, subject to, but not fully determined by natural laws. Who we are as free beings in the world is disclosed in the experience of respect of moral law ("Achtung vor dem Gesetz") which is a special kind of sentiment ("Gefühl"), namely the only one originating from a non-empirical cause. It is a "moral sentiment"[48] which signifies a sound marker and "motivating force" ("Triebfeder") that discloses our selves as not being determined just by egoistic interests. Moral sentiment

45 Kant 1975 A. 494 p. 61.

46 Kant 1975 A 485 p. 55.

47 Kant 1975a A 525 p. 280.

48 Kant 1974a A 131-133 pp. 194f.

shows itself positively, i.e. not just as opposed to egoistic interests, as *respect*, which is a human's own way of being in the world as a free person.

In pointing to the moral sentiment *within* us, however, Kant overlooks that he has not determined the *worldliness of the world* in which the individual subject finds itself always already *out there*, associating with others. The individual subject is determined in its whoness by Kant as a *moral* subject, an intrinsic distinction it bears as a mark of human dignity. Moral sentiment, then, is the hallmark also of the subject that, according to Kant, demands respect on the part of others. How moral subjects in the world have to do with one another is a question of intersubjectivity for which the worldliness of the world as a phenomenon remains invisible. In particular, that the subject *as who* it is could *itself* be constituted *through* the interplay with others, respecting, estimating and esteeming each other, including in privative modes, is not conceivable within Kantian subjectivist metaphysics.

Hence for Kant, the answer to the question, Who are we?, depends on how far we pay attention to the prior inner moral call in specific relations and situations, rather than it being the case that our valuing and esteeming each other in the interplay, through which we perforce share the world with each other, constitutes our very whoness, i.e. our very selves, in the world. Kant analyzes some negative forms of human interplay in which we do not respect the moral call, such as defamation ("üble Nachrede"),[49] which is to the detriment of the respect we owe to humanity. In view of others' faults, we should be not only cautious with our judgements, but even conceal them, instead of becoming obsessed with watching over other people's lives.[50] Respecting privacy in the sense of withdrawal from view is thus a moral question. Similarly, Kant stresses the role of moral respect in friendships in providing some kind of stability to those based mainly on feelings.[51] Even in what Kant calls "moral friendship" ("moralische Freundschaft"), where persons feel the

---

49 Kant 1977 A 145 p. 604.

50 Kant 1977 A 146 p. 605.

51 Kant 1977 A 155 pp. 610f.

need to disclose to each other in intimacy all their secrets, the possibility of abuse, particularly with regard to judgements about other people, should make us cautious, not only because people may be malicious but also because they may be indiscreet.[52] Discretion, however, is a mode of conduct that respects a person's *concealment*.

Kant's views on the autonomous moral subject in its interplay with others as well as with political, religious and military powers are an example of the tensions and compromises of bourgeois society looking not only for more social freedom and communication free of censorship, but also for an anchoring for the custom of respecting each other's free will. According to Habermas, Marx claims that public opinion is the mask of bourgeois society and its class interests.[53] This is the so-called Marxian critique of bourgeois class society as exploitative of the working class, a critique based crucially and untenably on the theories of surplus-value and the labour theory of value.[54] What *can* be said is that in Kant's time, the rights of the working class to participate in democratic (for Kant: republican) government were void due to *private property* requirements: only a man with a certain amount of property could engage in political decision-making at all. The same can be said *mutatis mutandis* concerning the bourgeois nature of some Kantian views on what should be the object of respect in the worldly interplay among free and autonomous subjects based on the respect of moral law. If the Kantian public sphere is merely a scholarly one, this is far from a democratic public sphere in today's sense. The private sphere is mainly related to social relationships in the context of family and friendship sharing some moral biases of its time.

As Nagenborg remarks, according to Kant, sexual relationships should not become fully explicit even within matrimony.[55] The private sphere is a separate domain with its own moral standards that could collide with the self's presentation in the public sphere. The fear of the citizen facing public scandal has its counterpart in the critical but idealized view of

---

52 Kant 1977 A 156-157 pp. 611f.

53 Habermas 1962/1990 p. 202.

54 Eldred 1984/2010 Appendix.

55 Nagenborg 2005 p. 92; Kant 1977 A 78 p. 558.

morality in private life as a source of criticism of public life. According to Nagenborg, Romanticism was a reaction against this kind of negation of natural customs in the private sphere.[56] Habermas' criticisms of Kant's conception of the public sphere "two hundred years later"[57] should now be revisited, not only because Kant could not foresee mass media, but also because he could not foresee the cyberworld[58] in which questions regarding privacy and publicness are posed anew. Such reposing demands not merely a re-examination of Kant's views on the public sphere as a republic of scholars but above all a recasting on the basis of a genuinely 'worldly' conception of whoness not shackled by theoretical constructions of intersubjectivity.

1.10 Privacy as protection of individual autonomy — On Rössler's *The Value of Privacy*[59]

"The question of whom I live with is a private affair, and so is what I think about my colleagues at work." This is the first sentence of Beate Rössler's *The Value of Privacy*.[60] The book ends with a story, *The Private Life*, by Henry James (1843-1916), "about the possible dissociation of the private and the public self, the private and the public person."[61] These two quotes provide a hint as to what is at stake for Rössler when discussing "the value of privacy", namely, the protection of the self or, more precisely, the protection of individual autonomy, which includes "the protection *of* relations and *within* relations, protection *with* others and protection *from* others. Each of the three dimensions therefore also includes the protection of the solitary subject from all others."[62] This protection concerns the three dimensions of privacy that she identifies and analyzes in her book, namely decisional, informational and local privacy. Although acknowledging that one's

56 Nagenborg 2005 p. 93; cf. also Ess & Thorseth 2008.
57 Habermas 1995.
58 Capurro 2003 p. 192.
59 This section is the final authorial responsibility of Rafael Capurro.
60 Rössler 2005 p. 1.
61 Rössler 2005 p. 188.
62 Rössler 2005 p 192.

personal life always includes relations with others, Rössler's concept of privacy focuses ultimately on the solitary autonomous subject. In the introduction she points to her use of the term 'private' as referring to "modes of action and conduct", "a certain knowledge" and "spaces", the third type being the view of privacy highlighted by Hannah Arendt on whom she later comments critically (cf. the following section). Issues of access and control — which she traces back to Warren and Brandeis' 'right to be left alone' as well as to Ruth Gavison and Alan F. Westin — form the core of Rössler's view on privacy. She writes, "Something counts as private if one can oneself control the access to this 'something'",[63] thus passing up the opportunity to distinguish between something and somewho. She broadens the issue of privacy beyond the classical notion based on spaces that I can control by discussing the value of privacy within the framework of liberal democracy that aims at protecting "individual freedom and the autonomy of persons in the face of inadmissible interference or regulations on the part of the state."[64]

According to Rössler, egalitarian liberalism is based on four principles, namely liberty, equality, neutrality of the state and democracy. Nonetheless, she is aware of the cultural differences in the normative conception of privacy and autonomy not only between Western and non-Western, but also within Western liberal societies such as in the case of the U.S. and Germany, which she scrutinizes. She maintains that the U.S. conception of privacy is based on the view that the state must keep a distance from the decisions and actions of the individual, while in Germany — she points particularly to the *Großer Lauschangriff* ('the great bugging operation') — it is less about state *intrusions* than about *inspections* of one's life.[65] She underscores that in both cases the ideal of a life "of one's own", understood as an autonomous and authentic life, depends upon privacy. A core issue in Rössler's view on privacy concerns the notion of freedom as individual autonomy, a concept that she traces back to Locke, Kant and Mill as well

63 Rössler 2005 p. 8
64 Rössler 2005 p. 10.
65 Rössler 2005 p. 14.

as to Rawls and Habermas. She analyzes the critique of the liberal tradition raised by feminist theories concerning the concept of privacy as being gender-biased.

The sphere of the household is "a place governed *only* by women and nature".[66] According to Rössler, the Aristotelean view of the οἶκος (*oikos*) as the place of women and family predates the gender bias of privacy in modern liberal societies, both being diametrically opposed. For Aristotle, the public sphere is the realm of political freedom, whereas the "genuinely *liberal* differentiation" is about "private freedom and public control."[67] This exclusion forms the core of feminist critique insofar as the gender-biased view of privacy is rooted in a pre-modern "natural" sphere and not in a conception of "equality of freedoms". She writes, "Such a concept of privacy and such a foundation for the concept is precisely what I am aiming for."[68] She discusses this gender bias in three classics of liberal thought, namely Locke, Mill and Rawls, and concludes by stating that "nothing is private in itself: the concept of privacy must be understood as a conventional and not a natural one".[69] This insight takes her straight to her concept of privacy as related to freedom and autonomy. To be a free subject means having "the basic ability to engage in processes of self-deliberation. If a person possesses nothing akin to concepts of choice, rational selection (at least in a broad sense of the term) and relevance, the idea of a free subject makes no sense."[70]

Freedom, she argues, does not centre on what I can do or not do, or what I have the opportunity to do or not to do, since such contingencies are beyond human influence. The lack of ability to do something does not equate to a lack of freedom. The notions of freedom and autonomy are taken from the classic liberal tradition of Kant and Mill. She does not reduce the concept of autonomy to the Kantian sense of *moral* autonomy but enlarges it to that of "*personal* autonomy in the sense of general

66 Rössler 2005 p. 22.
67 Rössler 2005 p. 22.
68 Rössler 2005 p. 26.
69 Rössler 2005 p. 41.
70 Rössler 2005 p. 46.

personal self-determination concerning how I want to lead my life."[71] Privacy has to do with the protection of this evaluative view of oneself, i.e. with our desires, goals and values and "*her own good reasons*" "to understand herself as the author of an action", as she remarks, following Gerald Dworkin and Richard Lindley.[72] She regards this critical attitude toward oneself as the core of the idea of authenticity as developed by Charles Taylor. She stresses that the question of giving oneself priorities with regard to projects and goals is not an easy task and that the range of options is determined by the cultural background as well as by the social context.[73] To be autonomous does not imply being exempt from such predeterminations, but being able to reflect on them. She rejects theories whose concept of privacy focuses solely on the protection of relations or on that of the person herself. The reason is "because neither of them is able to do justice to *all* the key aspects of privacy […] Special rights to privacy do not necessarily need to be based on the protection of "individual *freedom* or the *inviolability* of persons."[74] This is why she rejects the view of privacy as being primarily concerned with the protection of freedom and not of autonomy.

She summarizes her key insight as follows, "The thesis I am concerned with is that the true realization of freedom, that is a life led autonomously, is only possible in conditions where privacy is protected."[75] Privacy-protecting autonomy is said to be the basis of freedom, not the other way round. "Why do we like having 'a room of our own?'? Why do we want it to be in our hands what our colleagues know about our private life?" she asks. And her answer is, "Because all of this [...] would encroach upon our autonomy. To be able to ask oneself authentically who one is and how one would like to live, it is clearly necessary to have possibilities of withdrawing from the gaze of other people. To be able to conceive, develop and pursue goals, it is necessary to have dimensions in one's life that are free from the

71 Rössler 2005 p. 51.
72 Rössler 2005 p. 54.
73 Rössler 2005 p. 64.
74 Rössler 2005 pp.70f.
75 Rössler 2005 p. 72.

objections or control of other people."[76] Rössler does not see that the private, autonomous individual is always already in the world and that this world as a social world is sociated (vergesellschaftet) precisely by *reified social interplay* that provides the socio-ontological conditions of possibility of the historical modern individual *as* an individual (cf. *1.6 The private individual and private property as a mode of reified sociation: the gainful game (classical political economy, Marx)*).

Privacy as autonomy-protection means, for Rössler, being able to control the access "of others to me, to my person, to my (reflections on) decisions, and to information upon me"[77], just as control of access is an essential determination of the privacy of private property. This lays the foundation for the three dimensions of privacy, namely decisional, informational and local. Following, but also criticizing, ideas by Mill and Rorty, she deals with decisional privacy as being at the core of a self-determined life. Both authors separate the public sphere as the realm of liberal justice from the private domain where the individual's freedom and self-casting can unfold. Rössler criticizes not only the underlying assumption of a dichotomy between two separate spheres but rejects also the identification of privacy and freedom in the crude sense that to be free is ultimately to be private. She writes, "Yet what would, in certain circumstances, be violated is my (decisional) privacy, the opportunity for me to behave or live *unhampered* as I wish in social space. In such a conflict, one would appeal not to principles of liberty but of privacy."[78]

She goes even further by stating that the notion of decisional privacy "lies at right angles" to the distinction between negative and positive freedom as proposed by Isaiah Berlin.[79] Rössler claims that freedom as autonomy precedes this distinction. Although she acknowledges that "intersubjectivity" makes autonomy possible, the function of autonomy is to be able to distance oneself within such relations. This option of assuming a distance is implied, she maintains, when we speak about privacy protection. When dealing with forms of distance and withdrawal

---

76 Rössler 2005 p. 73.

77 Rössler 2005 p. 73.

78 Rössler 2005 p. 83.

79 Rössler 2005 p. 83.

she shares insights with Georg Simmel, Thomas Nagel ("civility") and Mill ("tolerance").[80] In this context, she discusses the difference between ethics and morality by defining ethics as dealing with personal reasons for one's own life, whereas morality deals with issues where others are concerned. She writes, "Ethical problems are the sort of problem concerned exclusively with the question of my own (good) life, while unambiguously moral, 'irreducibly intersubjective' problems are the sort, for example, concerned with justice in distribution."[81] One reason she gives for the separation between ethics and morality or between giving reasons to "ethical others" in contrast to giving reasons to "all others" is related to her criticism of Habermas' view that "ethical endorsement should be sought 'before the eyes of all.'"[82] Such pressure to justify oneself 'before the eyes of all' should not be confused with the fact that the ethical justification of personal projects is always done in a common or intersubjective language. The world for her is (or should be) populated by autonomous individual *subjects* whose relations are *intersubjective*, and precisely not the interplay among whos (cf. *1.1 The trace of whoness starts with the Greeks* et seq. above).

Her notion of autonomy becomes sharper when discussing Judith Butler's critique of the autonomous subject and Butler's view that relationality is inscribed in the subject itself as relational autonomy, while for Rössler the concept of autonomy and the idea of decisional privacy is not "substantially" but only "procedurally" relational.[83] Relationality "may be conceived and practised as a condition for the possibility of autonomy on the one hand, but also as an obstacle to a person's autonomy."[84] Although we live in relational contexts, autonomy, Rössler maintains, has to do with the option, "to break free from such projects and break away from such relationships" so as to reflect by ourselves upon our convictions, needs and desires.[85] This is

80 Rössler 2005 pp. 84ff.
81 Rössler 2005 p. 89.
82 Rössler 2005 p. 91.
83 Rössler 2005 p. 104.
84 Rössler 2005 p. 105.
85 Rössler 2005 p. 105.

particularly important, for instance, where women want to break with an imposed way of life, including ascriptions and assumptions based on a traditional gender-based hierarchy. The possibility of distancing oneself from given relationships does not imply conceiving the autonomous person as disconnected from them. Her concept of autonomy includes "a reflexive relationship on the part of the free person", freedom as autonomy being the key issue of privacy protection.[86] In this regard, she opposes her notions of privacy and freedom to those developed by Hannah Arendt (cf. next section).

For Rössler, Arendt's distinction between the private sphere of biological necessity and the public sphere of freedom is Aristotelean. Arendt describes a history of decline of this "unreasonably strict and essentialist social ontology".[87] But Arendt is also aware of the modern concept of privacy understood as "protection of intimacy" as opposed to social and political realms. Arendt regards a completely public life as "superficial" and a retreat into privacy as "indispensable".[88] Rössler, however, claims this separation implies that some activities belong *per se* either to the private or the public realm, which is an inadequate notion of privacy. Something similar happens with Arendt's notion of freedom. Although Arendt understands the separation between the public (free) realm and the private realm as being a functional one, "this separation blinds her to the fact that what is ostensibly private always plays a part in the public sphere: that women are women, for example."[89] Arendt purportedly has a reduced concept of freedom that "blinds" her also to seeing freedom as autonomy as being a condition of and not an exclusion from freedom in the public realm. An opposition between private freedom and public control as proposed, for instance, by Edward Shils, fails "to pay sufficient attention to the interplay of private freedom and public — social, political — space".[90] What sort of freedom does privacy protect? "For a precise answer to the question of what sort of

86 Rössler 2005 p. 107.
87 Rössler 2005 p. 108.
88 Rössler 2005 p. 108.
89 Rössler 2005 p. 108.
90 Rössler 2005 p. 110.

freedom is protected by privacy, these reflections can thus be no more than hints, because any such answer would necessitate a theory of the public sphere too. But this is not the place for such a theory."[91] She gives some indications for this issue at the end of her book.

The second dimension of privacy, namely informational privacy, deals with the question of the "control of what other people can *know* about oneself"[92] which means control over the "self-presentation" of individuals, a key phenomenon of whoness which, of course, does not come into Rössler's purview and which also signals implicitly that personal privacy has to do essentially with the interplay between self-disclosure and self-concealment in a shared world. Rössler truncates the phenomenon of self-presentation to individual *self-expression*, which requires no interplay among whos. She describes situations arising particularly from digital information and communication technologies such as "telephones, CCTV and video surveillance of shops and public spaces, 'tracing' on the internet, data transmission between firms or insurance companies, or the audiovisual supervision of houses and flats".[93] Informational privacy deals with protection of personal data for which she proposes the following typology: 1) "the privacy of thoughts and mental states, of feelings and views in general.", 2) data "that can be used not only to identify one person among all possible others, but also to ascertain a person's preferences, traits and habits", 3) data dealing with "everything (legitimately) done by a person within her own home" and 4) data relating "to activities and habits taking place outside the house and to the spatio-temporal facts about a person" (video and CCTV surveillance).[94]

She describes various contexts in which the principle of autonomy collides with other principles and interests, giving rise to various kinds of conflicts between a 'wanting to know' and a 'wanting to hide'. The others who want to know can be "unspecified others" such as state institutions, financial interests and the service sector or "specified

91 Rössler 2005 p. 110.

92 Rössler 2005 p. 111.

93 Rössler 2005 p. 119.

94 Rössler 2005 pp. 123f.

others" such as friends and intimates. She underscores that although "the self of a person is constituted dialogically", "self-consciousness" and "self-relationship", i.e., the capacity of a person to be autonomous, is the essential issue that privacy protection must take care of.[95] She writes, "Clearly, this dialogical dimension must not eclipse the *monological* component that must be provided by the subject if he truly wants to see himself as autonomous, possibly in circumstances when respect is denied to him," the dialogical dimension being a necessary but not sufficient condition of the self.[96] Nevertheless she points out that when dealing with these conflicts, ethical and moral perspectives cannot be strictly separated.

The third dimension of privacy, namely local privacy, involves the "private home", including "a room of one's own" and the family. In the last chapter "Interfaces: Public and Private" Rössler provides some hints on the public and private "interfaces", particularly with "the 'publicization' of intimate details that are traditionally still viewed as private."[97] While discussing Thomas Nagel's notions of "concealment and exposure"[98] Rössler agrees with the need for "a liberal culture in which civility and indifference in the social realm guarantee and organize each individual subject's scope for freedom and autonomy".[99] The separation between the private and the public spheres being conventional in nature, its function is to protect the autonomy of individuals in both realms. Again, that *reified* social interplay, a specific socio-ontological constellation of being (see *1.6 The private individual and private property as a mode of reified sociation: the gainful game (classical political economy, Marx)*) is an historical condition of possibility for such separation remains hidden to Rössler. At the same time, Rössler criticizes Nagel's view of a 'neutral' language in the public sphere. To understand something as a private or public matter is also a question of public "agenda-setting". But, she asks, "who puts what on

---

95 Rössler 2005 p. 132.

96 Rössler 2005 p. 133.

97 Rössler 2005 p. 173.

98 Nagel 1988 p. 1.

99 Rössler 2005 p. 180.

the public agenda?"[100] One can conceal or reveal a 'type', i.e. an issue concerning a particular kind of individual, by concealing or revealing a 'token', i.e. an issue concerning everybody, thus introducing a bias. Rössler summarizes the issue of autonomy that constitutes the core of her view on the task of privacy protection as follows, "A person is autonomous if she is able to identify authentically with the desires that govern her actions and with her objectives and projects, and if she is also able to pursue these objectives. She is autonomous if she in principle reflects on how she wishes to live and what sort of person she wishes to be, and is then able to live accordingly."[101] There remain "dissonant identities" between the public and the private person which she illustrates with Henry James' story *The Private Life*.

Although Rössler does not overlook the dialogical dimension of the self, she makes an appeal for a "monological" notion following the modern Western tradition. This forms the basis for her concept of autonomy as a capacity of self-reflection on one's life by distancing oneself from others and from a given morality. By doing this, Rössler apparently adheres implicitly to the Socratic tradition of taking care of oneself (ἐπιμέλεια ἑαυτοῦ *epimeleia heautou*) by giving reasons about what I think to be the case, and what and why I want to do something or not. But the Socratic tradition is a dialogical one. The Socratic self is not the modern subject distancing itself from others based on her autonomy as enabled by reified, money-mediated sociation. It is not based on its heteronomy vis-à-vis the divine but vis-à-vis the human other. It is a relational self, as Judith Butler remarks. The metaphysical tradition calls the ontological heteronomy of all beings as creatures *ens ab alio*. From a phenomenological perspective, the self is being *in* the world, which implies not only being-with-others but also being bodily and mindfully 'ex-posed' 'ec-statically' (lit.: out-standingly) to past, present and future. This temporo-spatial bodily and mindful exposure of human life (βίος *bios*) is limited by birth and death.

---

100 Rössler 2005 p. 183.

101 Rössler 2005 p. 185.

Natality and mortality — as highlighted by Hannah Arendt and Martin Heidegger — are the markers of human ontological heteronomy or contingency. None of this is addressed by Rössler. Gender duality signifies ontologically, among other things, gender diversity resulting from possible bodily responses to the call of others. From this perspective, autonomy is the self's response to the call of the world. It is not by distancing itself *from* the others and the world that the self contingently shapes itself but by taking a possibly dynamic stance in the interplay *with* others in a common, shared world-openness. A self's identity does not come from 'within' itself, but from identifying with offers of identity shining in from out there in the world, especially from certain significant others.

The original or ontological sense of privacy concerns not only the social interplay of concealment and unconcealment of the self but, more deeply, the event of concealment and unconcealment of world-openness itself that the self (the selves) mirrors in different 'cultural' ways. The possibility of withdrawal from the gaze of others and of shaping one's one private world is enabled historically above all by the 'eventuation' of a socio-ontological constellation of reified-value sociation. The value of privacy originates in and as the originary event of the opening of world, the bodily self being the temporo-spatial singularity of world-openness reflected in a plurality of whos for whom things can appear as *what* they are according, not only to changing semiotic and semantic interrelations among beings constituting a world, but also to changes in world-openness itself, through which and as which such relations are understood and lived. From this perspective, the 'normal' or 'conventional' social view of given customs or ethos is (socio-)ontologically open to questioning, since the self as being-in-the-world-with-others is open to different historical possibilities of shared being-in-the-world.

Rössler overlooks here and elsewhere the difference between the ontic-factual and this deeper ontological level, which latter she seems to understand solely, and mostly merely implicitly, in the sense of subjectivist metaphysics. For instance, she identifies the self with the single individual *as* separated ontic-factually, i.e. locally, from others and has problems admitting that this ontic-factual isolation does not imply that the self is not basically constituted by selecting and shaping an identity from a 'shining-back' from others and other 'things' (a landscape, a musical instrument,...) in the world. Rationality and self-reflection are not the originary way for the self to realize her autonomy but are responses to the ontological heteronomy of human existence, i.e. to the inextricable power interplay with other whos in the world. All are embedded in moods *as* which world-openness resonates rather than being properties of worldless subjects (such as their 'inner feelings'). There is an intellectualist undertone in Rössler's understanding of autonomy as based on rationality and self-reflection that indicates the dualistic heritage of modernity's separating reason and emotion within a worldless psyche-capsule.

The ontological heteronomy of the self, i.e. its ineluctable exposure to the interplay among freely self-casting selves and to its surroundings, is what constitutes, from a phenomenological perspective, the value of privacy as a play of self-revealing and self-concealing. Rössler's modern autonomous self needs the protection of a retreat from others and public openness to become aware of its autonomy and even become itself without, however, severing its being-in-a-shared-world. This gives rise to the problem of how to bridge the gap between the private, solitary, autonomous self and the public self, for which "interfaces" are needed. But "ruptures" — this is the last word of Rössler's book — remain nevertheless. The rupture that Rössler focuses on is "the solitude of one's private life history, in being-for-oneself in one's private thoughts as opposed to one's relationship to others".[102] The human self, however, itself brings an ontological "rupture" into being; it 'privatizes' and singularizes being to become an individual, singular source of freedom, instead of existing merely 'normally' in a fixed framework based on its present historical contours, human customs being legitimated on the basis of the weight and inertia of sheer presence. The value of privacy in a creative, philosophical, ontological sense is to protect individual creativity to question an hegemonic understanding of being so as to find

[102] Rössler 2005 p. 192.

the way out of (overbearing) metaphysical casts of being based, for instance, on the overwhelming presence of digital technology and digital ontology that forms today's ontological horizon (cf. Chaps. 2 and 3).

The autonomous private self in its solitude, who is at the heart of Rössler's "value of privacy", is only ever the converse side of the heteronomous, public self who is exposed to the finitude and vulnerability of human existence in the world. To *be* somewho requires showing off who one is in the world. A who is also endowed with the capacity, i.e. the power, as a self of sharing a common world-openness to provide different responses to the inexhaustible call(s) of being. This is the utmost task of the human evaluator, her ownmost, singular and inalienable personal task, which is proper (ἴδιος) or 'private' to her as a self but that she can forfeit, say, by either identifying or becoming identified with her (digital) data as a digital object of exchange in the cyberworld (cf. *2.5 The parallel cyberworld that fits like a glove* and *3.5.2 The gainful game unleashes its freedom in the cyberworld*). This is *one* way in which the self can lose its self to everyday averageness today.

Negative and positive freedom in Isaiah Berlin's sense are possibilities that, as Rössler remarks, do not constitute the realm of the self from the point of view of modern autonomy. Freedom conceived as the ontological eruption of free and contingent selves into world-openness, however, enables also 'autonomous', and indeed singular, responses to the way the world grants itself, or 'eventuates' historically. The value of personal privacy in the modern sense is that it keeps open the historical possibilities for individual, even singular, selves to 'erupt' in the world by enabling room for play of self-concealing and self-revealing. The interplay with others and the options for self-identification on offer in an historical world in a given situation, through which the self constitutes herself in a shared world, does not rely on her will to control and protect her autonomy, but above all on the mutual *trust* among the players as the fragile ontological ground upon which both positive and negative forms of mutual estimation situated in the spectrum between respect and disrespect are possible. Trust in this fundamental ontological sense as that which bridges the abyssal individual freedom characterizing human being includes, of course, also the deficient and privative modes of *mistrust*. By placing the issue of control at the core of her notion of autonomy, Rössler is blind for the issue of trust, which is not addressed in her book. The value of privacy within today's world addresses especially this possibility.

It is our 'ec-static' bodily and mindful existence that erupts into the open which is the historical time-space of ineluctably shared existential self-castings. Without a view of the value of privacy as a valuable play between concealing and revealing through which the players in the interplay enjoy also respite from over-exposure by being able to withdraw from the exertions of self-presentation as who, one succumbs to the illusion that the individual 'subject' could encapsulate itself in an autonomous solitariness and merely 'express' this self-formed self out there in the world. An individual self exists, however, only as a back-and-forth between withdrawal and exposure, showing off who one is in the interplay with others and also retiring into a more intimate, private world in which the play of showing off oneself as self to one's intimates plays out differently. Solitariness is only one, very specific, mode of personal privacy, and personal privacy does not amount to a privation of self-showing *tout court* nor to being 'outside' the world. Even solitary privacy involves showing oneself to oneself in the sense of pretending to be who one is for oneself, which, in turn, may be either mere pretence or genuine. Without an explicit view of the peculiar open human dimension of whoness, however, this cannot be seen.

The next section turns to an appraisal of Hannah Arendt's well-known study, *The Human Condition*, which in a certain sense is a richer and broader approach than Rössler's because Arendt attempts to articulate the phenomenon of whoness, which is *the* way out of modern subjectivist metaphysics.

1.11 Arendt on whoness in the world[103]

1.11.1 Arendt's discovery of the plurality of whos in *The Human Condition*

Perhaps the most exciting chapter in Hannah Arendt's major work, *The Human Condition*,[104] is the pivotal Chapter V on Action, completing the triad of the work's central trichotomy between labour, work and action. If labour for Arendt is the movement of the natural life-process of human being itself, based on biological need, and work is the movement of production that brings forth the works constituting an enduring, stable, material world, the realm of action is the movement of action and speech constituting what Arendt regards as the political realm proper. The chapter starts with an obvious, indeed seemingly trivial, observation, namely, that human beings exist in a "plurality",[105] thus taking up again an insight enunciated already in the first chapter, where Arendt pronounces plurality to be "the condition of human action" (1:9). This observation already offers the germ of the possibility of breaking with the venerable tradition of Western metaphysics of determining the human essence without recourse to the plurality of humankind as a determination that fundamentally affects any attempt to think human being itself.

Arendt passes up the opportunity to recast human being itself taking into account humankind's plurality, however, not only by making the distinction between "political life" (1:7) and "metaphysical thought" (1:9) and claiming the pertinence of plurality as the "conditio per quam" (1:7) only for the political sphere, but also by drawing a line between the "human condition" that is the subject of her study, and "human nature" (1:10), as constituted inter alia by "thought and reason" (1:10), which is left to one side. Behind this latter distinction lies that between who and what, which Arendt explicitly introduces with a reference to Augustine

---

[103] This entire section is the final authorial responsibility of Michael Eldred.

[104] Hannah Arendt 1958/1998.

[105] Arendt 1958/1998 Section 24 p. 175; hereafter cited in the form 24:175.

who, addressing himself or his god, posed both the question, "tu, quis es?" ("You, who are you?"[106]) and "quod ergo sum, Deus meus. Quae natura sum?" ("What therefore am I, my God? Of what nature am I?" x. 17) The answer Augustine gives to the first question is "A man", which is a what-answer in the third person singular, whereas the second question is claimed by Augustine to be unanswerable by man, but only by God, who knows everything of him (eius omnia x. 5). Arendt goes along with Augustine, without even noting that he gives a what-answer to the who question, and agreeing with him that "it is highly unlikely that we, who can know, determine, and define the natural essences of all things surrounding us, which we are not, should ever be able to do the same for ourselves" (1:10). In doing so, she capitulates doubly to the metaphysical tradition, firstly by obliterating the genuine question concerning whoness, and secondly by accepting the metaphysical pretension to determining "natural essences of all things", hence denying the historical nature of the casting of beings in their being. This metaphysical pretension extends anyway to human nature itself by giving metaphysical determinations of human being itself in terms of the soul, intellect and their essential qualities such as appetite, reasoning, etc., i.e., in terms of a what, a quidditas, an essentia.

It is strange in this connection that Arendt does not go into the significance of Augustine's *Confessiones* as a disclosure of the most intimate and 'secret' events and feelings from Augustine's life (whoness, quissity) through which one can see that the difference between quod and quis is at least immanent in his text, its very life-blood. Augustine is speaking intimately with his god in a you-and-me encounter, asking how he could meet him face to face. "Ubi ergo inveni te, ut discerem te, nisi in te supra me? ... Sero te amavi, pulchritudo tam antiqua et tam nova..." ("Where then have I found you to get to know you if not in you above me?" x. 26 "Late I have loved you, you beauty so old and so new..." x. 27) This is a passage from a love letter, written in the privacy of Augustine's heart. The intimate dialogical character of his *Confessiones*, however, does not impel Augustine to question the

---

106 Augustine *Confessiones* x. 6 cited 1:10.

determination of the essence of human being itself as composed of body and soul: "Et ecce corpus et anima in me mihi praesto sunt, unum exterius, et alterum interius." ("And here are body and soul present in me, the body more exterior, the soul more interior." x. 17), and Arendt follows him in this oversight.

Nevertheless, in the section on Action, Arendt does make use of the insight into plurality to introduce the problematic of how human beings "disclose" themselves "to each other" (24:176) as "who" (24:178) in "speech and action" (Gk: λέξις, πρᾶξις cf. 4:25), human plurality itself being "the basic condition of both action and speech" (24:175). She sees clearly that the question regarding "*who* somebody is" (25:181) has to be clearly distinguished from that concerning "*what* he is" (25:181), where this what is explicated as "his qualities, gifts, talents, and shortcomings" (24:179) that he "shares with others like him" (25:181). The shift of focus to what, that is determined in the third person singular, has "the result that his specific uniqueness escapes us" (25:181). By contrast, who someone is, is disclosed to others through words and deeds, especially works and deeds of love, that reveal this who's uniqueness, which is impossible "without a name" (24:180). Bearing a unique, proper name is hence a hallmark of whoness, but Arendt does not say as much explicitly, although this lies deep in the Judaeo-Christian tradition.[107] Nor does she use the term 'whoness' or 'quissity' to mark this dimension of social interaction among human beings off from the traditional category of 'whatness' or 'quiddity'. "Who" for Arendt is in any case explicitly a category or dimension of disclosure, of revelation, and that within the shared public realm in which name-bearing "men" show to each other *who* they are through word and deed.

There is, however, no ontological follow-through in Arendt's presentation of the phenomenon of whoness (and not only of whoness). What she offers is a philosophical anthropology interwoven with

---

[107] Already in Genesis (Gen. 2:7) it is said that Yahve created man (âdam; adâma=earth), thus making a normal word into a proper name in Gen. 4:25, und

historical observations from Western history, especially from Greek and Roman antiquity. Clearly defined ontological concepts determining modes of presencing do not shape up for the reader's mind; consequently, the phenomena being addressed are often obscure, implicit, mixed and open to surmise. Even crucial phenomena such as "speech and action" remain remarkably diffuse. They are alluded to countless times, but their ontological structure as modes of human being is never conceptually clarified. Such clarification presumably could be derived from Plato and Aristotle, to whom she often refers, although the Homeric Achilles would seem to be her chosen paradigm for word and deed, which does not provide us with any conceptual clarification, but rather with suggestive allusions to what phenomena she has in mind.

Nonetheless, Arendt's many novel and stimulating insights into the interplay that is human action deserve attention with a view to bringing them to their proper, elaborated socio-ontological concepts. To start with it must be noted that her use of the term 'action' (and 'interaction') is not a happy one because its difference from concepts of action and interaction, say, in Newtonian mechanics remains unclarified, and indeed, later on, gets thoroughly confused with them. A concept of interplay is entirely lacking and is at best only implicitly present, folded into the texture of her script, for instance, when she writes, "action, though it may proceed from nowhere, so to speak, acts into a medium where every reaction becomes a chain reaction" (26:190). It is inappropriate to employ, without warnings signs, a term so overladen and overdetermined with a meaning from modern physics. She continues, "Since action acts upon beings who are capable of their own actions, reaction, apart from being a response, is always a new action that strikes out on its own and affects others." (26:190) This observation hits the mark, and because it hits the mark, it is thoroughly inept to employ the term 'reaction' at all. But Arendt has implicitly already committed herself to this term by having chosen 'action' as a, if not *the*, key, albeit inadequately defined, concept in her work, whose German

---

5:3 (cf. the commentary to the Bible de Jérusalem, translated into French by L'Ecole biblique de Jérusalem, Paris 1961).

edition is entitled with the Latin, *Vita Activa* or *Active Life*.[108] The realm or dimension she is addressing, of "people ... acting and speaking together" (27:198) through which they show to each other who they are and perhaps come to "full appearance [in] the shining brightness we once called glory" (24:180), is not that of action and reaction, no matter (to employ Arendt's own words) how surprising, unexpected, unpredictable, boundless social interaction may be, but of *interplay*. It is the play that has to be underscored, not the action, and it is no accident that play is also that which takes place on a stage, for she understands the dimension of "acting and speaking" explicitly as the realm in which human beings "make their appearance" (27:199), revealing and disclosing their selves as *who* they are. On the other hand, interplay takes place also in private: in the interplay of love as a groundlessly grounding way to be who with another, where speaking easily becomes hollow.

It is the character of the movement of human beings' togetherness as interplay, whose explicit ontological structure I have presented in detail elsewhere,[109] that lends "human affairs" the "frailty" (26:188ff) that Arendt attributes to them. The "web of relationships" (25:181ff) among whos, which Arendt regards merely as a "metaphor" (25:183) and not as

108 Presumably in the tradition of actio vs. operatio and Thomas Aquinas' actus hominis vs. actus humanus, where the latter is with ratio (reason), or in the tradition of actio immanens (ἕξις) vs. actio transiens (ποίησις) which, of course, goes back to Aristotle's *Metaphysics* Book Theta, the West's foundational book on the ontology of *productive power*. And again an Aristotelean distinction: "Wo das Tätigsein etwas hervorbringt, ist ein doppelter Ursprung gefordert, der aktive Ursprung aus der Wirklichkeit des Tätigen und der passive Ursprung in einem passiv Bewegten." Engl.: "Where activity brings something forth, a double origin is required: the active origin from the reality of the active agent and the passive origin in something that is passively moved." *Hist. Wört. der Philos*. Bd. 1, Actio immanens/actio transiens, with references to the controversy with Johannes Duns Scotus: "operatio is a quality of the soul of the kind of fieri [happening ME], which is not movement in the proper sense", and also the distinction actus exercitus / actus signatus (the latter with expression of will).

109 Cf. Eldred 2008/2011. Cf. also Fink 2010 on play.

a fully fledged concept, is likewise, ontologically speaking, the interplay in which human beings willy-nilly entangle themselves with each other already by virtue of sharing a world with one another. Arendt herself has the germ of a more adequate concept with "to be among men" (inter homines esse)" (1:7).

1.11.2 The question concerning whoness as the key question of social ontology

The question concerning whoness is the key question of human togetherness in the world. Although Arendt refers to Augustine as the source for this question in the history of philosophy, it is Heidegger who puts the question on the philosophical agenda as an existential-ontological question. Heidegger's Marburg lectures on *Fundamental Problems of Phenomenology* in Summer Semester 1927[110] question in depth the traditional determinations of human being as some kind of being-at-hand (Vorhandenheit), such as res cogitans or a moral subject, and open up an alternative casting of human being as Dasein that allows a radically different ontological understanding of the selfhood of the self by marking off what from who:

> Das Seiende, das wir selbst sind, das Dasein, kann als solches mit der Frage, *was* ist das?, überhaupt nicht *befragt* werden. Zu diesem Seienden gewinnen wir nur Zugang, wenn wir fragen: *wer* ist es? Das Dasein ist nicht durch die Washeit, sondern [...] durch die *Werheit* konstituiert. Die Antwort gibt nicht eine Sache, sondern ein Ich, Du, Wir. Aber wir fragen doch andererseits: *Was* ist dieses *Wer* und diese Werheit des Daseins, — was ist das Wer im Unterschied von dem vorgenannten Was im engeren Sinne der Sachheit des Vorhandenen? Zweifellos fragen wir so. Aber darin bekundet sich nur, daß dieses Was, mit dem wir auch nach dem Wesen des Wer fragen, offenbar sich nicht mit dem Was im Sinne der Washeit decken kann.[111]

> The being that we are ourselves, Dasein [human existence, ME], cannot be *questioned* at all as such with the question, *what* is that? We only gain access to this being when we ask: *who* is it? Dasein is not constituted by whatness, but by whoness. The answer does not specify a thing, but an I, you, we. But, on the other hand, we ask nevertheless: *what* is this *who* and this whoness of Dasein —

---

110 Heidegger GA24 1975.

111 Heidegger GA24:169.

> what is who in distinction to the above-mentioned what in the narrow sense of the thingness of what is present-at-hand/occurrent. Doubtless we ask thus. But in doing so it is merely declared that this what with which we ask also for the essence of the who obviously cannot coincide with the what in the sense of whatness.

This long quote rubs the question concerning whoness under our noses, so to speak. It cannot be left in any sort of implicitness if the core of existential ontology is to be worthy of the name. Here, drawing on my other work, only a few brief indications will be given of how whoness as the mode of human beings sharing a world with one another can be laid out. Arendt mentions, for example, that making an appearance in the public realm, i.e. action, "without a name, a 'who' attached to it is meaningless" (24:180). A who has an identity, and the core of this identity is the who's proper name. A singular human existence must be identified with something that it is not, namely, in the first place, with a proper name, in order to *be* a who at all. Identity as who therefore presupposes difference and, more than that, an identity of identity and difference, since identity itself includes difference within itself. Who someone *is* as him*self* is only possible as an identity with something *other*. If the public sphere is a realm of appearance in which all whos are play-acting in an interplay with one another, the first mask they bear is their proper names that identify who each *is* — including for each who itself. Each who is a dramatis persona, i.e. a person bearing a mask in a drama, i.e. an action, played out with other actors, and this is not a metaphor, but, on the contrary, the ontological fundament on which such a thing as play-acting on a theatre stage is possible at all.

Actions out there in the world with one another are certain kinds of movements that bring forth some kind of change, some kind of μεταβολή, lit. over-turning. Arendt notes that "with word and deed we insert ourselves into the human world" (24:176) which implies, in particular, that such words and deeds bring forth a change in the world, if only in the sense of making an impression on the world through showing oneself as somewho. Such making-an-impression, however, is already the exercise of a *power* if power is understood broadly enough in the Greek sense of δύναμις as the potential to bring forth a change, an over-turning, a movement of some kind or other. The self-showing of whos to each other is therefore in the fundamental, neutral signification a *power play*, if only in the sense that appearances in the world through word and deed make some sort of impression on each other, even when they are otherwise ineffective in the sense of achieving a certain aim. That whoness as mode of existing in the world with others is essentially a power play is not seen by Arendt at all. It is, above all, a who's powers and abilities that are put on display through acting and speaking, and such display determines who that individual is in the shared world. The whoness of the who is a shining-back (Widerschein[112]) from the world in which a self is constituted precisely through a power play with others, not only for the others, but, first and foremost, for oneself. Without seeing that acting and speaking are fundamentally an exercise of individual powers, Arendt nevertheless can say, "Through [speech and action] men distinguish themselves [...]: they are the modes in which human beings appear to each other [...] qua men" (24:176). However, Arendt restricts this speaking and acting to a separate sphere of existence that she calls the public or political realm by distinguishing acting from labouring and working.

Arendt also restricts the human power to begin "something new on our own initiative" to acting: "To act, in its most general sense, means to take an initiative, to begin, (as the Greek word *archein*, 'to begin', 'to lead', and eventually 'to rule', indicates), to set something into motion (which is the original meaning of the Latin agere)," thereby bringing Greek ἀρχή into play, a concept that bears a heavy weight in Greek productivist metaphysics. "To set something into motion" in metaphysics means paradigmatically to be the starting-point (ἀρχή) for a *productive* activity as the power to bring about a change/movement of something ultimately into a finished product. From this ontology of productive movement/change, all philosophical and modern scientific understanding of movement is tacitly dominated, including Arendt's, even when she transplants the human power to be a beginning from productive activity to acting in the political sphere merely by omitting

---

112 Cf. Heidegger GA24:226, 229.

the end-product of productive movement, hence basically following Aristotle. 'Being a beginning', of course, cannot be limited to 'being born', i.e. to the natality that Arendt underscores, but means instead the power to cast oneself as a self into the temporal dimension of the future — at any time during one's existence.

Because she does not pay attention to the ontological structure of movement, Arendt also does not draw the necessary import from her insistence on the main thesis that action is always action among a *plurality* of "men", each of whom is a beginning, an ἀρχή.[113] If this is so, then the interactions among such men are the *interplay* among a plurality of ἀρχαί where the term 'interplay' is warranted to mark it off from the ontology of productive movement, which is an acting upon a physical thing (or a human regarded as a physical thing). Where a plurality of 'beginnings' are 'at play' with one another in action, what happens has the character of "inherent unpredictability", a character that Arendt sees only deriving from i) "the inability to foretell all the logical consequences of a particular act" (26:191) and ii) the inconclusiveness "of the story which, as the result of action, begins and establishes itself as soon as the fleeting moment of the deed is past", but can reveal "its full meaning [...] only when it has ended" (26:192).

Hence, for Arendt, the unpredictability of an action does not reside first of all in the very ontology of interplay among a plurality of players, but in the incalculability of the further ramifications of an action which gather finally into a story about *who* someone has been. For her, unpredictability of an action is overcome by making a story out of how the action's ramifications play out, a story that is unknown to the actor himself, but only 'fabricated' as a narrative told as a rounded whole by a storyteller: "what the storyteller narrates must necessarily be hidden to the actor himself" (26:192). The inconclusiveness of a life-story is contrasted with "fabrication" in which "the finished product" (26:192) is

[113] To be a beginning and thus free is a thought to be found throughout the metaphysical tradition, for instance with Kant (see above section) or Adam Smith: "...in the great chess-board of human society, every single piece has a principle of motion of its own..." Smith 1759/2000 Part VI, Section II Chapter II, penultimate paragraph p. 343.

already envisaged by the "craftsman". However, it is the *plurality* of players itself, the multiplicity of ἀρχαί, that already obscures the view of an outcome of interplay, not the inconclusiveness of the outcome per se. Hence, *pace* Arendt, the "frailty of human affairs" (the title of Section 26) derives in the first place from the ontological structure of the movement of *interplay* among a plurality of players and is, in this strict ontological sense, a *power play* whose ontology is distinct from that of productive movement.[114] Furthermore, it should be noted that Arendt's determination of the whoness of a who as a narrative related about him or her in retrospect by others, after someone's life-trajectory has concluded, is the *third person* perspective about who someone *has been*, i.e. with a retrospective look back into the temporal dimension of beenness (Gewesenheit in contrast to Vergangenheit or 'past'). For the first person, however, whoness is first and foremost the lead perspective of *who I will become*, of casting my self out of the possibilities offered to me arriving from the future, and is hence forward-looking. Because the future is always open for as long as I live, who I am is inconclusive, but therein lies also the *freedom* of my whoness. Here it is apt to cite Pindar: γένοι', οἷος ἐσσὶ μαθών. ("Become, learning who you are." *Pyth*. 2).

To recapitulate, for Arendt, the incalculability of action as an interplay among a plurality is not the issue. Rather, for her the issue is the uncertainty of the story of a certain who that will unfold from his actions. This inconclusiveness and uncertainty constitute for her the "frailty of human affairs" whose remedy, she claims, was sought by the Greeks in the founding a the πόλις as the "space of appearance" (27:198) in which "men" strive for "immortal fame" (27:193), i.e. a standing presence within togetherness with others whose standingness is given by the appreciative reflections from the others. The "prototype of

114 Both Friedrich Schiller and Johan Huizinga are famously associated with bringing the concept of play to the fore (cf. Huizinga 1939/2004), but neither works out the ontological structure of interplay as a groundless power play, in contradistinction to that of productive power, as laid out in Eldred 2008/2011 Chap. 5.

action for Greek antiquity" is imbued with "the so-called agonal spirit, the passionate drive to show one's self in measuring up against others that underlies the concept of politics prevalent in the city-states" (27:194). By *producing* the framework of a polis with its constitution and laws, as Plato and Aristotle proposed, a space for the standing phallic[115] presence of men as whos through speaking and acting was set up. Thereby, action, whoness and standing presence are brought into connection with one another in a way that remains hidden to Arendt, since she thinks not ontologically but rather socio-historically. The end of the πόλις, its raison d'être, is therefore to provide the space of togetherness for the contestation among whos of their phallic, standing presence through speaking and acting.

Phallic whoness as a mode of presencing is therefore the essence of the polis, i.e. of worldsharing, and this need not be taken merely as a state of affairs pertinent only to Greek antiquity. In *this* sense I can concur with Arendt's assertion that the "space of appearance [where] men are together in the manner of speech and action [...] predates and precedes all formal constitution of the public realm and the various forms of government" (28:199) when read not ontogenetically, but ontologically. Action, in Arendt's sense, is therefore, properly speaking, the *interplay of whos striving for phallic, standing presence in contest with one another* whose result is, hopefully, lasting, indeed immortal fame. Such interplay is a power play. The ontology of phallic whoness, of course, is only ever tantalizingly implicit in Arendt.

Power, in Arendt's use of the word, "is what keeps the public realm, the potential space of appearance between acting and speaking men, in existence" (28:200). This can be translated by saying that power is the potential for playing the phallic who-game of standing presence among men and hence, in this translated sense is a "potentiality in being

115 It goes without saying that 'phallic' is used here neither in a sexual nor psychoanalytic nor a pejorative sense, but points to the standing presence of a human being presenting him/herself as somewho which is behind the excellence (ἀρετή, more traditionally translated in moral philosophy as 'virtue', related to Latin 'vir' or 'man') of ἀνδρεία (literally: 'manliness', and more traditionally translated as 'courage'). Cf. Eldred 1999.

together" (28:201). Power in Arendt's sense is thus the potentiality keeping open the space for the who-game of standing presence. This *potential* is *actually* played out within this who-space as the *energy* (ἐνέργεια, at-work-ness) of mutual who-estimation and who-stand-contestation. Such potential is present above all in cities that provide a place for "men" to show themselves off to each other as who they are in a contest of mutual estimation whose ongoing outcomes remain incalculable. The "striving toward omnipotence" or "hubris" (28:202) can be interpreted as the striving for the highest stand as who, a futile striving insofar as an omnipotence would annihilate the potential for contestation among whos, as if other men were, or could ever be, entirely without power in the sense of lacking altogether the potency to make any change whatsoever in the world. Only dead men are impotent in this sense, and not even they are impotent insofar as their status, name and perhaps even fame as somewho *moves* those who are alive.

If power is conceived as "what keeps the public realm, the potential space of appearance between acting and speaking men, in existence", then such power is not man-made at all, but rather the enabling of the open clearing for the phallic power play among whos in which it is a matter of coming to a stand in the estimating presence of others. Such power, as the enabling of the open clearing for the who-game, is the granting of an historical mode of presencing among human beings conceived as the starting-points of their own movements in a contest of phallic estimation. Granting grants. In such an open temporal space, standing presence is possible and the names of some out-standing whos can also be remembered, especially in posterity's remembrance. In Arendt there is hardly a trace of such enabling granting of presence, but an implicit trace nevertheless, that is here uncovered and brought to light in an explicit explication. Instead, she regards the "public realm, the space within the world which men need in order to appear at all" as 'the work of man'"(29:208), thus denying the groundless granting of (an historical mode of) presencing itself. Without such enabling, granting power, as Arendt remarks unwittingly citing *Ecclesiastes*, "there is no remembrance". The open clearing for the who-game is ontologically prior to the political realm, which accounts for why Arendt does not speak of the contents of politics but instead of the "space of appearance [where] men are together in the manner of speech and action", i.e. the public sphere where they can attain, for a time, standing presence and perhaps outlast their mortal existence by establishing their proper names in collective memory.

Arguing against Plato's and Aristotle's thinking on politics, she explicitly excludes "legislating and the execution of decisions by vote" (27:195) because they are akin to men acting productively "like craftsmen"(27:195), i.e. according to the productionist paradigm of work tacitly adopted by Plato and Aristotle. She thus senses the one-sidedness of the productionist paradigm underlying all metaphysical thinking. Despite this, she is thoroughly misleading throughout the book by referring to and treating this public space of appearance as the political realm. She laments the historical loss of such a space for the who-game, which has given way to 'everybody' and 'people' counting without distinction in 'society'. For her, "action can be judged only by the criterion of greatness because it is in its nature to break through the commonly accepted and reach into the extraordinary" (28:205), i.e. the phallically out-standing, through which standing a who leaves his mark in historical remembrance. Such action is energy as the at-work-ness of a who's individual powers and abilities of whatever kind, including especially rhetorical powers, which Arendt restricts to "speaking and acting", that come to be estimated, reflected and affirmed in the open space of presencing and absencing for the who-game. It matters not so much *what* is said, but *how* it is said *as* a self-presencing and self-presentation of *who* somebody is. Arendt is right to mark off such "acting and speaking" from τέχνη ποιητική (cf. 28:207), which is specifically *productive* power and not the power at work in the "space of appearance". Her book is a plea for the dignity of the agonistic contestation of who-standing in the clearing of phallic togetherness vis-à-vis the 'mere' making of enduring things by the *homo faber* and the 'mere' labouring of the *animal laborans* to fulfil human biological needs.

1.11.3 The untenability of the distinction between labour, work and action

After having clarified what is to be understood by action, I turn to Arendt's postulation of "three fundamental human activities" (1:7) corresponding to three different determinations of human being itself, namely, *animal laborans*, *homo faber* and *homo publicus* (whereby Arendt does not employ this last term). She has an historical paradigm in view in drawing these distinctions, namely, the Greek polis. The sphere for the first kind of activity is that of private, hidden existence concerned with biological needs and functions of the body, including especially birth and death, whose need-fulfilment was achieved by the *labour* of slaves and women in the household. The second kind of activity is that of craftsmen's *work* making more durable things such as tables that are not immediately consumed in the satisfaction of need and therefore contribute to building a stable, durable world of things in which men live, i.e. a world's produced artificial infrastructure. The third kind of activity, as we have seen more clearly through the explication above, is that of *acting* as a who in a power play of mutual estimation, through which human existence comes to stand and shine in the shared world of the public realm.

Three different kinds of activity corresponding to three distinct, tacitly ontological, determinations of human being itself are already problematic, revealing a mixing of the ontic-factual with the ontological. Such hybrid presentations are enormously popular in philosophical and other kinds of writing in order to get one's message across by telling some kind of ontogenetic narrative in terms of beings taken purely in their onticity or historical facticity. Thus, for instance, the slave stands ontic-factually for labour, the craftsman for work and Pericles for action. Such a procedure makes things easy to understand, but pays the price of missing the always *simple* ontological point altogether. The first determination of human being itself as *animal laborans* is already shaky because it reduces human being to needy animal being. Thus, on that level, the labour of a man making bread can be compared with the labour of a bee making honey as a biological necessity of life *sans phrase*. "To labor meant to be enslaved by necessity..." (11:83). Human existence is then conceived as the striving to fulfil needs which, as biological, are dictated by the life-process itself of birth through to death and its reproductive repetition. But the way human beings live with one another is never simply a matter of fulfilling biological needs. Rather, biological need-fulfilment is sublated and embedded within the practices of everyday life that are always historical usages which themselves determine, in turn, what is needed. Naked biology in itself never defines need.[116] Furthermore, because needs are determined by the usages of sharing a world together, they are not limited to human 'species-being'. Hence, when Arendt argues in such a way, e.g. when she follows the well-worn ruts of theories of under-consumption and over-production in capitalism and argues that the "progress of accumulation of wealth" is subject to "the limitation imposed by the capacity to consume" (16:124), she is asserting a finiteness of human need. But needs are limitless because they grow out of the usages within which human beings share the world, doing things *for each other*. The possibilities of life-enhancing, mutually beneficial usages, however, are limitless and constantly changing through historical time. Hence there are no limits to so-called economic growth, whose purported limitation is a widespread misconception of our age.

Arendt laments that in the modern world, the activity of labour has been totalized to all of society. It has come out of hiding in the private sphere of the household and become the underlying category for society at large that is now become income-earning, consumerist society and conceived as an enormous household to be administered by "gigantic bureaucratic machines" (11:93). The realm of politics, she says, now becomes household management, and all human activities are evaluated according to whether they are productive or unproductive (cf. 11:85). A realm of appearances in which men present themselves to each other as outstanding whos, she asserts, has been absorbed by a determination of the human being as mere need-fulfilling labourer. Arendt thoroughly

---

[116] Cf. Eldred 2008/2011 Section 4 v) 'Aristotle on money and exchange — Money as a medium practically unifying social usages'.

misunderstands the distinction between productive and unproductive labour in Marx, claiming that productive labour is that labour which produces durable values (i.e. work in Arendt's terminology), that "adds new objects to the human artifice" (11:88)), whereas unproductive labour "leaves nothing behind" (11:87), producing only consumption goods that are immediately consumed in the social life-process. This is a very queer notion that has little to do with Marx's critique of capitalism, and Arendt does indeed then proceed to collapse this distinction by claiming that from a "social viewpoint, [...] all laboring is 'productive'" (11:89), where such productivity is tied exclusively to the "life process of mankind" within whose "frame of reference all things become objects of consumption" (11:89). But then, what was first understood as unproductive labour becomes productive labour, and what was understood as productive labour producing durables disappears altogether, leaving behind no distinction at all. How then is the distinction between productive and unproductive labour in Marx's analysis of capitalism to be understood?

The distinction concerns first of all the productive labour of commodity production and the unproductive labour required in the sphere of circulation *of capital* where the produced goods are sold and fresh means of production are procured. Arendt does not mention this important distinction in the analysis of capital at all, and it is inevitable that she neglects it because she suffers from a fundamental misunderstanding of Marx's main work, *Das Kapital*, whose title, she claims, following the German sociologist Karl Dunkmann, "is a misnomer and should better have been called *System der Arbeit*" (fn. 14:101), i.e. *System of Labour*, which, of course, would have suited her down to the ground because it dovetails with her own focus on labour and work. She shows that her understanding of surplus labour and labour power is incoherent when she claims that Marx understands "labor's surplus as that amount of labour power still extant after the means for the laborer's own reproduction have been produced" (14:106), thus confusing labour power, which is a potential, a potency, with its realization in performed labour, which may include a surplus beyond the labour necessary to generate the *value of wages*, and not a bundle of subsistence goods necessary for keeping body and soul together.

The key concept in Marx's *Capital*, namely, is *value* (cf. *1.6 The private individual and private property as a mode of reified sociation: the gainful game (classical political economy, Marx)*), which, again, Arendt entirely neglects. The concept of capital itself is that of the endless, augmentative, circular movement of reified value that is reified, first of all, in commodities and money. In particular, living labour that produces commodities of any kind is *indirectly* validated and estimated on the market through the finished commodities' exchange-value and *directly* esteemed and validated in the wages paid for the *hiring* of labour power, and this is the way in which human labouring activity is subsumed beneath the augmentative, circular movement of reified value as capital. It is only via this detour through reified value-forms that labour in capitalism rises "to the highest rank, as the most esteemed of all human activities" (14:101): the estimation of exchange-value on the markets, including the esteeming of labour as the human activity (involving the factors, human labour power itself working with raw materials, means of production and land) bringing about commodity products that are continually submitted to the markets' value-estimation. Such commodity production produces consumption goods and so-called consumer durables, as well as circulating and fixed capital goods. Hence, according to Arendt, since work disappears into totalized labour under capitalism, there would be no world of durable artifices produced by work. However, capital requires an infrastructure that includes above all its fixed capital goods which are the means of production that remain in the production process for many circuits of capital, being consumed only bit by bit, through so-called depreciation. Such fixed capital contrasts with circulating capital, such as raw materials and auxiliary materials, that circulates already in a single circuit of capital and in this sense is productively consumed in one fell swoop. 'Fixed' and 'circulating' are determinations of the movement of value as capital, i.e. they are forms of reified value.

Because of her thoroughly anthropological perspective from the *animal laborans*, Arendt demonstrates no knowledge of, or even acquaintance with, these signal features of the Marxian analysis of capital. The cyclical movement of value as capital disappears beneath her focus on the cyclical "movement of the living organism", the "cyclical life processes" that return "into the over-all gigantic circle of nature herself" (13:96). Since she conceives labour entirely in connection with the natural, biological life-process and its continual necessity to fulfil needs, she thoroughly misreads *Capital*, even to the point of confusing the biological reproduction process with the reproduction process of total social capital when she claims that "in the third volume of *Das Kapital* he [Marx] repeats that surplus labor beyond immediate needs serves the 'progressive extension of the reproduction process'" (13:99).

If, however, capitalism is to be understood ontologically rather than anthropologically, it must be conceived as an historical constellation of value in augmentative movement under which human being itself is subsumed in an interplay of value-estimation that I have called the *gainful game*.[117] This goes far beyond any mere obsession of certain people, or a certain class of people (capitalists, merchants, bankers, ...), with making money from which they could free themselves by being receptive to wise moral precepts such as we have from Seneca, "Dum de incremento cogitat, oblitus est usus; rationes accipit, forum conterit, kalendarium versat."[118], since everybody in this age is more or less a player in the gainful game.

Everything, including the labourer, that is useful to the usages of sharing an everyday world, enters into an interchange through which it is estimated, i.e. valued, in the value-form of money which itself must therefore be conceived as *reified social power* that, as capital, has the power to set and keep the economic process in motion. In particular, the individual finds its self-identity as a who also in a reflection from reified value itself, for instance, in how much it earns, how much wealth it has

---

[117] Cf. Eldred 2000/2010 and *1.6 The private individual and private property as a mode of reified sociation: the gainful game (classical political economy, Marx).*

[118] "While he is thinking of an increment [to his wealth], its use is forgotten; he accepts invoices, wears out the market, turns [the pages of his] account book" Seneca 1974 Ep. XIV.xviii.

accumulated, in what it can buy in exercising the reified social power of its earned income. Such an ontological conception is 'worlds' away from Arendt. Arendt's conception of value is fixated upon a notion of durability associated with work in contradistinction to labour, a conception she apparently adopts from her reading of Locke and Adam Smith. Their "difficulty" with regard to value, she asserts, was "their 'products' had to stay long enough in the world of tangible things to become 'valuable', whereby it is immaterial whether value is defined by Locke as something which can be kept and becomes property or by Smith as something which lasts long enough to be exchangeable for something else". (14:104) Value, however, does not depend on durability in either of these senses; intangible service commodities, for instance, are just as "exchangeable for something else", namely, money, and thus have exchange-value like any other tangible commodity, whether it be a consumption or durable good.

Arendt's distinction between labour and work becomes downright silly when she bases it on a quote from Locke, "the labor of our body and the work of our hands", as if labour were not performed with hands! For her, work is "fabrication" by *home faber* of something durable as part of the "human artifice" that is *therefore* a value. Things produced by work "possess the durability Locke needed for the establishment of property, the 'value' Adam Smith needed for the exchange market" (18:136). If durability is the hallmark of the products of work as values for Arendt, it is also the hallmark of the "objectivity of the man-made world" against which "the subjectivity of men stands" (18:137). This misconception of value leads then to a misconception also of "reification" (Section 19) which she conceives as the objectivization (Vergegenständlichung) achieved by ποίησις (explicitly equated with "fabrication" at 18:142), rather than the genuine reification (Verdinglichung) of a social relation of mutual estimation of performed labour in value-things (commodities, money). These value-things as reified social power (they have the power to move through exchange) then take on a life-movement of their own as capital moving through its circuit from money-value to commodity-value and back again. Capital is first and foremost the *movement* of value which therefore is anything but durable, but nevertheless never-ending in its form-transformations, and reified in a specific socio-ontological sense.

Arendt's distinction between labour and work collapses in the modern capitalist world where the labourers labour, producing not only the necessities of life in a given society in a given time (Arendt's labour), but also fixed capital goods that build the infrastructure of a stable world (Arendt's work). Furthermore, the distinction between labour and action, too, starts to leak when the character of labour as value-generating and being estimated as valuable is taken into account, because value is that phenomenon which comes about when performed labour (commodity products) and labour power itself (the living wage-earner, from production line work to top executive) are estimated and valued on the various markets through being *paid* for. Such payment is an indirect, reified valuing, esteeming and estimating of the labourers' (wage-earners') labour, which is a kind of indirect who-recognition for which wage-earners *vie*. This may be very far from the striving for "immortal fame" in the ancient Greek world through "speaking and acting", but the striving for reified estimation of one's worth in society through earning wages, is nevertheless akin in the sense that both amount to showing oneself off *as* who one is and being estimated and esteemed for this display of individual powers (cf. the next subsection). Hence Arendt's threefold distinction among human activities is only approximate and plausible, and beset by certain confusions.

1.11.4 Whoness and the gainful game

If Arendt's postulation of three distinct and fundamental kinds of human activity and three distinct determinations of human being itself is untenable, then, in particular, action and economic activity (which Arendt places under the rubric of labour and work) can coalesce. "Speaking and acting" through which "men" show themselves and show themselves off *as* who they are within the plurality of a shared world are not separated off in a separate political or public realm. Rather, as Arendt herself concedes, the public realm includes also economic action: "exchange itself already belongs in the field of action and is by no means a mere prolongation of production" (29:209). Unfortunately, she does not take this thought further to bring to light how market exchange itself can be conceived as part of the action through which men estimate and esteem each other as *who* they are. The exchange of commodity goods on the market is, namely, already an *indirect, reified* way through which, in particular, "men" display their labouring and entrepreneurial abilities to each other and estimate them through the products (including services) offered on the market. Not a word from Arendt on this aspect. The reason is that she neglects exchange-value as a phenomenon of mutual estimation and reified power play. Already with the phenomena of advertising and salesmanship, a kind of speaking and acting is seen to be inherent in economic activity as associated with realizing reified value in the money-form.

For Arendt, somewho's identity is who he reveals himself to be through speaking and acting in the shared world. She claims that this identity does not lie in the hands of the individual himself, but instead in those of others who are able to tell the life-story in retrospect. Who-identity is a narrative told by others about how the who in question acted and spoke in life, a story that comes to closure only with death. This is very much the third-person perspective on an individual assessed and estimated by the others. From the first-person perspective, I experience my *self* also from the resonance I hear from others in the shared world, whilst also being as self the source of spontaneous movement, i.e. action in Arendt's sense. If my identity is ultimately the story told about who I was after my death, then whoness is irretrievably out of my hands; my identity is defined posthumously by others. This is the aspect of the *striving for immortality* that Arendt underscores. Each who strives to anchor his identity in posterity's remembrance. My lived whoness, however, is intimately tied to my actions and choices in life, i.e. it depends on whether and how I grasp or fail to grasp the potential for existing open to me in my time in my particular situation, including choosing those with whom I am to intimately share my life. Out of this particularity I forge my unique singularity, which may or may not be affirmed through the validating, esteeming reflections from the shared world.

The playing field for identity as somewho is the shared clearing for self-presentation, which includes also economic activity. In the modern capitalist age, economic agents are defined by the character-masks of the four basic income-sources that are the value-forms assignable to the economic players: wages, rent, interest and profit of enterprise, corresponding to the hired employees, the land-owner, the financier and the active, organizing entrepreneur, respectively. (cf. *1.6 The private individual and private property as a mode of reified sociation: the gainful game (classical political economy, Marx)*) These four figures are socio-ontological determinations of who one can be in a capitalist economy, occurring empirically in all sorts of hybrids and gradations. For instance, the economic identities of a salesman or buyer for a firm and a production-line worker are existentially very different, although both are subsumed under the income-source value-form of wages as the hiring price for labour power.

Arendt neglects the economic power play among a plurality of economic players. In fact, as we have seen, she neglects the power play among a plurality of whos altogether. This power play is the socio-ontological source of uncertainty and unpredictability in the striving to be somewho in the world. For Arendt, however, unpredictability arises from not being able to foresee the consequences of an action. An action sets a chain of reactions in train that are unforeseeable, and may reach beyond an individual life. But the power play is not to be conceived like a chain reaction allowing analogy with processes in the physical world, as Arendt indulges in in Section 20 'The Process Character of Action', in particular, employing the example of potentially uncontrollable nuclear chain reactions, but as a play in the sense both of play-acting and a fathomless game among a plurality of spontaneous starting-points of movement, i.e. players.

As an answer and "remedy" to the unpredictability inherent in action, Arendt proposes the "faculty to make and keep promises" (33:237). She insightfully claims that, "binding oneself through promises, serves to set up in the ocean of uncertainty, which the future is by definition, islands of security without which not even continuity, let alone durability of any kind, would be possible in the relationships between men". (33:237)

This insight has significance especially for the gainful game, where it translates not only into the form of intercourse called *contract* that plays a key role in all discourse on modern political economy, but also into significant phenomena such as credit, creditworthiness, *credibility* and *trust*, without which the interplay of economic life — not to mention the power play of politics — grinds to a halt.

1.11.5 Public and private realms?

Arendt develops her distinction between the public and the private realms from the paradigm of the Greek city-state in which the household was the hidden, private realm for the fulfilment of needs by women and slaves as a necessary precondition for the head of the household to be free to show himself off in the public realm (the agora) in a contestation among equal, free men. "The political virtue par excellence" (5:36) was therefore "courage", i.e. ἀνδρεία, literally 'manliness'. In this clearing of togetherness, men strive for "immortal fame", a striving which, Arendt claims, has become alien in the modern world where everybody is merely a consuming wage-earner ("jobholder" 5:31). For Arendt, the public realm is that of the "disclosure of the 'who' through speech, and the setting of a new beginning through action" (25:184) whereas the private realm is "the sphere of the household and family ... related to the maintenance of life" (5:28). She therefore grasps the crucial aspect of the distinction, namely, as that between *disclosing* oneself as *who* one is or *hiding* oneself in the privacy of the household. The play of disclosing and concealing who one is, however, cannot be tied down to separate "realms" or "spheres". Nor can the disclosure of who one is be restricted to "speaking and acting", as Arendt herself concedes when she writes that "men disclose themselves ... even when they wholly concentrate upon reaching an altogether worldly, material object" (25:183). This amounts to an admission that in modern *society*, too, which she marks off from the Greek city-state, there is who-disclosure in economic striving.

This shows up a weakness in Arendt's narrative, historical mode of presentation of her thoughts, for the play of showing off and concealing one is the essential feature of whoness itself, that is not tied to an historical paradigm. Rather, even when, as Arendt says, the Greek division between the private household and the public realm no longer pertains, and instead the household has come to be writ large as modern society, in which the economy (οἶκος), earning a living in the economy and economic management by the state become all-dominating, the play of whoness is not overcome historically, but assumes a new guise. It plays out now also within the *gainful game*, which is the socio-ontological structure underlying the modern market economy that remains hidden to Arendt. Therefore, when she determines the "privative trait" (6:38) of Greek privacy as a deprivation of being able "to enter the public realm" (6:38) where free men could "reveal actively their unique personal identities and thus make their appearance in the human world" (24:179), she is restricting her conceptual determination of privacy to a particular historical situation. Rather, modern society provides a new scenario for the play of revealing and concealing who one is, i.e. of *being* public and private. Public and private refer originarily to *modes of human presencing and absencing which are both marked by the play of disclosing and concealing* in many subtle ways, not to (ontic-factually) separate spheres. To anyone blind to the meaning of being as presencing and absencing in time-space, the preceding statement must seem meaningless.

Arendt's remark — namely, that what the Greeks regarded as an "idiotic" life of "one's own (idion)" (6:38) in the privacy of the family, because it was cut off from the common, shared life of the polis cannot easily be understood today in a society in which privacy as the "sphere of intimacy" (6:38) has appreciated in value — is historically plausible. The key, underlying distinction between disclosure and concealment of who one is, however, is socio-ontologically of greater, deeper import. Concealing or disclosing who one is, of course, amounts to concealing or disclosing one's own life-world which, however, is not a separate "sphere", but rather the two aspects of whoness itself as a play of concealing and disclosing, including both when one is *outside* "the four walls of one's private property" (9:71) *and within*. By identifying a specific local "hiding-place from the common public world" one runs the risk of confusing the privacy inherent in the who-game of self-disclosure and self-concealment with the privacy of private property or with a kind of *physical* disclosing and hiding.

Arendt herself traces the shift from the Greek counterposition of the private household to the public realm for free men to show off who they are, to the modern counterposition of the private sphere of intimacy to the society of 'everybody' with its conformism. In private intimacy, the modern individual unfolds a richness of sensibility in "ever-changing moods and the radical subjectivism of his emotional life ... born in this rebellion of the heart ... against what we would call today the conformism inherent in every society" (6:39). Modern private intimacy offers a new setting for the play of revealing and concealing who one is to the intimate other, which is different from the who-games the person indulges in out there in society when one must be careful to choose the right who-masks (personae) for the occasion. The games of intimacy between you-and-me are perhaps even a fourth kind of human activity besides Arendt's proposed (faulty) tripartite division of human activity into labour, work and action.

To recapitulate this crucial point on the nature of privacy: If the Greeks depreciated the household as a private, hidden place for the performance of what was necessary for living (the labour of slaves and women, including childbirth and child-rearing, the shameful necessities of the body), "the modern age, in its rebellion against society, has discovered how rich and manifold the realm of the hidden can be under the conditions of intimacy" (9:72). This richness of intimate privacy resides above all in the who-games that intimates can play with one another, concealing and revealing, and even *becoming*, who they are, through which they also esteem and appreciate each other. The who-play of intimacy, of course, is different from the who-play in public where a who must come to a stand and show him- or herself off in the full glory of his or her powers and abilities.

As just noted, to shore up the idea of a private realm or sphere, Arendt makes a misleading tie between personal privacy and private property. It is true that the privacy of private landed property implies a restriction of accessibility to the privacy of the home (even a rented home has of private property right to limit access), and so personal privacy does in part rely on the privacy of private property. But, as we have seen in earlier sections of this chapter, private property itself is a much broader and qualitatively different phenomenon from the play of showing oneself off or concealing oneself *as* who one is. In our modern society, with its fully developed private property intercourse, private housing can also be *rented*, which affords, under the terms of the *lease*, the same private-property protection as a hiding-place, without actually having to own the house itself or the land on which it stands. For those loser income-earners in the gainful game who become homeless, the lack of income leads also to a lack of privacy in the sense of having a place to physically withdraw. A homeless person's whoness is mercilessly exposed to public view.

Despite the misgivings articulated in the above appraisal, Arendt is to be praised for placing the phenomenon of whoness as self-disclosure at the centre of her major work and also for putting her finger on the essential aspect of (personal) privacy, namely, the withdrawal from exposure to public view, although who-games of revealing and concealing are played precisely also in public spaces, even before 'everybody', with all kinds of subtle intermediate shades, such as deceptive, misleading disclosure of who one is. The possibility to withdraw to the country (Cicero's *Tusculum*...) and to live in concealedness (cf. Epicure's λάθη βιόσας) was always, and still is, threatened by the power of the state (Roman Empire, the modern state's surveillance apparatus, secret service, etc.). Ovid lamented publicly (*Tristia*) in banishment. The correspondence between Cicero and Atticus is also an example of the fragility of private messages, i.e. epistles, written first of all not for the public gaze (already for political reasons). Today personal privacy is under threat, in particular from large corporations whose business is intimately tied to making and shaping the cyberworld (cf. *2.5 The parallel cyberworld that fits like a glove* and *3.2 Digital privacy: personal freedom to reveal and conceal* et seq.). Here and now, the eery power of digital cybernetics (a pleonasm) makes itself felt.

1.12 Recapitulation and outlook

With the preceding section, we have concluded the presentation of the elements of a phenomenology of *whoness*, its relation to *personal privacy*, and marked personal privacy off from that of *private property*. A sketch of private property in the modern world in its essential value-structure has led to a determination of the essence of market-capitalist society as the *gainful game* of *reified value in movement*. All these preparations will serve us well when we come to consider today's world which is permeated by digital technologies of all kinds, and even increasingly enveloped by them. Whoness, privacy, private property each assumes a different character in a digitized world. Before being able to approach these questions, however, it is necessary to first provide a sketch of what the digital means, not merely superficially as a new kind of technology, but as a way in which the very being of the world is cast and presents itself. The following chapter will culminate in a concept of the *cyberworld* that will facilitate consideration of privacy in today's fast-emerging and consolidating digitized world. Instead of remaining on the ontic-factual surface of the phenomenal world, discussing this or that technology and its benefits and/or dangers in terms of 'trade-offs', and the need for new norms, we must ask what the deeper socio-ontological structures of a digitized world are. Hence the necessity of a detour through digital ontology to learn to see where we are — not something for the impatient seeking pragmatic solutions and fixes.

2 Digital ontology

Michael Eldred

Here ontology is not to be understood in the insipid signification it has come to have in modern science, namely, as a complex taxonomy of terms and their interrelations in some subject area: "Ontologies therefore provide a vocabulary for representing and communicating knowledge about some topic and a set of relationships that hold among the terms in that vocabulary."[119] Rather here, the ontology practised still breathes in the inspiration from Aristotle's *Metaphysics* as an investigation into the being of beings in four distinct dimensions.[120] Whereas, however, in Greek philosophy, being itself was tacitly understood as standing presence, here being itself is overtly understood as coming-to-presence within three-dimensional time-space, and beings are likewise conceived temporally as that which comes to presence and presents itself in this time-space. Beings are the 'presents' that present themselves in and absent themselves from time-space, either as present or as absent in two distinctive ways. But I am jumping ahead of myself by introducing at the outset a still unheard-of understanding of being that has been around for less than a century. So let me go back very briefly to the beginnings with Plato and Aristotle.[121]

---

119 Ontology Working Group 2002 http://www.cbil.upenn.edu/-Ontology/#ontology.whatis This is in line with the prevailing understanding of ontology in analytic philosophy as "The basic question of ontology is 'What exists?'" (Chalmers 2009). Note also the developments in the area of the semantic web, which is based on such taxonomic ontologies; cf. Capurro 2006 that draws attention to the connection between the hermeneutics of texts and the so-called ontologies of the internet.

120 Very briefly, these four dimensions are with respect to i) the categories, ii) movement, iii) truth and falsity, iv) intrinsicality and contingency.

121 Cf. Eldred 2009/2011 or Capurro 2001 for an in-depth treatment.

2.1 From the abstraction from physical beings to their digital representation

Plato famously located the being of beings in the εἶδος or ἰδέα or 'sight', 'face' or 'look' that a being presents of itself to human understanding. A being takes a stand in presence and presents itself in a well-defined sight. It can only be seen *as* a being through its 'ideal sight'. In Aristotle, the Platonic 'sight' becomes the μορφή or 'form' that is impressed on the material and brings it to a visible stand in presence *as* a being that can also be addressed by words.[122] As is well-known, however, Plato's metaphysical thinking was influenced by a close proximity to Pythagorean geometry; the visible geometric contours of a being that is present are akin to the 'sight' that a being presents of itself. The affinity of metaphysics and mathematics from the culmination of Greek philosophy is the beginning that will maintain its hold on Western thinking, and thus Western history, up to the present day with its own culmination in the digital dissolution of the being of beings. Only by understanding where the digital comes from in the history of Western thinking will it be possible to assess and critique present-day attempts to come to terms philosophically with the digital world (cf. in particular the critique of Floridi in Chap. 3).

Aristotle rethinks some of Plato's key insights in an alternative language. In particular, he thinks through the mathematical entities starting from physical beings. Both the geometrical and the arithmetical are the result of abstracting from physical beings which, for Aristotle, are beings that are subject to movement, i.e. to change or 'over-turning' (μεταβολή). Such abstraction is a separating-off (χωρίζειν) in thought that results in independent geometrical and arithmetic entities, namely, geometric figure and arithmetic number. A physical being has a place (τόπος) which Aristotle thinks as the 'skin' enveloping a physical being, thus enabling it to present itself in the space of presence. Separating off this skin and regarding it as something separate results in geometric figure, which therefore no longer has a place, although the points within

122 Cf. Capurro 1978.

the figure have position with regard to each other. For instance, a triangle resting on its base has a different position from a triangle poised on one of its angles. A further step in separating-off or abstraction is to simply count the physical beings present: 1, 2, 3, etc. Such counting reduces the counted being to a mere number in a sequence of counted numbers (ἀριθμοί), completely abstracting from the being's qualities and even from its geometric shape. Counting requires only the pure difference between presence and absence: if a being is present in the sequential counting, it is marked by a 1, and if not, it is marked by 0 and left out of the counting. All that 'counts' is the string of 1's. At best, the being is given an ordinal number in a sequence of counted numbers, i.e. its own unique number in that sequence. A number not only does not have a place like a physical being does; it also has no position like a geometric figure. Number is both placeless and positionless, and it is also *discrete*, in contrast to geometric figure, which is *continuous* in the sense that all the points that go toward making it up hang together very tightly. This distinction has momentous consequences for the history of mathematics and mathematical science up to the present day, including in mathematical logic and quantum physics, in which disciplines there are still unresolved antinomies directly relating to discreteness vs. continuity.

An abstracted number is very different from the λόγος that is given to a being as its name (ὄνομα). A physical being presents itself and offers itself to view *as* such-and-such, e.g. this being presents itself *as* a bottle. Hence 'this' gathers itself (λέγειν) in the sight of a bottle that is presented to human understanding that takes in this definite sight. Such understanding taking-in is what the Greeks mean by νοεῖν, the activity of νοῦς (intellect, reason). A physical being presenting itself *as* such-and-such in its λόγος (word) is clearly much richer than its presenting itself merely as an abstract counting number, as one thing among a set of counted things. A being's name says much more, in a more differentiated way, than a mere ordinal number. Nevertheless, there is an affinity between word and number insofar as both are discrete, placeless and positionless. The discreteness of words means that they are countable, and therefore each can be assigned a number. Any kind of text is a finite series of words, which may be characters, as in Chinese, or composed of letters, and therefore this ordered sequence can be replaced by an ordered sequence of numbers, where each number in the sequence stands for a definite word, words in any given language being regarded as part of a finite vocabulary on that language. If the words themselves are composed of syllables or individual letters, they can be further decomposed into numbers standing uniquely for individual syllables or letters. Hence, by virtue of its countable discreteness, any text at all can be represented uniquely by an ordered string of numbers. Numbering and counting result in full *determinacy* of presence.

The next step is that any number at all can be represented to the base 2, i.e. in binary code, because any counting number can be uniquely and determinately expressed as the sum of powers of 2, just as it can be expressed uniquely in the decimal system as the sum of powers of 10. In base 10, ten symbols are required to represent the base, whereas in base 2, only two, the binary digits or 'bits' 0 and 1, are required. Hence, anything that can be said 'logically', i.e. in words, can be represented uniquely and determinately in a finite, ordered sequence of bits which, although composed perhaps of billions of bits, remains countable and finite. The deep affinity between number and word can be called the 'arithmologos', which is discrete, placeless and positionless. (This affinity is essential for mathematical logic's results in the work, say, of Gödel, Church and Turing.) Furthermore, due to its arithmetic character, the arithmologos is *calculable*.

2.2 Mathematical access to the movement of physical beings

The discrete, digital, arithmological representation of the logos in itself is not world-shaking, because performing arithmetical operations on a digital sequence as such is not all that useful. It first becomes useful when the logos is a text saying calculably how physical beings move in a calculation or computation (λογισμός). It must be said that the logos itself speaks continually of movement, for λόγοι themselves speak of movement already in the most elementary of statements, such as 'Socrates walks', consisting of a named subject (noun, ὄνομα) and a verb (ῥῆμα from ῥεῖν 'to flow'), as proposed by Plato and Aristotle, which gave the starting-point for thinking about grammar. So the logos may describe movement, as when the subject-noun is given a predicate-verb describing its movement, but how could it calculate this movement so as to control it? Aristotle already had an ontology of movement that represents the apex of his thinking, since it brings to a climax Greek philosophy's attempts since Parmenides and Heraclitus to come to terms with the manifold phenomenon of movement/change. Although Aristotle's ontology of movement was a *productive* conception of movement according to which a starting-point or point of origin (ἀρχή) has control over a change in something else to bring forth or pro-duce an end-product, this ontology was not yet mathematized and therefore not yet a calculating logos. Instead, Aristotle employed his ground-breaking conception of energy (ἐνέργεια, Aristotle's own neologism meaning literally 'at-work-ness') to conceive how a power (δύναμις) actualizes itself in movement toward an end, the state of perfected presence (ἐντελέχεια).

Aristotle's ontology of movement and change in terms of his famous concepts is by no means done away with in the modern age and indeed, without Aristotle's concept of energy, and its associated terms such as 'force', 'work', 'action', there would be no modern science. Rather, with Copernicus, Galileo, Kepler and Newton, Aristotle's ontology of movement and change gains an increasingly mathematical formulation expressible ultimately in simple mathematical equations, namely, Newton's three simple laws of motion that make motion, at least, i.e. change of place or loco-motion, calculable. This is the momentous breakthrough that allows physics to become a mathematical science, above all by regarding all sorts of movement as *change of place* (e.g. in the nineteenth century, heat comes to be conceived as the motion of molecules) and all sorts of causality as *effective* causality where a caused effect can be expressed in a mathematical equation involving linear-causal time.

To be able to do this, physical beings themselves must be cast as mathematically accessible, as Descartes lays down in his famous *Regulae*. This text may be regarded as the metaphysical blue-print for the modern age as dominated by the mathematical sciences. Geometric access to physical beings practised already by the Greeks was the first port of call, but geometric figure itself cannot be subjected to a calculus. Theorems in geometry rely crucially on the intuition of spatial figure that cannot be reduced to mere calculation. Therefore, the points of a geometrical figure had to be expressed in number to become calculable. The points thus lose their position, but, in exchange for this loss, they become arithmetically calculable — in Cartesian geometry. Number, however, is intrinsically discrete, whereas geometric figure is continuous. How was continuity itself to be mathematized? This problem was solved more or less by Newton and Leibniz with the infinitesimal calculus that was able to calculate with infinitely small quantities 'as if' they were mere numbers. The gaps in the linear continuum between the rational, countable numbers were thus filled by the irrational, but real numbers.

The intuitive approach to infinitesimals was put on a sounder mathematical footing in the nineteenth century by the German mathematicians, Weierstraß and Dedekind, by making continuity approachable through an *endless* sequential counting called the mathematical limit, but the basic ambiguity between physical continuity and mathematical, calculable discreteness resurfaces in the twentieth century in the foundations of mathematics (Weyl), mathematical logic (Gödel incompleteness) and mathematical physics (quantum indeterminacy, ambiguity between wave and particle). Such problems in the foundations, however, have not prevented mathematicians and scientists from calculating further and extending the mathematical access to the physical world. Perhaps the most ingenious step in forcing open this access and the reach of mathematical calculation was the shift to abstract algebra that freed mathematics from arithmetic number.[123] Equations could then be written and solved algebraically with mere

123 Cf. for more detail Eldred 2009/2011 § 2.7.

symbols representing magnitudes in general, no matter whether they were discrete, continuous or merely symbolic (as in the abstract algebra of, say, groups or categories).

On the back of advances in mathematics, the formulation of physical mathematical laws of motion could forge ahead into more subtle types of movement beyond the mechanical motion of physical bodies, including signal transmission that heralded in today's information society. Movement itself could be mathematized as energy regarded as a flow of particles, especially electrons. Engineering science, for instance, depends crucially on its being able to write and solve equations for the motion of electrons (circuits). Chemistry is able to write equations for chemical reactions and calculate how much energy is released or absorbed by a given reaction. The modern age as based on the mathematical physical sciences unleashes a calculating power over physical movement and change which, of course, take place in *time*.

2.3 The mathematical conception of linear, continuous time

Aristotle already conceived time as a number lifted off movement by counting in which a later now is counted after an earlier now. Time is cast as an endless sequence of counted nows in a row. With the discovery, or rather, the casting of mathematical laws of motion, this counted nature of time, that can be counted by the ticking of a clock, no long suffices because motion itself takes place continuously, and the Newtonian laws of motion are expressible as equations in continuous variables according to which the state of a physical system can be calculated at a later point in time given the initial state at an initial point in time. Hence time itself, must be cast as a continuous linear real variable t that occurs in the relevant equations of motion. The rate of change of a physical system can be calculated only by differentiating with respect to the continuous variable t. And so on. Mathematical calculability presupposes *continuous* linear real time, whereas the determination of time as a quantity is only ever a clock-time that is always *discrete*. This is a further antinomy that haunts modern physics.

Nonetheless, equations of motion written in terms of a continuous linear real variable t give Western humankind a hitherto unimaginable control over movement of many different kinds. Moreover, the totalizing tendency of the mathematical sciences is to cast *all* possible movement in the world, including social movement and change, in terms of (perhaps highly complex, including statistical) effective-causal motion that can be mathematically calculated, today by stepwise calculations (algorithms) in computers, perhaps using statistical techniques to draw regularities out of masses of data. Hence the attempts over centuries to establish also social sciences according to the paradigm of the mathematical physical sciences, that has long since reached human being itself with the running controversy over freedom vs. determinism that today assumes a neuroscientific guise.

2.4 Outsourcing of the arithmologos as digital code

If the mathematical physical sciences have unleashed seemingly unbounded calculable control over all movement in linear time, this arithmological will to power over physical beings takes on a decisive new quality when these equations themselves are digitized in binary code that is then impregnated in its own electromagnetic matrix.[124] The digitization of texts may open possibilities of representing them not merely on paper but via an electromagnetic medium itself. Such an impregnated electromagnetic matrix, however, only becomes legible to a human being if it is shown on an electronic display. To achieve this, the

124 It is crucial here not to confuse the generality of an electromagnetic medium with, say, superseded technologies such as magnetic core memory. Any medium for inscribing bits must take advantage of electromagnetic phenomena in the broadest sense of Maxwellian electromagnetic force-field theory. It is force-fields that are mobilized for inscribing, processing, transmitting and storing bits. An electromagnetic medium in the present context is not restricted to employing magnetism, nor is it to be understood only electronically, i.e. as the movement of electrons. A photon digital processor, for instance, still employs electromagnetic phenomena, since light itself is an electromagnetic phenomenon, but neither simply magnetic nor electric. Chemical bonds holding molecules together are also electromagnetic in nature.

mathematical laws of physics are required that allow a transformation of digital representation from ordered bits in an electromagnetic medium to the illuminated representation of digital pixels on a screen, and vice versa, to be calculated. This transformation is then put into effect by a physical process driven by energy, i.e. by the controlled motion of electrons. The representation of the text on the screen can then be changed by altering the digital code, which again relies on causal laws of motion linking movements on a keyboard with changes to the digital code in the electromagnetic medium. Hence the digital-electronic word processor is born. This is only the start, because there are many, many other kinds of movement that can be digitally controlled.

The digitized, outsourced control over movements in the physical world comes into its stride in our own time. The mathematical scientific logos that encapsulates laws of motion of many different kinds can be employed to understand countless situations involving a change of circumstances of whatever kind, and this understanding can be written down in a *digitally coded text*. This digital code itself can then be outsourced to an electromagnetic medium where it is employed to process digital data fed in. These digital data may be, for example, the digitized sense data received by a high resolution video camera that are entered into and processed by face-recognition software, which is nothing other than code written in line with a physical theory of how human faces are to be distinguished from each other under many different circumstances. If the face-recognition software makes a hit, a signal is automatically emitted to alert an operator to take a closer, 'human' look. In this way, physical movements in the world, e.g. people moving through an airport, are subjected to automated surveillance in the sense of recognizing certain human 'particles' in that movement. Only this outsourcing of digitized code opens up the prospect of automated control of movements of all kinds. The limits to such control lie only in the limits of human ingenuity in applying laws of physical motion of various kinds to understand a certain state of affairs so as to gain a precise, mathematizable understanding of its movements which can then be digitally coded and outsourced as *executable code*. Other names for executable code include software, routines, algorithms, source code, computer program.

The mathematician, Alan Turing, must be attributed the ingenious insight that a (Turing) machine that can algorithmically process, i.e. compute, digital data fed into it, can first be fed with the program code that encapsulates the algorithmic rules for processing all the data that will follow in sequence on the endless 'tape'.[125] This is the Universal Turing Machine that stands at the portal of the digital age by serving as the mathematical blue-print for the electronic computer that is becoming more and more ubiquitous in more and more guises today. Indeed, it would not be too much to say that, if Aristotle's *Physics* is the fundamental book ("Grundbuch", Heidegger) for the West as a whole, and Descartes' *Regulae* the fundamental blue-print for the modern age, then Turing's 1936 paper ranks as the blue-print for the digital age of the cyberworld. In such a machine, digital code directs the machine to move one move to the left or the right and to either print or not print a digital bit. This machine motion is the ultimate digital motion in the world upon which the digitized control of physical movements of all kinds in the world may be imposed.

After this concise overview of digital ontology and the digital cast of being that is coming increasingly to hegemony in today's world, it is time to turn to consider the cyberworld that has arisen out of the outsourcing of digital code into its own medium. The digital cast of being has given us a world parallel to, and gradually permeating, the physical world in which digital beings consisting of strings of bits circulate. They have their effects, both within the cyberworld and, through the interfaces to this world, back on the physical world, including on ourselves as physical beings.

2.5 The parallel cyberworld that fits like a glove

Cyberworld is the name not for some merely ontic-factual, artificial thing, but the existential-ontological name for the ontic-factual internet plus other interlinked networks *insofar as* this global technical thing also

[125] Turing 1936.

represents an (electromagnetic) *medium for the movement of digital beings* (bit-strings) in which we human beings participate and through which we also steer, either directly, or indirectly through automatically executable digital code. This gives rise, say, to the possibility of robots, which are artificially 'animated' machines that, once programmed, have the source of movement within themselves, even though they need a current of electrons to drive them. Robots with an interface to the physical world in which they control some movement/change or other may be termed *hard robots*, whereas those that control some movement/change within the electromagnetic matrix of the cyberworld itself may be called *soft robots*.

Even if, in a certain way, all tools and machines are a materialized outsourcing of our productive world-understanding, what is new and unique with the digital cast of being is that it enables a digitally coded segment of world-understanding (misleadingly called 'symbolic Artificial Intelligence') to be outsourced as *automatic* machine code. The cyberworld, as the materialization of the digital cast of being, is an artificial world produced by outsourcing the arithmologos as (executable, automatic) digital code that moves in its own global medium. The cyberworld is populated by countless trillions of bit-strings that are either 'passive' digital data or 'active' executable program code. These two kinds of code copulate with each other in countless billions of Universal Turing Machines,[126] generating new bit-strings that continue to circulate throughout the cyberworld, which itself is nothing other than a never-ending concatenation of Universal Turing Machines impregnated in the electromagnetic matrix.

The strange character of this artificial digital world is that we encounter our own materialized, digitized logos and world-understanding in such a way that, with clever programming of the human interfaces, this mimetic world also assumes natural, physical traits. It is only for this reason that we can also move through this artificial world in a genuine sense as cyberspace, or share this world with one another in a genuine sense, i.e. not merely 'virtually'. We are

---

[126] Cf. Eldred 2012a.

ourselves logical beings for whom the world is gathered into a stand for understanding, and therefore we well understand this materialized logos and can easily orient ourselves and even carry out actions in it and through it. The physical world and the digital cyberworld are by now so seamlessly intermeshed with one another that the everyday life-world is already a physico-digital world. This trend will continue under headings such as 'ambient intelligence' and 'ubiquitous, pervasive and invasive computing'. The term 'cyberworld', as introduced above, is used in preference to 'internet' because the latter is the name for a specific network that does not include even digital mobile telephony, which must be regarded as an important segment of the cyberworld today. Only in this broader context can issues around privacy and trust be properly approached. Cyberworld is also philosophically appropriate because the very word raises the issues of control (cyber-) and the specific worldliness of this artificial, networked thing.

Even though the digital horizon as outsourced digital code is not merely something ontic-factual, but an existential-ontological phenomenon in the sense of a *materialization* of the digitized, controlling access to the being of beings as a whole, it is important to handle the word 'world' here very carefully, because the world is the unique, singular, unified timespace of human existence. The point is not that the cyberworld is a special, parallel world separated from the world, but, as the materialized digital cast of being, a certain way in which the world shows itself to human being today *as* a world. Otherwise we would be living in two (or more) 'worlds'[127] and would have to seek the world encompassing these worlds, which would lead us to postulate

[127] For a critique of thinking in terms of spheres, see Capurro www.capurro.de/operari.html e.g. in English translation: "Insofar as being-in-the-network manifests itself as a flight from the everyday world and caring for one's togetherness, including caring for one's own bodiliness, it is a sign of Dasein having closed itself off within the digital cast of the world. And conversely: enclosing oneself in the everyday world prevents the process of (digital) *nearing*, i.e. of the extension of those relations which, liberated from physical beings, are possible in the medium of global digital networking."

some sort of transcendent world.[128] In keeping to the unity and singularity of being-in-the-world, which is what human being per se *is*, the cyberworld is simply a way in which we are in the world with our own materialized, outsourced, digitized world-understanding which confronts us *as if* it were a parallel world. With the digital cast of being, not only does an other hermeneutic and apophantic AS[129] emerge historically as a way of understanding the world, but this AS, the digitized arithmologos, materializes itself technically in executable digital code and *circulates* in its own medium. With this caveat, we can speak of the materialized, outsourced, digitized arithmologos *as* a parallel cyberworld which now will be further discussed.

Digital beings are nothing but digital code, i.e. strings of bits. A bit is pure binary difference that can be represented by, say, 1 and 0. To write a bit, a stable difference in the inscription matrix between two unambiguous states[130] is required, and this is provided by electromagnetic states of the medium that can be changed in a controlled way by electromagnetic force fields, including currents of electrons or laser beams. Digital program code must be 'legible' to a processor as a set of step-by-step instructions (the algorithm) about what to do with digital data input. After processing, other bit-strings are output, which are signals sent to destinations to trigger electromagnetic effects. Thus, for instance, a keyboard inputs the digital code for a certain letter that is sent to the processor in which the already loaded word-processing program interprets the code as a letter and in turn sends a signal to the

---

[128] Hence the rise of cybermysticism or cybergnosis, and deficient ways of living with the cyberworld; cf. Capurro & Pingel 2002e.g. "Within the digital casting of Being we look at humans as they are online instead of embracing the digital within the 'life-world' (Husserl). The online casting pervades our lives, including our lives as researchers. Its predominance has led to the idea of not only displacing, but even replacing bodily existence (Moravec 1988, Kurzweil 1999). We may call this thinking *cybergnosis*, i.e. the expectation that we will be able to redeem ourselves from our mortal condition through (digital) knowledge."

[129] Cf. Heidegger SZ 1927 §§ 32f. on the hermeneutic and apophantic As.

[130] Quantum computing endeavours to employ an ambiguity, or indeterminacy, of the bit to do parallel calculations simultaneously.

text-file, another digital string, and to the display screen, where certain pixels are electrically excited to display the letter in question. The cyberworld is so called because it is the matrix in which bit-strings circulate and change under the control of program code and input by a plurality of human beings and physical sensors. 'Control' is here the operative word; hence the prefix 'cyber-' that comes from the Greek word for 'control', 'steer', 'govern'. The English word 'govern' has the same Greek root 'cyber' (Latin 'guber').

The various digital computing devices of all kinds can also be linked electromagnetically so that program code instructions and data can be sent among many digital devices, each of which is basically a Turing machine. This network has been set up as the internet, a network among (inter) computing devices. The hardware for this network is dispersed physically all over the globe, allowing global cybernetic control and transmission of data of all kinds. Insofar, the term 'cyberworld' is justified, indicating a globe spanned by an interconnected electromagnetic medium enabling total digital control which, however, is exercised by a plurality of programmers and bits of executable code. Hence, the totality is splintered into many control centres. This cyberworld has human interfaces or 'windows' with the physical world, such as keyboards, graphic display screens, microphones, loudspeakers, keyboards, touchscreens, etc., that enable human beings to look into this digital world, input data and program code, receive messages of various kinds output from it.[131] The cyberworld also has both passive-receptive and active-productive interfaces with the physical world, receiving data through devices such as cameras or thermometers, and producing controlled changes in the physical world, such as when a computer program controls traffic lights, or moves a robot arm on a production line, or changes the settings on a dialysis machine according to patient's current data which the program has analyzed.

131 With inventions and refinements of the 'mouse' pointing-device, the graphic interface, the touchscreen, etc., Steve Jobs was a genius in understanding the importance of the 'handiness' of the interfaces between the human body and the materialized digital. On digital 'handiness' (Zuhandenheit) cf. Capurro 1992, Capurro 1986 and Capurro 2008a.

Total cybernetic control in the cyberworld breaks down, or rather splinters, due to the *plurality* of users who can inject digital code into this digital world that is designed to subvert the envisaged effect of other code.[132] The digital movements designed to be controlled by a certain program code can be negated, neutralized, subverted or exploited by additional program code. Strife arises among the various digital programs designed to control certain definite movements. Computer viruses, Trojans, etc. are written and disseminated to countermand other pieces of executable digital code, e.g. to overwrite a digital message displayed on a web-site or for purposes of industrial espionage. Such power play played out in the cyberworld raises the spectre even of *cyberwar*. In this way, the cyberworld itself becomes a playground for the power play among human players, including politically organized players such as states or armed guerillas. The global cyberworld fundamentally changes the power plays, because now so many players are playing, and the power itself is digitized and outsourced in automatically executing algorithmic code. This counteracts the other tendency of the cyberworld to bring under control movements of all kinds, including in the physical world, through clever digital code. The subjectivist metaphysics of the modern age was cast (first of all by Descartes) to realize the calculable mathematical-scientific control of movements of all kinds. Only with such control's palpable materialization in the digital cyberworld, where technical knowledge itself has gained autonomy as automatically executable code, does the under-lying, controlling subject become dethroned, so to speak, both by the power plays among the plurality of players[133] and the autonomous automation of control to which human beings themselves are now *subjected*. The human subject is becoming subjugated to its own artificial digital world, in a way that parallels its subjection to the economic movement of reified value (cf. *3.5.2 The gainful game unleashes its freedom in the cyberworld*).

---

[132] Cf. Winograd & Flores 1986; cf. also Capurro 1987

[133] Cf. Capurro 1995 Kap. V 'Die artifizielle Unterwanderung der Interpretationsgemeinschaft' and Eldred 2009/2011 § 3.5.

2.5.1 Cyberspace

The spatiality of the cyberworld is curious. People speak of cyberspace as 'virtual reality', but this term is not justified insofar as the cyberworld as a genuine medium has its own spatiality through which human being itself can navigate. The two essential characteristics of spatiality for human being are orientation and approximation (in the sense of 'bringing into proximity' or 'nearing'[134]). Since the cyberworld is 'inhabited' solely by digital code (i.e. bit-strings comprising passive data and active, executable program code) which is nothing other than outsourced calculating human logos of an arithmetic, algorithmic nature, it is a homogenous space whose places are specified purely numerically in a kind of mathematical vector space of finite dimensions. Each place in the cyberworld is simply a co-ordinate position specified as an n-tuple of whole numbers. These co-ordinates can also be given names and these names graphic interface representations which are called web-sites. The cyberworld can thus be navigated by human beings who take their orientation from the co-ordinate places suitably re-presented visually as a graphic 'site'. Behind these sites, however, is simply a string of digital code, i.e. a (usually very long) number enabling digital control. If necessary, one can also do without the comfortable graphic interface. From such sites, bit-strings can be brought into proximity by the human user. The human user thus moves in cyberspace 'as if' in a physical space, employing the same existential characteristics of orientation and nearing as in the physical world. This is only possible because digital code itself can be translated back into a graphic re-presentation that 'looks like' the physical world. To this extent, the term 'virtual reality' is justified, but the digital code behind the graphic re-presentations is 'really' distributed throughout the physical world on countless pieces of hardware (servers), and a user sitting in Helsinki 'really' can bring digital data on a device in Sydney into proximity on his own digital device.

Even though discrete bits-strings that inhabit the cyberworld are different in their mode of being from continuous, physical beings, the

---

134 Cf. Eldred 2009/2011 § 4.2.

parallel cyberworld is remarkably permeable and does not represent a separate sphere. It is indeed striking that we human beings have scarcely any problems moving back and forth between the cyberworld and the physical world, which has above all to do with the fact that we are of our nature 'logical' and are not alienated when the logos now materializes itself as a bit-string and confronts us. We understand the logos because beings themselves come to stand and show themselves to our understanding through the defining gathering that is the logos. Especially since programmers have also written visual, audio and tactile interfaces for the average dumb user which impressively imitate the physical world, we move through the cyberworld 'as if' literally handling everyday paraphernalia. These 'easy' interfaces are cleverly adapted to our bodily constitution and bodily movements in the world. Only the programmers have to know about the translation of digital code into beguiling visual, audio and tactile interfaces, and this translation has been crucial for the explosion of the internet. Moving in cyberspace has become a 'natural' everyday movement.

2.5.2 Cybertime

What about the temporality of the cyberworld? Is there a peculiar cybertime to be distinguished from the time-space in which human being itself exists? Cybertime is the clock-time digitally registered automatically within the cyberworld of occurrences taking place within it. Every movement within the cyberworld is a change in digital bit-strings of some kind or other, e.g. when a digital message is sent or received, or when the processing of certain data has been completed, or when a cybernetically controlled process breaks down. Each of these occurrences can be given automatically a time-stamp according to global clock-time (Greenwich Mean Time/UTC). Cybertime is thus a globally co-ordinated, digital counting of now-moments that can be used to date any occurrence in the cyberworld. Due to the cybernetic surveillance and control of all occurrences in the cyberworld, the *dateability*[135] of all occurrences is total, automated and indelible, unless the time-stamp data

[135] Cf. Heidegger SZ 1927 § 79 and Eldred 2011a § 6.

are deleted. Digital beings embedded in the global electromagnetic matrix are there 'forever' as long as the necessary electrical energy is supplied or the magnetic media are intact, and as long as they are not deleted by an electromagnetic force acting on the force-field that is the electromagnetic medium. These time-space data in themselves, however, have no memory; it is only the human players in the cyberworld who remember and can recall.

Time-stamped occurrences in the cyberworld are recorded by data that in themselves are timeless.[136] Only a human being inhabiting time-space with its three independent temporal dimensions is *in time* and can therefore also use time-stamped data to construct other digital beings, i.e. software, that employs these data for a definite purpose, e.g. tracking the progress of a postal delivery. By outsourcing the temporal understanding of the world to digital code, it seems as if this code itself were 'in time', but this is an illusion today often indulged in. In particular, any user's activities in the cyberworld are automatically registered as cyberworld occurrences, providing, on (human) recall, a complete timeline profile of where and when the user in question has been in the cyberworld. The digital trace of users' movements is one important aspect of being-in-the-cyberworld arising from its totally cybernetic character. In the physical world, the trace of an individual's movements can never be so complete. Hence other individuals, companies and the state can construct temporal profiles of users' movements, either of specific users or of types of users, depending upon how specific the time-stamped data are. E.g. the state's taxation arm can effectively invade privacy by acquiring and evaluating time-stamped data of an individual's financial transactions.

With respect to the temporal dimension of the future, dateable cybertime proves itself to be invaluable by providing endless amounts of time-stamped data on digital occurrences in the cyberworld that can be analyzed or 'mined' using mathematical statistics to discover regularities and correlations which, in turn, can be extrapolated into the future. In this way, future occurrences in the cyberworld can be predictably

[136] Cf. Eldred 2012a.

modelled in linear time, especially with a view to uncovering future *trends*. Where the movements of many users in the cyberworld are available as time-stamped data, mining these data is a valuable tool both for the state and private companies as we shall see in more detail in the next chapter. The attempt to mine and extrapolate the plethora of time-stamped data is based on a *linear, one-dimensional* conception of time, for otherwise, the regularities and correlations uncovered in the data could not be extrapolated. After all, such predictive data mining is a matter of mathematically connecting and extending the dots.

With this section, the crucial concept of the cyberworld has been developed, which will enable us in the next chapter to bring together a phenomenology of whoness focused specifically on personal privacy and private property, on the one hand, with today's specifically digitized nature of being-in-the-(cyber)-world, on the other. Only by preparing the ground carefully in this way is it possible to clearly conceptualize digital whoness in connection with privacy, publicness and freedom, thus avoiding misconceptions engendered by preconceptions.

3 Digital whoness in connection with privacy, publicness and freedom

Michael Eldred[137]

The two preceding chapters have provided a sketch of a phenomenology of whoness with special regard to privacy, publicness and freedom as well the rudiments of a digital ontology that allows today's cyberworld to be seen as the consummate way in which the digital cast of being comes to presence and presents itself today. The task for the present chapter is to bring these two strands together so that specifically *digital* whoness, privacy and publicness come to light.

3.1 Digital identity - a number?

Who someone *is* is a way of manifest presencing in the world. To be somewho means to be a *self* which comes about through an individual's *identifying* with, i.e. adopting as his or her own, certain chosen possibilities of existing that shine back from the world. Personal identity (selfhood) is therefore always an identity of identity and difference. On the other hand, we have seen that the digital cast of being, i.e. the way in which all beings shape up and present themselves as decomposable into bits, precipitates today in an artificial cyberworld in which digital beings, i.e. bit-strings, circulate. One can view this historical event as a consummation of the productivist metaphysics that started with the Greeks, especially Aristotle, whose *Physics* and *Metaphysics* paved the way for mathematical access to the world. The mathematico-physical sciences have become the hegemonic way in which today the world is understood — in a realist, materialist, causal way. The invention of the computer, which fulfils a Leibnizian dream, enables this mathematically cast world to be represented *as* bit-strings and digitally computed.

[137] All sections of this chapter are the final authorial responsibility of Michael Eldred, apart from the section 3.7 by Rafael Capurro.

People living today, however, do not have to know anything at all about this mathematico-metaphysical background. Instead, they are confronted with and grow up in a world in which their immersion in the cyberworld is increasingly becoming quotidian normality. The human interfaces with the cyberworld make it fit like a glove, so that the borders between being-in-the-cyberworld and being-in-the-physical-world become increasingly blurred. 'Like a glove' here is neither a metaphor nor a simile, but an English turn of phrase that points to and says how human bodiliness fits with the artificial cyberworld. The two intermesh seamlessly into a unified everyday being-in-the-world. What does this signify for individual selfhood, i.e. individual identity?

The digital beings 'inhabiting' the artificial cyberworld are nothing but strings of 0s and 1s, i.e. a finite binary number. These binary numbers, however, are 'magical' in the sense that they unfold into all sorts of data or information about the world, on the one hand, and, on the other, into executable program code that processes data to bring forth calculable effects both within and without the cyberworld. As far as the human user or denizen of the cyberworld is concerned, the cyberworld presents itself to him or her through the various interfaces that today have been well-adapted to the human body and mimic the physical world. Such interfaces are technical, requiring a technical device of some sort: desktop, laptop, hand-held, implanted chip or whatever. This device itself is assigned a number automatically (e.g. IP address) by the cyberworld; it is identifiable through this number, which may be combined with other numbers such as location and time co-ordinates. The human user of a digital device interfaced with the cyberworld is willy-nilly identified with this device's number so that, in a certain way, the user's identity itself becomes this number as far as his or her presence in the cyberworld goes.

The cyberworld denizen both sends messages through and receives messages from the cyberworld via the convenient technical possibilities put at her or his disposal by the programmers.[138] Such messages are themselves digital beings, i.e. a binary number or bit-string, despatched

[138] Cf. Capurro & Holgate 2011.

through or received from the global electromagnetic medium, which are data of some kind that themselves have to be processed by the appropriate executable code to become 'presentable', e.g. the voice of a person speaking through a microphone has to be converted into bits that are transmitted through the hardware comprising sound card, PC processor, internet interface, internet router, etc. so that finally, by being processed along the way by the appropriate executable code, this voice signal is reconstituted as an audible voice at the receiver's end. Thus, for instance, I hear my friend speaking, who is part of my personal world, or a customer making an inquiry, who is part of my business world. This was the problem posed to Shannon when developing his 'Mathematical Theory of Communication'.[139] A cyberworld denizen can call up data from all over the world, according to his or her interests, which are a reflection of personal identity, i.e. of who this individual understands him- or herself to be in the world. A cyberworld denizen can also present him- or herself as who s/he is by posting data at some site within the cyberworld. These data, of whatever kind (text, image, sound, video) are *identified* with the individual posting them, who may use a pseudonym.

What is a pseudonym in the context of the cyberworld? In the first place, it is a string of bits which, by virtue of the cybernetic computability of the cyberworld, may be linked to the identifying number of the device the user is using, location and time co-ordinates. As a pseudonym, this bit-string is supposed to disguise the genuine proper name of the individual concerned. Since the proper name is at the core of any who's identity, such covering-up amounts to a measure to keep that individual's private world private, i.e. hidden from view. *Anonymous* postings in the cyberworld are possible, just as they are outside it, in which case the identity of the person posting is identified only indirectly through the (stored) data of the internet log logging the user's movements in the cyberworld. Because all sorts of data circulating in the cyberworld can easily be stored, i.e. recorded automatically, this opens up many opportunities for processing those data, in particular, with a view to establishing the identity of a particular

[139] Shannon 1948.

user and his or her movements. The individual is identified with a piece of code (an IP address, the ID of a digital device) that enables also cyber-surveillance and cyber-tracking, amounting to 'überveillance'.[140] All the digital data in the cyberworld relating to a certain individual can be pieced together, through the appropriate executable code, in an individual profile that inverts the first-person perspective of what someone does in the cyberworld into a third-person perspective of a reified digital data profile through which others, in a certain way, have disposal over who the individual concerned *is*. The cyberworld is a cyber-space-time with digitized Cartesian space-time co-ordinates recording movements within it, and not the time-space of a world in which human being exists ec-statically stretched toward three independent temporal dimensions.[141] Hence the third-person, 'objective', 'scientific' view of an individual that is enabled through the linking of digital data, clashes with the first-person view of an individual living his or her life in and out of the cyberworld or the first-and-second person viewpoints of sharing a world.[142]

The cyberworld also offers a space for individual whos to present themselves *as* who they are by placing bit-strings (mostly data) in and sending them through the cyberworld. With its visual and audio interfaces, the internet has opened untold possibilities for self-presentations of all kinds which can be called up globally by anyone. Any who's identity becomes potentially global through the medium of the cyberworld, with the consequence that who any self is as a shining-back from the world becomes malleable also through the feedback received back from the cyberworld. Who I am for myself can differ crassly from the third-person identity circulating in the cyberworld. The game of who-presentation takes on a digital guise with a quality different from showing oneself off as who one is in other public media, by virtue of the ease and global scope of such self-presentation via a bit-string with which the who in question identifies.

---

140 Cf. Michael & Michael 2010.

141 Cf. Eldred 2009/2011 for more on three-dimensional, ecstatic time.

142 Cf. Capurro 2011 and Chapter 5.

The striving of any who to be somewho in the cyberworld is to receive as much *appreciative feedback* from other cyberworld denizens as possible, which can happen fairly directly due to the accessibility of the cyberworld to everybody. In the case of other public media, there is usually a gatekeeper that watches over who is to have a say, to make an appearance in that medium. The who-game thus comes to be played on a larger, global, digitally mediated scale, a cyber-stage. Nevertheless, the stakes remain, firstly, being noticed at all, and, secondly, gaining others' attention, being esteemed and estimated highly by others (positive feedback). What Plato called φιλοτιμία (love of esteem) thus takes on a different garb in a different scenario in the internet age, but remains the same in that it is still the who-game which, of course, is played not only in the West. The lure of being esteemed as somewho is amplified by the ease of self-presentation in the cyberworld.

Another aspect of finding one's self in the internet age is that, due to its global reach, the cyberworld reflects many different possibilities of living in the world, from all the world's different cultures. Ease and cheapness of access to the internet for billions of people open up a vast space in which to find one's self, thus perhaps causing friction with the expectations within the ethos of a given culture. Especially entertainment media such as film and music proffer identity masks to anyone who'll put them on, adopting a life-style and self-understanding that may be promoted by a culture industry. The ease with which digital beings disseminate throughout the cyberworld leads to a fast merging of possible identities, especially for youth who are still finding themselves, also in what the cyberworld offers by way of quickly circulating identity masks that inevitably induce also a certain levelling of youth-identity. One of the more trivial of such masks is fashion, i.e. how somewho dresses to present him- or herself to the world. With the cyberworld, youth fashion especially spreads very quickly around the globe, with youth fashion strategies demarcating who one is from one's parents' identities becoming adopted rapidly. The typical different local cultural identities also become more visible in their differences via the cyberworld.

3.2 Digital privacy: personal freedom to reveal and conceal

One could see everything in the little square-shaped boxes; there was no privacy; none of those lingering shadows and odd corners that there used to be;
Virginia Woolf *Orlando* p. 543

As discussed in Chapter 1, there are two basic kinds of privacy: personal privacy and the privacy of property. The former has to do with disclosing and concealing *who* one is, whereas the latter concerns access to, use and disposal of various kinds of property. In this section the focus will be on the former, and in the next on the latter.

It is paradoxical that to be somewho implies a striving for *showing* oneself off *as* who one is in the world, the very opposite of a withdrawal into hiddenness. These are games of self-presentation, of pretending to *be who* one is through the adoption of one mask rather than another, which is by no means a matter of mere pretence, because to be somewho at all, some kind of *fitting* mask or other must be adopted with which one genuinely identifies or with which, through sheer unconscious habit, one has unwittingly identified. Without a mask of self-identity, no self-presentation at all. Showing off who one is can go through a gamut of gradations, even to the point of such diffidence or modesty that one would rather not put oneself on show at any price, but instead lead a quiet, undisturbed life in seclusion. With the advent of the cyberworld, the possibilities for revealing and showing off who one is multiply exponentially, and the possibilities of tracking somewho's movements in the matrix of the cyberworld are immense, since every movement leaves a digital trace embedded in the matrix. In this sense, it is virtually impossible to remain hidden as who one is in the cyberworld. One has to go to extraordinary technical lengths to cover one's tracks in the cyberworld, an effort most people do not want to make, if only because they have no clue about how to achieve it technically. Since the cyberworld, by its very cybernetic nature, offers such strong technical possibilities of tracking anyone's movements in the cyberworld, including any data an individual deposits on any public site within the cyberworld, issues of personal privacy come to the fore. Above all, it is the easy technical options for recording data of all kinds that are problematic and must be curtailed. The issues surrounding personal privacy in the cyberworld are therefore not merely technical nor only a matter of normative restriction and regulation but, first and foremost, of learning to see that digital personal privacy is itself an historically new socio-ontological phenomenon in which the digital control that the cyberworld affords hits back at human individuals themselves leading their private lives.

One way — perhaps the *key* way — of concealing who one is in the cyberworld is to encrypt one's data. Another is to keep one's data, whatever they may be, at a site in the cyberworld to which access is limited and controlled. Since, within the cyberworld, one *is* (identified with) one's data, data encryption amounts to a powerful way of veiling one's identity and one's movements in the cyberworld. *Encryption* itself is a technology relying crucially on mathematics, especially pure number theory of the prime numbers and, more recently since the advent of the *idea* of quantum computers employing quantum decryption algorithms, other cryptographic theories such as code-based, hash-based, lattice-based, multivariate-quadratic-equations and secret-key cryptographies.[143] All cryptography is a race to keep ahead of decryption techniques, which are the other side of the coin to cryptography and become more powerful, the faster computers themselves become. The strength of an encryption technique is assessed by its ability to withstand (today: quantum-algorithmic) decryption attacks. In the computable cyberworld, even encryption techniques are computable. There is an irony in the fact that the immense power of calculation unleashed in the cyberworld simply through digital beings themselves being bit-strings gives rise to the converse problem of *preventing* certain bit-strings (keys) from being computable by practical standards, i.e. within a reasonable amount of computing time, which is

143 Bernstein et al. 2009 pp. 1, 17.

the problematic of complexity theory.[144] It is also ironic that, whilst efficient algorithms may be found to crack encryption techniques, the converse is not possible: there is no mathematical proof that a given encryption technique is unbreakable, but rather, only practical experience gathered over many years trying to crack an encryption technique allows an assessment as to whether an it is practically safe. This is a consequence of the insolubility of the Entscheidungs-problem.[145]

Private sites in the cyberworld, to which access is controlled, must go hand in hand with encryption techniques because data must be transmitted back and forth between a user and a private site in the cyberworld (that is, a certain server in the internet). Concealing who one is, i.e. maintaining one's privacy, thus becomes a matter of digital technical finesse. Private sites in the cyberworld are protected by passwords or some other technical means such as card readers or iris scans. These techniques work according to the principle of matching two parts of a symbolon in the Greek sense, like a key with the lock, which now are simply two bit-strings that must match to gain access to a site where certain data can then be 'seen'.

Encryption techniques and limited access to data on certain sites are both technical achievements which, however, have their counterparts in likewise technical ways of breaking or subverting codes, thus gaining access to data supposed to be hidden from view, if only in the sense of being illegible. Invasions of digital personal privacy hence become a matter of cleverly developing the right anti-code that will break an encryption or gain access to a private web-site, e.g. by computing myriad possible keys. Theft, in particular identity theft, gains a new meaning in the cyberworld; it becomes *hacking* which is a computing task. The protection of digital personal privacy has to be approached in a technical manner related to digital data protection. If the core of somewho's identity is her or his proper name, this digitized name, which is merely a binary number, is connected with other bit-strings (data) that

144 Penrose 1999 pp. 181ff.

145 Turing 1936.

add up to give a full digital personal dossier on the person concerned. Today the possibilities of collecting data and processing them into person-specific dossiers are immense. This is data mining in its person-specific variant. Digitally there's hardly anywhere to hide, except behind a screen of encryption that may or may not hold up under hacking attack.

3.3 Protection of private property in the cyberworld

The other aspect of cyberworld privacy, which must not be confused with personal digital privacy, are the digital, cyberworld aspects of private property. This concerns both digital data that are *themselves* private property and digital data *about* private property. The focus here will be on the former. Protection of digital private property has an eminently economic aspect and importance. Insofar, it concerns the gainful game, as introduced and outlined in *1.6 The private individual and private property as a mode of reified sociation: the gainful game (classical political economy, Marx)*. In the area of personal privacy, digital private property concerns a person's private life-world which needs to be protected, i.e. kept hidden, by limiting access to personal digital data on that person, an issue discussed in the preceding section. Here, therefore, we will concentrate on the economic aspects of digital private property which, at the same time, are then of juridical importance.

Every player in the gainful game is an income-earner of some kind. The aim of involvement in the economic game is always money-related, money itself being the reification of value whose movement through its various forms *is* the capitalist economy. Each of the four basic income-types is the price of buying or hiring an income-source. The reification of value as money and price is *arithmetically quantitative*, and thus discrete, which enables easy digitization and hence also almost unlimited scope for calculation, starting from bookkeeping through to models of whole economies running on super-computers. The movement of a capitalist economy, which is, in its hidden essence, the movement of value in myriad circuits of capital, can be captured mathematically and hence also digitally, and that in countless phenomenal forms such as supply control, logistics, personal finances, financial accounts of companies small and large, market transactions of all kinds from consumer retail through company turnover to stock exchange transactions in highly derivative products. Money itself can become digital, i.e. a jealously kept bit-string kept in an electromagnetic purse, access to which is controlled by some kind of digital security procedure. Payments can be made in the cyberworld simply by transferring a bit-string for a certain amount from one digital purse to another.

Private property in the form of *personal* income also has a connection to personal privacy because the individual income-earner is also an individual spender, i.e. a *consumer* (along with family members who help spend what the breadwinner has earned). Consumption is an important, if superficial, aspect of personal identity-formation and -cultivation insofar as consumption reflects how an individual shapes his or her private world and understands him- or herself as some particular who from among the countless self-defining possibilities on offer, thus marking him- or herself off as who from others. Being a consumer, however, brings an individual into contact with firms selling consumer goods. The firm itself may be located in the cyberworld, giving rise to *digital retail commerce* , i.e. *e-retailing*, in the digital retail market-place, which is one kind of market among many that exploits the medium of the cyberworld. The consumer enters into a relationship with an online (digital) retailer through the medium of the cyberworld and hence becomes digitally identifiable, with all that implies for digital retailers' attempts to market (advertise) and sell retail goods from toothpaste to real estate. Issues of personal privacy arise massively because a consumer's movements in the cyberworld provide the basis for building a profile of individual consumer behaviour that may be used cleverly to enticingly market goods. Debates on internet privacy to date focus very strongly on this ease of invasion of personal privacy, but this is, to a large extent, the other side of the coin to privacy as private property, the other major issue being the incursions of the state into both personal privacy and the privacy of private property.

Corresponding to the four basic kinds of income-source property as discussed in *1.6 The private individual and private property as a mode of reified sociation: the gainful game (classical political economy,*

Marx), it can be asked what their digital cyberworld counterparts are, viz. what is a digital labourer, what is digital land, what is digital money-capital and what is a digital enterprise. Let us consider each of these in turn.

Since the labourer (*wage-earner* of any kind) as a living human being is also the bearer of (the right to) life and liberty, this income-source is not for sale (although its labour power, whatever it may be, can be *hired* out and expended in labour of some kind or other), and also cannot be digitized, despite the suggestive analogy with robots or, perhaps, avatars. The former are complicated, cleverly programmed kinds of machines, whereas the latter are digital representations of an individual with which this individual identifies, a kind of digital who-mask (cf. *1.2 Selfhood as an identification with reflections from the world*). If human beings themselves are conceived as some kind of highly complex neurobiological data-processing machines, as some are wont to do in the area of artificial intelligence, then conversely it is seductive to conceive robots, too, as humanoid. If, however, human being is thought through outside of today's hegemonic, scientific, subject/object paradigm, it is hardly possible to confuse human being — whose hallmark is freedom — with any sort of artificial being. The question concerning the historical cast of human being itself is a fundamental one lurking in the background to discussions of the ethical implications of the cyberworld for human living.

Land in the cyberworld (*cyberland*) can be regarded simply as a binary number, like anything else in the cyberworld. Digital land is nothing other than a numerical address (or several) in the 'universe' or cyberspace of all possible cyberworld addresses. Such addresses are generally called IP (Internet Protocol) addresses which are an n-tuple of integers, hence countably finite and also rational in the mathematical sense. Having an address, position, *digital location* or *digital place* in the cyberworld is the precondition for posting any digital beings there (data and executable code), and for any other digital beings (such as a user's command) reaching it. Compared to places in the physical world, arithmetic digital 'places' are both placeless and even positionless.[146] Since cyberland is merely a bit-string address, and such addresses are available without limit and at almost zero cost, there is no absolute ground-rent[147] to be had for it and hence also no price for a cyberworld address, which are as plentiful as grains of sand. A mere numerical address is all that is needed for a location in the cyberworld. This number even enables users to spend time there, perhaps even a lot of time, chatting, exchanging, constructing artificial identities called avatars, moving through artificial 3-D worlds, etc. etc. Strictly speaking, the cyberworld is the materialized, digitized arithmologos, but the average user need know nothing at all of this arithmologos because the programmers have constructed the necessary sensuous, handy interfaces.

Although digital locations are merely a binary number, this number is associated with a (domain) name, which is of crucial importance for presenting who one is in the digital world, whether it be an individual person or a company. Therefore, certain names and their associated cyberworld locations (domain names) are jealously guarded, especially for commercial reasons, and therefore command a price, which may be called *digital (or cyber-) differential ground-rent*. In the case of an individual, having a location in the cyberworld for showing off who one is may be important for that individual (one of its who-masks for self-presentation comparable to one's proper name), and he or she will pay for that stable location where he or she is to be found in the cyberworld. For an enterprise of any kind, an internet address is a digital business location that likewise must be paid for, or rather *leased for cyber-ground-rent*, especially when the associated name is good for doing business. Hence there are auctions for desirable cyberworld locations, that is, for the names that can be associated with a firm digital location. A company can only set up business in the cyberworld by first securing a digital location where it can locate its data, program code and perhaps its digital goods as well, if they are of the digitizable kind, such as music or movies.

---

[146] Cf. Eldred 2009/2011 § 2.2.

[147] For more on ground-rent, see Eldred 1984/2010 §§ 44ff.

A *digital business location* must have a shop-front where prospective customers, who may be consumers or other businesses, can enter. Hence some of the digital code at that location must be made accessible to prospective customers, i.e. it must be public, whereas the back-room remains private. A significant issue in private property rights concerns the data and the data track that prospective customers or simply visitors to a commercial digital business location leave behind. To whom do these data *belong*, and to whom and for what purposes may they be *employed* and *disclosed*? Issues of personal privacy here clash head on with commercial private property interests. Hence the importance of clearly having in view the two different primary phenomena of privacy. May a digital business, such as a social media web-site, rightfully anonymize these data and use them for data-mining purposes regarding, say, consumer behaviour? To whom do the commentaries belong that the user of a commercial blogging web-site leaves behind? In the physical world, such questions do not arise in such profusion because a private user's movements in the physical world are not immediately recorded as digital code which, in principle, can be stored 'forever' (a bit-string never 'dies'). With the deployment of digital technologies in the physical world, however, new issues regarding the privacy of personal data arise when e.g. a customer to a shop is recorded on a video camera or, more generally, when a member of the public is filmed on a public street. The latter example illustrates a conflict not between private property rights, but between the private citizen and the state's surveillance measures in the name of public order and security.

The equivalent of *means of production* and *means of circulation* in the cyberworld is the software (executable code) kept at the cyber-business location to generate or make available *digital products* for customers. Digital products can consist of data of various kinds that may be legible (fairly) directly (e.g. a journal or 'newspaper' article, an e-book) or more indirectly (e.g. the audio file of a song, the video file of a movie which must be processed by the appropriate software in the appropriate hardware) or executable digital code (software of any kind for both personal entertainment and business purposes). To do *transactions* in the cyberworld, the customer must be able to securely transfer data to the online shop for the order to be filled. If the product purchased is itself digital, specific access must be granted to the customer to download the purchase. A commercial transaction online hence requires encryption technology, especially to keep the customer's financial data secure.

Cyberworld banking is a case in point where secure intercourse with the bank is paramount. Money itself takes the form of a bit-string recorded in a customer's account from which withdrawals can be made by transferring digital data across the cyberworld to a recipient's own bank. Commercial transactions in the cyberworld thus combine aspects of both personal privacy and private property. Personal privacy is involved insofar as the individual making transactions does not want this to become common public knowledge. In the physical world, a transaction is usually fairly private, even if performed publicly in a shop, but in the cyberworld, the digital data relating to the transaction can circulate freely through the electromagnetic medium and be misused for questionable purposes. The privacy of private property is of concern because of the danger of digital theft and digital fraud which arises everywhere where digital data pertain to financial accounts such as bank accounts or credit cards. A company's cyberworld location may be also productive in the sense of being part of its operations in the broadest sense, including internal data-sharing & communication, accounting, research & development (involving intellectual private property), (secret) business & marketing strategy, etc. etc. All these cyber-activities of a company must be kept private in the double sense of hidden and non-manipulable by outsiders. Hence, once again, encryption technology is of the utmost importance for maintaining the integrity of private cyber-property in a company.

A special problem arises with regard to *commodity products* that are themselves digital, such as texts, music, film and software, because these are simply (perhaps extremely long) bit-strings that can be copied in the electromagnetic matrix almost without cost, i.e. given that one has a digital device of some kind for storing bit-strings. The *production* of such a bit-string may have cost an enormous amount of labour (e.g. years spent by an author writing a book or by programmers developing a piece of software such as a game), technical means of production (e.g. a recording or film studio), invested money-capital, ground-rent for a production site, but the *reproduction* of the digital product costs almost nothing. There is thus a glaring discrepancy between production and reproduction costs. Hence the attempts to protect digital products through encryption techniques, which can only be partially successful because, in the end, any encryption code can be cracked by clever hackers with fast computers, which today are ubiquitous.

In the case of executable digital code (i.e. software), this represents human intelligence that has been digitized and materialized (i.e. outsourced) in a digital electromagnetic matrix that can easily be joined seamlessly to the cyberworld where it can be executed (i.e. used) anywhere. The same holds true for any other digitized intellectual product insofar as it is materialized human intelligence which, in its outsourced form can, at the very least, be easily copied, even though it is not automatically executable. A digitized treatise, for instance, may not be much use to many people, because it has to be read and understood by someone who is suitably educated, but a piece of software that unfolds its effects automatically is useful for 'everybody' and hence up for grabs. No wonder then, that the protection of *digitized intellectual private property* becomes a major issue with the emergence of the cyberworld where, as with personal identity, the very powerfulness of computability itself becomes a problem.

Digital loan-capital in the cyberworld is simply money loaned via the medium of the cyberworld. An individual or company with credit from a bank or some other lending institution can call down credit lines online, or an online bank account is supplemented with an additional balance over which the lender can dispose. Money-capital is also used to purchase shares in private companies publicly listed on stock exchanges, and such share-trading is done via the cyberworld today as a matter of course, as if it had never been done in any other way. The deep affinity of money as a mere discrete quantity to a digital representation has meant that banking and financial markets have led the way in exploiting the opportunities offered by the cyberworld, in particular, with regard to *cost-savings*, and that on a *global* scale. Money and share entitlements easily assume the form of bit-strings and can be transferred quickly through the digital electromagnetic medium. Money-capital also may be invested in commodities or foreign exchange for the sake of making a trading profit. The cyberworld enables a scarcely conceivable *acceleration* in the speed of financial transactions on the world's financial markets as well as the *automation* of trading by means of digital code (trading algorithms). This acceleration is just one facet to the acceleration in the turnover of capital as a whole and thus the acceleration of time in capitalist societies, since the allocation of money-capital to public companies through the stock market also has effects on each company's turnover time.[148]

Trading on all sorts of financial, commodity, foreign currency markets via the digital medium must be surveilled cybernetically to prevent market manipulation, which is an aspect of the protection of private property. The employment of trading algorithms can also distort the functioning of financial markets by exacerbating price fluctuations, especially when the trading algorithm turns out to be highly inappropriate for the current market situation, or simply contains a disastrous bug. Thus losses (and hence an 'injury' to invested capital) may occur simply through 'dumb' software being deployed in the wrong situation. That executable digital code in the form of trading algorithms automatically executes trades on a given market amounts to this code acting as an agent of the company (usually a broker, a bank or some other financial institution). The algorithm is legally entitled to make transactions in the name of the company. Insofar, the private property title is alienated or outsourced to a kind of robot as legal agent. The company's programmer who wrote and deployed the trading algorithm, however, remains the human legal agent. Infringement of private property rights can therefore also occur when the code of a trading algorithm is interfered with by a third party, which may even cause major disturbances on a given market.

Another aspect of digital privacy concerns the relationship of individuals and companies to the *state*. This concerns not only surveillance of an individual's or a company's movements in the

---

148 For more detail cf. Eldred 2009/2011 § 5.5.

cyberworld, but also, and especially, the disclosure of digital financial movements for *taxation* purposes. Driven by an insatiable appetite, the state invades the privacy of financial data to ensure and enforce tax collection. Digital code also opens up new possibilities for tax surveillance, tax collection and even completely new taxes (e.g. financial transactions tax, satellite-based road tolls) that would scarcely be collectible without the aid of the appropriate software and hardware. The new digital world stimulates also politicians' powers of imagination for inventing ever new sorts of taxes, which invariably are associated with incursions into the privacy of private property not simply by appropriating it as taxes, but by forcing disclosure of financial data.

3.4 Cyber-publicness

The global electromagnetic matrix that we have dubbed the cyberworld (in preference to 'internet'), provides places to bit-strings of all kinds that can be inscribed in it, where they can also change co-ordinate places, i.e. circulate in this vector space. Those bit-strings that can be taken in and understood without further ado by human beings, such as written texts, images, audio recordings, digitized movies, etc., may be called *(immediately) intelligible code*, in contrast to executable digital code (programs, software, apps, routines, algorithms) and *processing data* that are 'read' only by digital programs to produce automatic effects that are not immediately taken in by human beings. For the sake of clarity and simplicity, we introduce the distinction between *digital messages*, which are (immediately) intelligible code circulating exclusively among human beings and legible to them, and *digital signals*, which are processing data sent to a digital device for processing to effect some change, from either another digital device or some physical source (e.g. incident light, ambient air).

Processing data are essential for programs that automatically and algorithmically process data-input, including in so-called machine-to-machine 'communication' and the 'internet of things',[149] through which the eery automated control through the medium of the cyberworld

[149] Kranenburg 2008.

extends to become not only 'ubiquitous' and 'pervasive' (these terms being used interchangeably in the current discourse on the subject), but all-pervasive and downright invasive of personal freedom. Through the prospect of an all-pervasive and invasive ambience of interlinked, cybernetic devices, human beings themselves are willingly delivered over into a cyberworld which they themselves have made and continue to build and extend, apparently for the sake of their own convenience of living.

There is a problem in making the distinction between messages and signals because of the tendency to regard computer programs and computers themselves as 'intelligent' or 'smart', or even to conceive of 'messages' and 'information' being sent back and forth among all kinds of physical beings. Thus, e.g. 'data' received by a radio telescope from a galaxy can be regarded as 'information' emitted by that galaxy, or temperature data received by a machine via a thermometer are regarded as the machine's receiving a 'message' which it 'interprets'. Behind this utter confusion between human being and artificial being lies the oblivion to the ontological difference, namely, that it is only human being that is capable of understanding data *as* data, information *as* information, a message *as* a message and is hence *intelligent* in the sense of being open to the *being* of beings.

The modern age, however, has been cast by Descartes dualistically as res cogitans and res extensa, and this remains so to the present day, despite all the critiques of Descartes within modern metaphysics that have only modified or varied his basic dualism. In particular, today's science, which is out to achieve control of the world through effective causality, both *relies* on this dualism and then proceeds to *collapse* and confuse it. In particular, today's science is utterly oblivious to the distinction between who and what, and its will to power depends on its being blinded to it. Science thinks within a realist, materialist metaphysics that strives for control even over the soul and the ideal through the real. Hence, for example, real, physically present, sense data are (conceived as) processed in the brain into ideal representations of real objects out there, and the science of psychology turns the soul into a real object of research that can be measured and tested. The immaterial human mind comes to be conceived as materialized in the brain[150] so that it is completely natural today to speak of brains 'thinking' and, say, of the right and left hemispheres of the brain 'thinking' differently, the one half analytically, the other holistically, emotionally. The billions of neurones in the brain come to be conceived as the seat of consciousness (in preference of Descartes' pineal gland), as if consciousness itself would be generated spontaneously by enough artificially cultivated neurones interacting. Who is to say, however, that the human mind is (in) the brain or in the head or in the body at all? Why isn't the brain conceived as a physical *condition* of the mind which is by no means confined to a human body? This is not to suggest any sort of mysticism; on the contrary, we experience very directly all the time that *in* our minds we are always already *out* there in the world.[151]

The perplexing, astonishing and distinctive hallmark of the cyberworld is that human understanding of aspects of the world has been digitized and outsourced materially into its own artificial medium where it automatically produces effects and insofar seems to be 'alive'. Along with this outsourcing of human understanding, we have become seduced into speaking of computers' 'intelligence', of machines 'interpreting' code, of 'messages' being sent back and forth between digital devices themselves, of 'smart' phones, etc. etc., all of which results in endless confusion and further oblivion to the distinctiveness of human being itself. By having outsourced the arithmologos to an artificial world of artificial devices, it is as if we were looking in the mirror of our own intelligence. Hence modern science comes to model human thinking itself as 'computable', i.e. as reproducible by a computer that is large and fast enough, and such research is supported by extremely generous grants precisely to further science's will to effective control. *Digital artificial intelligence* is presently enjoying a revival in interest from all sides.

In this section, the focus is on those digital beings, immediately intelligible code or digital message, that human beings can take in and

---

[150] Cf. Roth 2003, Singer 2004, Fuchs 2009.

[151] Cf. Eldred 2012.

understand and appreciate, starting with written messages, but including of course also photos, music and film. Such messages can be either private or public. Private messages are addressed and circulated to those friends and acquaintances who are part of one's own personal life-world; they may be posted at a location in the cyberworld to which only these friends have access. With such messages back and forth, friends show themselves to each other *as* who they are, thus sharing a private world. They may indulge in shows of self-presentation that are not intended for the world at large, in which they adopt other masks for their public personae. An important aspect of personal privacy as a valued aspect of living one's life has thus become the protection of private messaging in the cyberworld against intrusion of all kinds, whether it be from other persons, from companies or the state. Such messaging is an aspect of the play of revealing and concealing who one is oneself, which amounts to the play of revealing and concealing one's own private life-world. Having control *oneself* over this who-play of disclosure and exposure is today an important issue for personal freedom which is very difficult because the cyberworld by its very nature enables digitized control *by others*. The autonomous 'data-subject' is an illusion.

Conversely, the cyberworld offers hitherto unknown potentials for presenting oneself as who one is to others in general, i.e. to the public, since an individual can post almost any digital message at some location or other in the cyberworld or send it through the cyberworld to many recipients, as with a public e-mail discussion. There is thus a specifically *cyber-publicness* based on the circulation of digital messages freely through the cyberworld to 'anyone who'll listen'. This cyber-public-sphere already encompasses the entire globe, providing a platform for anyone to present themselves as who they are through digital messages sent out into the cyberworld. Given the economic, technical and political prerequisites, the cyberworld is freely accessible and thus represents a public medium to be distinguished from older public media such as newspapers, journals, radio, television and film, because now *everybody* can show off who they are in the cyberworld.[152] There is no gatekeeper

[152] Cf. Scheule et al. 2004.

to having your say, and the costs of sending out a message are minimal, even though it may have taken more or less considerable resources to make the 'message', e.g. a video. There is a new quality to cyber-publicness thanks to easy accessibility, which gives 'freedom of speech' a new meaning, although 'speech' has to be understood in a very broad sense to include all sorts of digital messages.

Circulating messages in the cyberworld is a kind of movement whose source can be an individual, an association, a company, an organization, a government agency, etc. Here we consider only individuals as the sources of messages. To be the source of a message is to spontaneously control a movement of one's own life and is therefore an expression, an exercise of human freedom. Who one shows oneself to be through the messages sent out into the cyberworld can be estimated and esteemed by others through the entire gamut of estimation and appreciation, which passes into negative modes such as being derided for one's message (it was not appreciated, so the sender is depreciated) or being completely ignored (and thus not having one's existence as somewho confirmed by the world at large). To receive an echo from others through the cyberworld requires sending messages that 'say' something to somebody. The louder the echo, the more popular the message. The more popular the message, the more it has been tailored to what people in general already understand and appreciate. Presenting oneself as who one is by sending out messages into the cyberworld is double-edged insofar as one can receive confirming feedback that bolsters one's who-stand in the world, on the one hand, or, on the other, that one becomes exposed to unwanted publicity in being gossiped about by others in the third person, over which one has no control.

Digital messages of all kinds have to be taken in and interpreted in one way or another by others, giving rise to *differences of opinion*. This is the *controversy* generated by what a message discloses about the world, no matter whether it be a trivial matter or one of great import. Insofar as it is open to everybody, the cyberworld is a neutral medium that lets both shallow and deep messages through.[153] There is always

[153] Cf. Eldred 2011b in Capurro & Holgate 2011.

strife over truth, especially over the deeper truths of the world. Consumers expressing their opinions about products they have used (e.g. a stay at a certain hotel) may disclose a useful truth for other consumers that has very little to do with the identities of those posting such consumer-goods' assessments. A musician posting a digital audio-file of his or her own music, by contrast, is exposing herself to an appreciative or depreciative estimation by others in her very identity *as* a musician. Sending out political messages into the cyberworld may be an endeavour to engage in controversy over the deeper justification of a political viewpoint, or it may be merely an effort to find like-minded supporters for a political worldview or action or specific policy decision. The former is a search for a measure of truth, the latter a search for confirmation of political convictions. And so on. The artificial medium of the cyberworld offers analogously the same possibilities for exchanging or publicizing messages of all kinds as the other media do. Its easy and cheap accessibility to everybody draws praise for its so-called 'democratizing' potentials.

Here it is important to distinguish democracy as a certain form of rule (-cracy) by people (demos) over the people (demos) as (democratic) government from democracy as power (dynamis) enjoyed by the common people, for 'everybody'. If 'every' individual has the power to freely send out and receive all sorts of digital messages through the cyberworld, 'everybody' is in this sense freer. Perhaps this should be called *demodynamics* (people power) rather than democracy. Such a dynamism of the people at large to engage in digital messaging does not amount to 'power to the people' in a political sense, but to a general freedom of everybody to engage freely in sending messages back and forth to each other in public, a kind of *public digital angeletics*[154] that bypasses the gate-keeping power of other media and also easily eludes the power of government to control the formation and dissemination of public opinion, especially on volatile political issues.

---

154 Angeletics is a phenomenology of messaging first developed by Capurro; cf. Capurro & Holgate 2011.

The circulation of digital messages in the now global cyberworld contributes to the formation of a *global public opinion* that is not uniform, but marked by segments and a back and forth of opinions on issues of the day. This global public opinion goes hand in hand with *global moods* that permeate the global medium of the cyberworld atmospherically, ranging from uplifting to downcast through all possible gradations from momentary euphoria through to fear, anxiety, despondency and utter resignation. News with a global relevance is now 'there' within seconds or minutes, accompanied by commentary and chatter and different moods in different cultural situations. The uprising of a people in a part of the world, for instance, will be accompanied by a mood of the celebration of freedom in one country, and by a mood of fearfulness over national security in another. Each historical culture resonates differently with the current global news situation. As an artificial, technical thing, the cyberworld has no mood, but the people who send and receive digital messages through it do.

3.5 Freedom in the cyberworld

> 'Don't you wish you were free, Lenina?'
> 'I don't know what you mean, I am free.
> Free to have the most wonderful time.
> Everybody's happy nowadays'
> He laughed. 'Yes. "Everybody's happy
> nowadays." We begin giving the children
> that at five. But wouldn't you like to be free
> to be happy in some other way, Lenina? In
> your own way, for example; not in
> everybody else's way.'
> 'I don't know what you mean,' she repeated.
> (Aldous Huxley *Brave New World*)

3.5.1 The cyberworld frees itself first of all

The cyberworld is the artificial, global, electromagnetic medium for the movement of bit-strings of all kinds through it. Freedom of movement relates first of all to bit-strings themselves, which are free to move in the same sense employed in physical dynamics for the motion of physical bodies. Freedom of movement for bit-strings thus signifies a technical enablement of their motion through the cyberworld.[155] Freedom in the cyberworld is therefore, in the first place, a freedom for the cyberworld itself to unfold its digital powers of control over changes within and without the digitized electromagnetic matrix. The cyberworld unleashes its cybernetic powers of control upon the world as a whole. Such bit-strings may be message data for communication between and among human beings, or they may be processing data, or they may be program code itself, including malicious executable code or 'malware'.

The cyberworld, which includes the internet, has caused excitement worldwide for the technical ease with which messages can cross the globe at minimal cost. This seems to be the greatest boost to freedom of expression in a long time. One is enthusiastic about how digital communication has enabled and pushes toward democratic government from below in contrast to earlier times when despotic regimes had an easy time of it in suppressing dissent, simply by controlling state radio and television. The one-to-many construction of the mass media has been undermined and altered by the many-to-many communication in the Web. Social web-sites excite private individuals with the possibilities for extending their personal life-worlds through easy exchanges with friends, sending digital messages back and forth almost instantaneously. People *en masse* form a kind a global, cyber-connected We, thus making talk of 'people in general' as a universal, undifferentiated category and appellation more and more pertinent and palpable as a *reality* mediated precisely by this technically sophisticated, artificial *res* (thing) called the cyberworld.[156]

'People' are also very enthused by the possibilities of working from home or from shifting, self-chosen workplaces that have opened up through the technologically enabled option of sending bit-strings through the cyberworld. People, or at least some segments of the workforce, are less tied to specific workplace locations and have become

155 Cf. Shannon 1948 which aims precisely at such technical enablement.

156 Cf. Eldred 2011 in Capurro & Holgate 2011.

freer in that sense. The movement of bit-strings can substitute to some extent for the movement of human bodies by means of transportation. Business communications have become quick, easy and highly mobile, not just for personal communication, but also for sending business data back and forth for informational purposes or to be processed further. From a personal and business point of view, the cyberworld seems to enhance our being in the world. As a drawback, there is only the danger that privacy, in the double sense developed in this study, will be violated, such as when the personal data of private persons are 'hacked' or surreptitiously gathered, or business secrets stolen from internal company data-servers. Therefore there is great concern and discussion in the media over privacy issues, and these privacy issues all revolve around the security of bit-strings in the cyberworld, whether they be digital messages, processing data or executable program code. All three kinds are open to unwanted disclosure or damage and manipulation. Infringements of data security are seen to be a threat to freedom in the cyberworld. This is the view from the surface of everyday life, both personal and business.

But there are deeper issues of freedom here relating both to technology itself and to the economic mobilization of the globe. Digital technology implemented in the cyberworld seems to be for the convenience of its users, to make their lives easier, but the converse is also the case: the more digital technologies are incorporated into everyday lives, the more living becomes dependent upon these technologies. Mobile telephony, for instance, seems to be a boon for humankind, but it also turns human beings into the appendages of their mobile phones and other mobile digital devices to receive all kinds of digital messages from voice messages through text messages to photos and videos. People start to add up and weigh the pros and cons of having a mobile phone. Many decide they need one for this or that reason. Such needs arise only from the changing complex of customary usages constituting their daily life practices. People's lives are thus being shaped by digital technologies of the cyberworld. It is appropriate here to speak of 'people' because these technologies are perfectly general and designed for 'everybody'. Like the electronic mass media of television and film, the ubiquity of the cyberworld starts to engulf everyday life itself. The all-surrounding cyberworld grafts itself onto the everyday world as a natural part of it which 'nobody' can do without. The movements of bit-strings through the cyber-matrix starts to dictate the pace of everyday life and invade life-time day and night wherever the cyberworld pervades.

'Surrounding cyberworld' is a synonym for so-called '*ambient intelligence*' that is one of the emergent technologies which will immerse people in an environment 'populated' by networked digital devices into which human intelligence has been outsourced, thus making the devices themselves seem intelligent. 'People' develop an 'intimacy' with their ambient cybernetic devices that control certain aspects of their everyday lives and they thus become dependent on them for shaping their lives and directing their lives' movements, which increasingly conform to the movement of bit-strings driven by currents of electrons. Again there is the ambivalence between making our lives easier through digital gadgets, on the one hand, and becoming more and more dependent on their so-called intelligence, on the other. Only the software developers and the engineers truly have the knowledge about what these devices do, because they designed and programmed them. Their design is life-shaping.[157] The ubiquity and everydayness of the cyberworld depends enormously on the work of software developers and engineers who have catered to making the devices 'handy'[158] (conforming to the human body) and also very simple to operate (so that users need know nothing at all about the digital code that controls them). To live in the everyday world enveloped by the cyberworld requires no knowledge whatever, even in principle, of what a digital bit is, thus opening and widening a gap between those who know and those who don't that has broader social implications.

With regard to the public media, especially the speed with which digital messages are disseminated throughout the cyberworld generates the illusion that the latest news bit-string is the best and most important.

---

157 Cf. Winograd & Flores 1986, Coyne 1995.

158 In German, the very word for mobile telephone is 'Handy'.

Under the impact — or onslaught — of the budding cyberworld, the news media are sucked increasingly into the vortex of the 24x7 news cycle. Bit-string speed seems to be of the essence, supported by fast-shifting public curiosity that easily turns to boredom in microseconds. To be in the cyberworld-infiltrated world seems to require that 'one' is up with the latest. Thoughtful reflection on newsworthy events takes time, much more time than it takes to report that they have happened. Taking the time to reflect requires having the leisure to do so, a space in time that must be financed somehow by the media to support their best journalists. Because the latest news is available in the cyberworld at any time and mostly for free, quality journalism requiring an investment in good journalists is increasingly under threat. The media agglomerate and aggregate to save costs, which leads to a blunting of the edge of a serrated, critical journalism.

Today's developments in digital information technologies are not merely a matter of new technologies, but come at the climax of a long historical trajectory in which Western thinking has prepared technological access to control the movements/changes of beings of all kinds. To comprehend this eery destiny, it is necessary to step back from current issues surrounding digital information technologies that seem so pressing today and take the long view. Hence it is worthwhile quoting thoughts from some years back:

> Today, with the information technologies and the information set-up (*Informationsgestell*: cf. Capurro 1995), human beings are being inundated on a planetary scale by beings in the shape of in-formation. We are continually being impressed and thus brought to stand by information. Western humankind has thus come to fulfil its metaphysical destiny in a superlative manner of being the beings that produce beings and has dragged into this destiny the rest of humankind to boot. We are totally absorbed in and saturated by beings in the way of in-formation. The information set-up is the im-pressive gathering of all possibilities of in-forming. The role of humans in this set-up is that they are called upon, i.e. challenged, to stand in the clearing of impression by in-formation. Beings in the age of information take on the shape of the barest outline, i.e. the 'digital difference'. Humans are used by being in being susceptible to difference, i.e. the de-limiting outline of beings. Today this de-limiting outline, the ἰδέα, is nothing other and nothing more than a string of 0s

and 1s. Being informed means nothing other than noticing the difference between 0000110001000000 and 0001100001000000. To say that being is computation (*computari est esse*) means that everything that *is* is translatable into a digital form. Being in-formed and im-pressed by binary code is the ultimate metaphysical destiny of Western humankind.[159]

3.5.2 The gainful game unleashes its freedom in the cyberworld

There is also an intimate connection between the fluidity of the cyberworld and the inherent tendencies of a global economy to mobilize everything and everybody gainfully. As we have seen (*1.6 The private individual and private property as a mode of reified sociation: the gainful game (classical political economy, Marx)*), the capitalist economy can be conceived as the movement of reified value in self-augmenting cycles. Money-capital is advanced with the expectation that it will return augmented with profit after all costs have been defrayed. All the various sorts of income-earners are players in this now globalized gainful game. The cyberworld as a powerful technology provides the opportunity i) for massive cost reductions in all sorts of ways, especially through automating production and circulation processes and ii) for increasing the rate of turnover of capital, and thus profits, especially by facilitating communications with employees, customers, suppliers. In particular, the cyberworld enormously enhances the movement of money as cyber-digits. Transactions of all kinds can now be done more speedily, including receipts from customers, payments to suppliers and employees, loan transactions with banks, and so on, thus reducing turnover-time. Today's banks have profited enormously by the introduction of digital automation, saving labour costs, cutting workforces and pushing the costs of transactions onto customers, who now have to purchase the digital equipment to communicate with their bank accounts and learn the ins and outs of their banks' software without the banks incurring any training costs.

Work productivity can increase through automated processes outsourced to the cyberworld and especially through the ease of

---

[159] Eldred 1996/2002.

communication with employees anywhere, anytime that turns employees themselves tendentially into appendages of their digital messaging devices, on constant stand-by for instructions from their superiors or new tasks to do. An important aspect of the protection of personal privacy is to keep in place barriers to employees' becoming permanently contactable through the cyberworld, at their employer's, business associates', customers', etc. beck and call. Such constant availability as a 'labour power' amounts to an invasion of a personal life-world and a blurring of the line between work and private life. For an income-earner of any kind, there is always the temptation to succumb to the siren calls of gainful opportunities offered by the cyberworld. Workoholism is encouraged by the ease with which work can continue digitally. An investor, for instance, can easily search the cyberworld for investment information and investment opportunities during his or her entire waking life. Managers can keep their digital device next to the bed at night to respond immediately to customer queries.

Hence it can be seen that the gainful game can be played in and through the cyberworld which, as a global medium, can lubricate and speed it up. The gainful game and the cyberworld are affine, and because the latter is becoming more and more ubiquitous and all-pervading, the players can be drawn more tightly into the gainful game's play. One could say that the cyberworld is an excellent medium for the *freedom of the gainful game* itself, which is dissociated from its pawns, the income-striving players themselves, and under the control of nobody, especially not within the grasp of state controls or subject to a wished-for 'primacy of politics'. Politics and the state can only try to regulate the rules of play. The cyberworld extends the reach of and accelerates the gainful game also known as capitalism. This is a two-edged development since, on the one hand, it enables many to earn an income who have been excluded from the gainful game and can even contribute to fostering entrepreneurship and alleviating poverty. On the other hand, the gainful game itself strengthens its hold on human life-movements, drawing them more and more into conformity with moves in the gainful game, now mediated and lubricated by the movements of bit-strings. To be able to draw back from this tendency to be sucked in, human beings need to *learn to see* the gainful game in its essential nature, which is not at all the case today, in particular, because even the social science of economics is lacking a foundational concept of value and proceeds from the ingrained preconceptions of subjectivist metaphysics.

3.5.3 Human freedom in the cyberworld

In view of the freedom enjoyed by the cyberworld to unfold its potentials and the freedom of the gainful game to extend its reach and intensity, both of which rely on a restricted meaning of freedom as a freedom to move, it has to be asked what *human* freedom in the cyberworld means. In view of the above, it would seem to be ambivalent because, apart from being encroached upon by the cyberworld, human lives also are enhanced by the convenience it affords, in much the same way as Adam Smith refers to the "conveniencies of life". The sheer cybernetic powers of the cyberworld offer the potential for shaping one's own life in many hitherto inconceivable ways including especially the possibilities for sharing one's world with others either privately or publicly. Keeping in touch with family, friends and acquaintances globally becomes an easy matter of course. The possibilities for presenting oneself in the public space increase exponentially.

Kant's community of scholars, for instance, becomes less exclusive through the ease of communicating and publishing via the cyberworld. Institutional power to play the role of gatekeeper, with regard to which scholar or thinker has something worthwhile saying, lessens, and along with it the peer pressure of peer review. Prestigious institutions embodying and defending the status quo of today's 'success-ful' thinking are still at the forefront in presenting themselves, but the cyberworld niches for alternatives widen, similarly to how the possibilities of printing cheaply opened up the public sphere long ago for alternative ways of thinking that found no place in the conservative learned institutions or were even repressed by governments. This seems to be one of the greatest potentials for the cyberworld: to enable and further the freedom for the dissemination even of thoughtful thoughts on the questionableness of the cyberworld itself and the gainful game. Ironically, this possibility goes hand in hand with a trend toward thoughtlessness, as the intelligent control over life-movements is outsourced to cybernetic systems about which most users are clueless. Bit-string torrents threaten to dictate the movements of human lives, including by skilfully manipulating human curiosity.

We turn now to consider alternative approaches to issues of privacy in the cyberworld.

3.6 Assessing Tavani's review of theories and issues concerning personal privacy

Private life-worlds as considered in *1.4 The question concerning rights: personal privacy, trust and intimacy* are prior to privacy conceived as "physical/accessibility, decisional, psychological/mental, and informational" as discussed by Tavani,[160] who provides a review of various theories of personal privacy under these headings. *Physical privacy* is a crude criterion because a private world cannot be tied down at all physically, and indeed, the very term "physical" (res extensa) is metaphysically loaded vis-à vis the 'psychic' (res cogitans). Rather, personal privacy is a social phenomenon. Not even the privacy of private property (cf. *1.5 The private individual, liberty, private property (Locke)*) can be conceived simply as restrictions to or control over physical accessibility, since use and disposability also come into play. Personal privacy need not imply a physical isolation at all, but 'merely' the hiddenness of one's affairs, even in public. Both "access to persons (and their possessions)" and "informational privacy" confuse two aspects of privacy, namely, personal privacy, which is a matter of disclosing or concealing a personal life-world, and the privacy of property, which is an issue of access to, and use, disposal and transfer of property.

Decisional privacy is a misnomer for the individual existential freedom to cast one's self, thus shaping one's own life-world, which is deeper than and provides the existential-ontological ground for making

[160] Tavani 2008; cf. *1.10 Privacy as protection of individual autonomy — On Rössler's The Value of Privacy*. Interestingly, although Rössler has a somewhat similar categorization of types of privacy, Tavani does not mention her book.

decisions. Decisional privacy is linked to an individual's having *control* over access to (ontic-factual) information about him- or herself[161] which, again, is an aspect of personal privacy in the sense of being able to withdraw one's personal world from view to others and of being able to choose those to whom one wants to reveal and share one's own personal life-world.

Psychological privacy proceeds from the notion of the encapsulated subject with a psyche 'inside' the body (this bodily location usually being imagined to be, more specifically, the head), and thus remains captive to subjectivist metaphysics with its notions of consciousness generating representations of the outside world inside the head. It is the obvious counterpart to physical privacy within metaphysical thinking. If psychological privacy is to mean non-intrusion into a subject's mind, then it is impossible anyway, because, speaking from the phenomena themselves, there is no encapsulated subject and the mind is always already out there in the world[162] where it is subjected to various influences, including attempted manipulations or prying. The human psyche *is* simply the openness to being-in-the-world.

Informational privacy, finally, is a superficial misnomer for the concealment of a personal world itself, i.e. that not everything about a personal life-world be exposed to public knowledge. If the focus is on "information", which is kind of entity, then it would seem that personal privacy would be protected by protecting data "both stored and communicated",[163] which, in the same breath, are[164] regarded as a person's private property, which is here not the issue and from which personal privacy should be conceptually distinguished, but most often isn't. Personal privacy is invaded also, say, when rumours are circulated about an individual's private life, and data and information capture only

---

161 Cf. *5.4 The Council of Europe Resolution on the protection of the privacy of individuals vis-à-vis electronic data banks in the private and public sectors*

162 Cf. Eldred 2012.

163 Tavani 2008 p. 139.

164 Here we do not go along with the ongoing degradation of the English language by treating words with Latin plural endings, such as 'data' and 'media', as singular nouns.

the *third-person* aspect of an individual as a what, not as a who. Personal privacy can be violated also in a *first-and-second* person encounter between *you-and-me*, when you overstep the bounds of what I would freely reveal to you about who I am, i.e. about my own life-world. Such first-and-second person aspects of the phenomenon of personal privacy, such as trust, are necessarily overlooked by theories of privacy that are in search of 'objective' criteria instead of taking the play of revealing/concealing in the world as the hallmark of personal privacy. A world cannot be rendered 'objective' anyway, since it is first and foremost an open temporal clearing within which beings, including human beings, present themselves *as* what and who they are, and also absent themselves.

The false lead of conceiving personal privacy as informational privacy, which has been blindly followed by today's debate on privacy and the internet, goes back to Alan Westin, who lays down that "privacy is the claim of individuals, groups or institutions to determine for themselves when, how, and to what extent information about them is communicated to others".[165] This misconception of privacy rests on a misconception of truth itself, which is originarily a phenomenon of disclosure, and not the so-called 'truth value' of statements.[166] Even the broader definition of privacy offered by Hauptman et al., "Generally, we can state that privacy is closely related to the concept of intimacy including physical integrity, but there are a lot of other dimensions of privacy (spatial, emotional/inner life of a person) that privacy incorporates",[167] misses the concealment of a personal self's life-world as the kernel of personal privacy. Moreover, in its captiveness to subjectivist metaphysics, it confuses what is called the "emotional/inner life of a person" with a mooded life-world that is not 'inside' a person at all, but 'out there'. Hauptman et al. cite also the "probably most famous definition [...] by the American judge Thomas M. Cooley, who defined privacy as the 'right to be let alone'.[168] This broad definition included

165 Westin 1967/1970, cited by Hauptman et al. 2011.

166 Cf. Heidegger SZ 1927 § 44.

167 Hauptman et al.2011.

168 Cooley 1888.

the protection of life and (intellectual) property as well as feelings[169] and is the starting point for many definitions of privacy that were developed later". This definition, too, misses the play of disclosure/concealment as the core of personal privacy and also confuses it with the privacy of private property, which is a distinct phenomenon (cf. *1.7 Trust as the gainful game's element and the privacy of private property*).

Tavani discusses also Moor's "restricted access/limited control (RALC) theory" of personal privacy that at least has the merit of introducing privacy "in a *situation* with regard to others",[170] rather than merely the privacy of information or data. Situations only come about in a world. A world affords both concealment and disclosure of a situation. Moor makes the distinction between "natural privacy" and "normative privacy". Properly speaking, natural privacy refers to the play of concealment and disclosure that any who plays out in the world. To be a self, a who has his or her own, personal world whose enjoyment has essentially to do with not being constantly or arbitrarily exposed to others' gaze. A who's world is often concealed from others, but without any restriction to its disclosure in the sense of wanting to preserve one's privacy, as when a person is accidentally not seen in a public place such as a park. So-called normative privacy has to do with privacy *protection* through "privacy policy and laws",[171] but, prior to and deeper than that, the issue concerns *personal power* over the play of concealment and disclosure of one's own world. A private conversation carried on in public, say, on a mobile phone is still private, even when the individual is careless about whether he can be overheard (cf. *3.7 An appraisal of Nissenbaum's Privacy in Context*). An infringement of his privacy takes place if someone takes measures to overcome concealment to intentionally eavesdrop on the conversation, perhaps through technical means (e.g. by intercepting the call). Such an infringement of privacy is prior to any consideration of normative protection.

---

[169] Kleve and de Mulder 2008.

[170] Moor 1997.

[171] Tavani 2008.

Hence what personal privacy *is* of itself is skipped over in favour of considering norms applicable to contexts; the basic ethical issue, however, is the former, for this concerns private individuality as a valued, customary way of life which is an exercise of individual freedom in the sense of a power-over... Since individual freedom is the power over one's own life-movements of all kinds, to be a *free individual* means also to be the spontaneous origin of control over one's own *who-game of concealment and disclosure* with the world, which is not captured by the phrase "management of privacy" "involving *choice, consent, correction*".[172] Talk of "management" is also conducive to reducing issues of personal privacy to providing "individuals with some control regarding who has access to information about themselves in particular contexts" by means of "normative privacy policies" (ibid.). Hence there is a bias in the theory toward making 'useful' policy prescriptions that can be translated into legislation regulating access to "information", which is not the basic phenomenon of personal privacy at all. To speak of "situations" was an improvement when looking at the phenomenon of personal privacy, but there seems to be a slippage back into considering merely how access to information and data is to be controlled. Situation comes to be understood merely as in what situation access to data is to be normatively, legislatively controlled. E.g. Moor discusses whether access to data on professors' colleges salaries is to be allowed or disallowed depending upon the criterion of whether the college is large or small.

Tavani then goes on to discuss three "benchmark theories of informational privacy", viz. Nissenbaum's conception of "privacy as contextual integrity", Floridi's "ontological interpretation of informational privacy" (cf. *3.8 Floridi's metaphysics of the threefold-encapsulated subject in a world conceived as infosphere*) and Vedder's "categorial privacy".[173] "Benchmark" here is supposed to indicate the rough, schematic nature of these theoretical models. With the focus on "information", the personal, private world itself is lost from sight.

---

172 Tavani 2008.

173 Vedder 2004.

With Nissenbaum (2004), once again there is an emphasis on "normative protection", to the neglect of the phenomena themselves (cf. also *3.7 An appraisal of Nissenbaum's Privacy in Context*). The discussion is devoted to "information such as medical records and financial records"[174] and the "contexts" in which it is normatively appropriate or inappropriate to divulge such information. Contexts here are similar to Moor's "situations". By focusing on norms and information, Nissenbaum overlooks that the situations pertinent here are at base the situations in which an individual discloses or conceals her or his personal life-world or aspects thereof, i.e. the showing-off as who one is through to the concealment of who one is in multifarious situations. Nissenbaum does take up issues associated with an important new phenomenon that arises through the *enormous powers of digital technologies* within and on the periphery of the cyberworld to *disclose personal worlds*, in hitherto unimaginable ways.

Whereas showing oneself in public places, such as a public street or square, used to be an innocuous act without consequence for preserving the privacy of one's personal world, with the advent of, say, surveillance cameras connected to a network (the cyberworld), the possibilities of disclosing personal worlds through data collection and automated data analysis, including the dissemination of the results of such analysis, increase exponentially. Such personal data can be collected automatically both within and without the cyberworld, and they all can be fed into the appropriate location in the cyberworld (perhaps a police database, or a private company's data analysis unit). Publicly available information such as land or company ownership can be combined with other data to build individual profiles of a person's life-world. In a sense, one could say that digital technology has become 'too smart'.

Before, however, rushing to consider consequences and issues of normative protection, it first has to be seen that the cyberworld with its internal and peripheral digital technologies brings about a qualitatively new phenomenon of *calculable cyber-disclosure* of individual life-worlds that represents a danger to the *freedom of a private individual to*

---

174 Tavani 2008.

withdraw from the public gaze. The state, private companies and other individuals[175] now have other, enhanced technological powers to pry into personal lives by employing data on private persons in public that used to be innocuous or were not collected at all (such as a person's route to work on a certain day). Large parts of the cyberworld itself are public spaces insofar as the communication between a user and publicly accessible servers is unencrypted. Such communication data can be intercepted by anyone having the appropriate digital program code at hand (e.g. search-engine logs), even without resorting to stealthy software that decrypts data traffic in order, say, to tap an encrypted digital telephone conversation. This is akin to having one's movements through public streets automatically recorded in a digital medium and these data later analyzed by a computer located somewhere in the cyberworld. In this sense, private life-worlds and who individuals are from an outside, third-person perspective (i.e. as information) become digitally *calculable*.

With his notion of "categorial privacy", Vedder (Vedder 2004), picks up on the qualitatively new phenomenon of the *cyber-disclosure* of individual life-worlds that threatens privacy in new 'calculating' ways. He takes on issues of "Knowledge Discovery in Databases" and "data mining" in cases where automated analysis of digital data allows conclusions to be drawn about individual personal worlds which can happen, of course, only if there are personalized data in the database. If data are both aggregated and anonymized, this danger is not imminent, but there is still the issue of how aggregated data on personal life-movements can be 'mined' to surveil, influence or manipulate, particular groups or "categories". Vedder extends the issue of protecting individual, personalized data to protection against personalized data being aggregated into databases to derive certain statistical regularities from them. Statistical analyses of aggregated data are what insurance companies have been doing for decades and centuries to derive estimates of risk probabilities. Automated gathering of digital data and their processing enhance possibilities for statistical risk calculations, making

---

[175] Cf. Ganascia 2009.

them more accurate and refined. If, on the basis of such statistical analyses of databases, an individual finds himself in a risk category with negative consequences for taking out some kind of insurance (health, life, motor vehicle, etc. etc.), that is hardly an issue for personal privacy, since an individual cannot even claim that his data ended up in the aggregated database. The issue of so-called categorial privacy seems to be confused with an issue of *protection against discrimination* on the basis of certain individual features, such as living in an area with the 'wrong' postcode, which thus become stigmata.

Tavani also discusses issues of employee privacy, especially that of surveillance of employee activities through the deployment of digital technologies that can automatically record employees' movements in the cyberworld, such as e-mail correspondence or duration, or even content, of telephone conversations. Here there is a clash between personal privacy and the privacy of private property insofar as the employee has hired her or his labouring powers to the employer for a specific job and therefore has an obligation, within limits, to carry out employers' instructions and perform duties within the job description. Within the terms of the employment contract, the employee has a right (and even a duty in the case of a public company) to supervise and monitor an employee's activities, but how far does this right extend? Digital technologies make it easy and cheap to check on what employees are doing, e.g. if they are wasting company time with personal activities, but such surveillance is also an infringement of *trust* in employees and also an invasion of personal privacy insofar as employees also have to manage their private affairs from the workplace. Where is the line to be drawn between *trust* and *control*?

The employer also has an interest and a right to monitor work *efficiency* as an aspect of measuring cost-productivity, but here, too, limits must be drawn. Measuring the duration of telephone conversations or the number of keystrokes per minute an employee types may be useful for measuring work efficiency, and easily implementable, but these practices are also repugnant in the sense of reducing the employee to a mere efficient agent of the employer's overall work organization. The interface between personal privacy, which is an important aspect of human freedom and dignity, and the private rights of private property becomes rich in conflict in the case of employees and employers, since employees are necessarily in close, live contact with their employers via the organizational hierarchy and, within limits, must do their employers' bidding. This perpetual *power struggle* is not simply an issue of personal privacy, i.e. of the extent to which the life-movements of employees are revealed to employers, but is embedded in the larger issue of employer-employee relations, which brings into play questions of private property rights, personal trust vs. supervision, human dignity and the freedom to be the responsible 'master' of one's own life-movements.

One kind of movement that individuals perform within and without the cyberworld is *change of place* or *locomotion*, which is one of the kinds of movement analyzed long ago ontologically by Aristotle (Aristotle *Phys.*). Tavani discusses this phenomenon only on an ontic-factual, empirical level, and with a bias toward normative protection. Within the cyberworld, change of place amounts to what has come to be known as 'surfing', which is a 'nearing' of digital locations (co-ordinates within the cyberworld such as IP addresses) through cybernetic commands (e.g. given tactilely by a mouse-click or a touchscreen). Such movements, of course, can be automatically recorded in the electromagnetic matrix. On the cyberworld's periphery with the physical world, change of place can also be automatically recorded and analyzed by means of technologies such as GPS, mobile telephony or RFIDs. This is a Janus-faced development that opens up both good and bad possibilities. On the good side, it can afford more mobility for old people, children or even prisoners; on the bad side it enhances the 'creepy' options for following innocent people. It is apparent that digital technologies of many kinds enable a huge increase in the potential for tracking movements in the physical world, including of individuals using all sorts of means of transport. Individual privacy of a personal private world, however, includes the concealing of physical movements from place to place. Again there is a clash between personal privacy and private property, on the one hand, and between personal privacy and the state's interest in public security, on the other. E.g. a toll company collecting tolls on an expressway has a pecuniary interest in recording vehicles' movements, which data can also be misused for purposes of tracking individual persons by private companies or by the state. Digital technologies and their embedding in the cyberworld, where data can circulate quickly, make Big Brother a palpable reality that endangers personal liberty.

In section 6.5.1 of his 2008 article, "What Kind of Value is Privacy?", Tavani discusses this question without saying what privacy is or what a value is. Rather, privacy is put simply into a series along with "security, autonomy, and so forth". Tavani introduces a distinction between "intrinsic" and "functional" values, the latter being valuable as a means to an end, whereas the former are valuable in themselves. But valuable for what? Tavani adduces the connection that Moor (Moor 1997) makes between privacy and the "core value" of "security". Both of these "values" are said to be essential for "human flourishing" which is increasingly under threat from "information technology" because of its encroachment upon privacy. But what, exactly, are security and human flourishing, and what connection do they have with human freedom in the world? In discussing "Why Privacy is Valued?" (6.5.2), Tavani makes a connection between privacy and "freedom and democracy", "autonomy" or the need for a "shield" against "intrusions", again without digging any deeper. The core question of what human freedom *is* is left to one side, i.e. it is begged. Instead, Tavani and the authors he cites are content to proceed from pre-philosophical notions of these phenomena. This contrasts starkly with previous sections and chapters of the present study devoted to a phenomenology of human being itself as whoness, including the question of the freedom of human beings cast thus socio-ontologically as individuals striving to be somewho and to shape their selves through interplay in the openness of the world. Because foundational socio-ontological questions are invariably skipped over, there is no mention of privacy conceived as the concealment of a personal life-world.

Instead, Tavani reviews a discussion among certain authors in which there is a weighing of the pros and cons of individuals' freedom to selectively disclose "facts about themselves". An "individualist agenda" of personal privacy is thus set against concealment of information that "can be harmful to the social good". Does the social good demand, for instance, that individuals reveal their bank accounts to the state? This is a thorny, controversial question invariably evaded in discussions of privacy. Instead of clarifying in a phenomenological way the connection between personal privacy and freedom, Tavani's discussion focuses on arguments for privacy under certain epithets that are pitted against one another: "individual value", "public value", "collective value", "common value", as if the "value" of privacy could be weighed on functionalist scales as an "individual good" against "the larger social good", or even placed on the other side of the scales, thus begging the question as to how and in what sense, if at all, "society" has precedence over the individual. The issue of how something like a "social good" can conform with freedom is not raised.

Tavani cites Regan's (Regan 1995) argument for privacy itself as a social good in terms of its being valuable not *per se*, but for something else, viz. for the "democratic political system" which, of course, begs the question as to the value of democracy as a form of government that must be justified, if at all, in the context of a clarified philosophical conception of human freedom. This has been a principal concern of political philosophy since Locke, with Hegel's *Philosophy of Right*[176] being a certain culminating point, in which a concept of freedom is at the core, serving as the touchstone for assessing how a social order with its state can be compatible with freedom. Values are not merely "goods", but must be anchored in an ethos, a customary way of life that is held dear by people sharing a world with one another (cf. *1.3 Values, ethos, ethics*). In any case, privacy as an individual freedom to conceal or reveal a personal life-world does not have to justify itself to "society", but rather, society as a way of sociating and living with one another has to justify *itself* as compatible with freedom, which can never be dissociated from its core: individual freedom, since it is in the first place human individuals who are the points of origin for their life-movements, free or otherwise.

[176] Hegel RPh 1970.

The following, final section (6.5.3) of Tavani's article discusses how policy can be framed to protect "informational privacy", thus moving into territory that will be reconnoitred later in this study (Chap. 6).

3.7 An appraisal of Nissenbaum's *Privacy in Context*[177]

Helen Nissenbaum criticizes the private/public dichotomy as a presupposition for the idea that making personal data public means that such data can be used by anybody for whatever purposes without people being aware of it and/or giving their consent.[178] She is aware that, although it is "both unrealistic and unreasonable" to strive for protection of privacy in public, it makes sense nevertheless to exercise control over what one exposes for observation.[179] This distinction provides the basis for measures securing intellectual property such as patents and copyright. If the realm of the private is conceived as divorced from the public sphere, then the problem of privacy in public has no meaning whatsoever. As Nissenbaum remarks, this dichotomy has influenced the philosophical discussion by placing values such as "autonomy, liberty, personal relationships and trust" on the side of the private sphere alone.[180] Obviously, such a conception is the heritage of modernity and its view of the self as an encapsulated subject separated from the outside world. This separation gives rise to the right to privacy in the sense of a right to control information in an area strictly separated from the public realm, whose content may vary in different social and cultural settings. Commercial as well as political interests are particularly amenable to such a dichotomy, regarding any restriction of their actions with private information in the public realm as an unacceptable restriction of (their) liberty. Nissenbaum calls this view of privacy from the perspective of liberty the "knock-down argument".[181]

---

177 This section is the final authorial responsibility of Rafael Capurro.

178 Nissenbaum 1998.

179 Nissenbaum 1998 p. 32.

180 Nissenbaum 1998, p. 9.

181 Nissenbaum 1998 pp. 10ff.

On these premises Nissenbaum develops a new conception of privacy based on what she calls "contextual integrity", a concept that she considers to be "the same idea" as that proposed by Jeroen van den Hoven, who uses the term "spheres of access",[182] as well as Michael Walzer's "spheres of justice".[183] Personal information in the public sphere is not "up for grabs", where no norms of privacy apply.[184] Obviously, the defenders of "data aggregation" and "data mining" are not interested in "contextual integrity". According to Nissenbaum, by taking information from one context into another, persons themselves are concerned. She points to "wide-ranging" individual values "such as autonomy, liberty, individuality, capacity to form and maintain intimate relations, mental health, creativity, personal growth; as well as social values such as free and democratic society".[185] She writes, "The picture of a person that a profile provides can, for the reasons given, be broad, deep and traverse time. These pictures may be rich enough to reveal aspects of an individual's character, to ground predictions about their propensities, and even suggest ways of manipulating them".[186] Nissenbaum's conception of privacy as dealing with the personal integrity of the self is related to Alan Westin's notion of "personal autonomy"[187] and Ruth Gavison's view of privacy as promoting liberty of action.[188] She refers also to Jeroen van den Hoven for whom the privacy of persons, which he calls "moral identification", is what is missing "when personal data are piled up in our databases and persons are represented in administrative procedures".[189] Moral identification "presupposes knowledge of the point of view of the data-subject and a concern with what it is for a person to live that life" (ibid.). Following the idea of the modern "liberal individual", van den Hoven considers

---

[182] Nissenbaum 1998 p. 37, van den Hoven 2001 p. 431.

[183] Walzer 1983.

[184] Nissenbaum 1998 p. 22.

[185] Nissenbaum 1998 p. 30.

[186] Nissenbaum 1998 p. 27.

[187] Westin 1967/1960.

[188] Gavison 1980.

[189] van den Hoven 2001 p. 440.

privacy as a kind of "moral time out" for "moral reflection and self-improvement".[190] This view of the moral self is understood as related to the Aristotelean ethics of self-improvement.[191] But the modern categories of morality and legality as well as the idea of the modern self as detached from the world cannot be identified with the Aristotelean formation of individual character (ἦθος ethos), nor with the relationship between the individual and the *polis*.[192]

In her recent 2010 book *Privacy in Context*, Nissenbaum further develops[193] her views on privacy as "contextual integrity". She uses a spatial metaphor pointing to the gap between the "heavens" of universal human principles and values and the "hard ground of concrete, gritty, detail" that contextual integrity is supposed to bridge.[194] The book begins with an overview of contemporary technologies such as monitoring and tracking, massive and deep databases, the capacity to disseminate and find everything, that everywhere threaten privacy. The second part of the book is devoted to currently influential approaches to privacy, dealing particularly with the value of privacy and the threat to or "encroachment" (van den Hoven) upon moral autonomy. She reviews the classical view of privacy based on the public/privacy dichotomy and questions it from the perspective of "privacy in public". "The dichotomy theories," she writes, "are spared having to explain why video surveillance of public spaces or trawling public records for purposes of aggregation is problematic because, according to them, they are not in the private sphere and therefore are not a privacy problem".[195] She does not reject totally the insights arising from the dichotomy, but states her own view as follows: "The central thesis of this book is that a right to privacy is neither a right to secrecy nor a right to control but a right to *appropriate* flow of personal information".[196] "Contexts," she writes,

---

190 van den Hoven 2001 p. 442.

191 Swanson 1992.

192 Bien 1985 p. 225.

193 Nissenbaum 2004.

194 Nissenbaum 2010 pp. 9f.

195 Nissenbaum 2010 p. 113.

196 Nissenbaum 2010 p. 127.

"are structured social settings characterized by canonical activities, roles, relationships, power structures, norms (or rules), and internal values (goals, ends, purposes)".[197] Contexts are "essentially rooted in specific times and places" that reflect the norms and values of a given society.[198] Hence, for her, contexts are not *situations* that are constituted and constantly evolve and dissolve in experiential time-space.

Nissenbaum's view of norms is basic for her approach of "contextual integrity". She adopts as a default position the view of norms as prescriptive, and not just descriptive, with regard to human action. She further distinguishes "informational norms" as related to individual contexts from "context-related informational norms" as referring generally to the former. But this difference is not an opposition, since informational norms are "co-constitutive" of the second type.[199] Informational norms, including now both types, are common to senders, subjects and recipients of information that might be individuals and/or organizations, although she concentrates on single individuals. Not being restricted to defining information as belonging either to the private or the public sphere but to different contexts, Nissenbaum remarks that "attributes" or "information" types arise within an "indefinite array of possibilities".[200] This implies that privacy, for Nissenbaum, is not an attribute of a particular kind of information, but depends on the context in which it is shared, privacy being then a second-order attribute, to use the terminology of systems theory. Contextual integrity might then be used as a "decision heuristic" in order to find out context, actors, attributes and transmission principles. The last might include reciprocity, deserving to receive information, entitlement to know something, compulsion to reveal information, knowledge and/or permission to share information and so on. Nissenbaum consequently questions the alternative between a right to control versus a right to constrain access to information as based on the public/privacy dichotomy.[201]

---

197 Nissenbaum 2010 p. 132.
198 Nissenbaum 2010 p. 134.
199 Nissenbaum 2010 pp. 140f.
200 Nissenbaum 2010 p. 143.
201 Nissenbaum 2010 p. 147.

Contextual integrity as dealing with or presupposing given norms and principles, i.e. what is usually called customs or ethos, could be considered as being essentially conservative or even subject to the "tyranny of the normal", particularly because norms and principles are supposed not only to be considered as descriptive but also as morally normative.[202] To avoid this, Nissenbaum writes that "a theoretical account of social contexts ought to leave room for the possibility that a society may, on occasion, revisit and scrutinize contexts and their respective values, potentially concluding they are unsound or unworthy".[203] She thus makes an appeal for the critical function of ethical thinking on a given morality. Another problem concerns the issue of the plurality of spheres, that might lead to the domination of the norms and values of one sphere over the others, the result being tyranny. Following Michael Walzer, Nissenbaum proposes that the principles operating in all spheres are to "be inferred from the meanings of the relevant social goods".[204] But she also remarks, "I do not believe there is a fleshed out general theory on how best to match principles to goods within spheres; instead each sphere demands focused investigation to draw out the connection".[205] And further, "There are other regularities that might usefully be studied across spheres, as opposed to within".[206] This problem seems to be not only a methodological one but concerns the very idea of a plurality of contexts as detached from a common shared world. Nissenbaum summarizes her thesis as follows: "We have a right to privacy, but it is neither a right to control personal information or a right to have access to this information restricted. Instead, it is a right to live in a world in which our expectations about the flow of personal information are, for the most part, met; expectations that are shaped not only by force of habit and convention but a general confidence in the mutual support these flows accord to key organizing principles of social life, including moral and political ones. This is the

202 Nissenbaum 2010 p. 160.
203 Nissenbaum 2010 p. 180.
204 Nissenbaum 2010 p. 168.
205 Nissenbaum 2010 pp. 168f.
206 Nissenbaum 2010 p. 241.

right I have called contextual integrity, achieved through the harmonious balance of social rules, or norms, with both local and general values, ends, and purposes".[207]

A critical appraisal of Nissenbaum's concept of privacy as contextual integrity from the perspective of whoness and a shared world approvingly acknowledges the change of perspective proposed by Nissenbaum with regard to the traditional dichotomy between the private and the public as well as to the view based thereon of the relation between an encapsulated and worldless 'I'-subject matched to private data. This is what we call the *what* in contrast to the *who* perspective. Nissenbaum crosses out this relation by calling attention to the underlying relation between individuals and their worldly life-contexts. Nevertheless, neither the question concerning the whoness nor the interplay between whoness and a common shared world is explicitly stated, let alone conceptually worked out. Instead, Nissenbaum's ethos-based view of privacy as "contextual integrity" rests on the presupposition of overarching and meta-contextual moral principles and values being pragmatically addressed from a contextual perspective. Eventually she has to acknowledge the limits of the contextual approach when facing the danger of tyranny arising from the predominance of one sphere and its values over the others, and look to the "heavens" of meta-contextual values and norms.

Nissenbaum fails to see that my lived whoness or ethos, and not just the ethos of the normal and/or the normative, is intimately tied to my actions and choices in life, i.e. it depends on whether and how I grasp or fail to grasp the potentials for existing open to me in my time *in* my particular situation and not detached from it. Out of this particularity I forge my unique singularity through an intertwining with others with whom I share a common world. I am who I become through the mirroring interplay with the world of others in myriad formative, temporally dynamic situations. The normal as well as norms are forged in this common existential context that we call the world and hence are not themselves originary. Without such a shared world, we are faced

---

[207] Nissenbaum 2010 p. 231.

with a plurality of contexts related to some kind of universal norms that contextual integrity is supposed to perceive from a bottom-up perspective. A situation, however, is not a static and separate "sphere" but a dynamic process of our temporo-spatial existing. Nissenbaum, as well as van den Hoven and Walzer, overlook this temporo-spatial dimension and, in order not to get lost in a plurality of contexts, look for some kind of elevated principles and goods overarching and encompassing all spheres, although not in the same respect.

Principles and values are not primarily related to the good, but self-related if we keep in mind that the self is not an isolated and worldless *ego* but always already intertwined in an interplay of showing-off to each other, sharing the world and *therefore* being capable of delimiting contexts, common values and rules of action. The basic commonality to which all values and norms refer is not in the meta-contextual "heavens" addressed by Nissenbaum in her spatial metaphor. Nor can such values be primarily fixed with regard to some common goods that can be seen *as* common, because we share a common world from whose habitual usages the common good emerges, and not the other way round. In other words, privacy is basically a dimension of the interplay between self and world, in which the who *finds* its self-identity shining back from the opportunities the world offers, and not a relation of self and contexts. It is the integrity of the disclosive/concealing interplay between self and world that is at stake when discussing issues of privacy in different situations and contexts, and with regard to different norms and values. Self-related norms are not ego-related or context-related, but world-related, and this means that they emerge within the open temporo-spatial horizon of shared human existence.

This is the reason why we can question an established morality within as well as beyond a given context and/or culture, as pointed out by Nissenbaum, not only in order to avoid "conservatism", but also to respect the basic openness of human existence to the temporal dimension of the future. This gives rise to the question not only of distributive justice with regard to different "spheres", but also of commutative justice in the interplay of human freedom that in this perspective turns out to be just another word for privacy; that is, if it is not conceived in terms of the isolated moral individual whom van den Hoven aims to protect so that he or she might take a rest outside the "encroachment" of the digital sphere where the big players are not only national states, but as private players conversant with digital technologies. These private enterprises possess huge amounts of data that are the objective residue of commutative processes, as if it were separated from the interplay between self and world that goes on also within the technologically enabled cyberworld.

The question concerning privacy in the cyberworld pertains to the self's data within specific contexts only secondarily. Primarily, it is a question concerning the relation of the cyberworld to the shared world where selves, and not egos, are an integral part of the game, showing off and displaying their abilities to each other. *Hence we should be focused on the integrity of self-world interplay as being endangered by the encroachments of the global digital environment: the danger of being thoroughly pervaded and invaded by the requirements of the freedom of movement of bit-strings, and the danger of being engulfed by the digitally enhanced gainful game.* This means ethically more than the pragmatic approach of pluralism and less than the appeal to meta-historic norms and values coming from the "heavens", but rather a turn to how we become and evolve as 'we' in dynamic situations of reciprocal interplay.

This implies also more than "spheres of trust"[208] since it concerns the interplay among selves in a shared world, and not just of (encapsulating?) "spheres", such interplay relying as it does crucially on *trust*. Trust can be engendered or regained neither by technical means nor by moral and/or legal principles and values, particularly not if they are rooted in "heavens". Trust in a basic existential sense is an originary phenomenon among free selves sharing temporo-spatially a common, culturally attuned world, open together toward an unforeseeable, but nevertheless shapeable future in which its open abyss is bridged by mutual trust. An individual and common ethos is based on trust in this basic sense, which is more a matter of a *culturally mooded ethos* than of

---

[208] Nissenbaum 2010 p. 198.

'effective regulation' or high moral norms. Trust makes it possible for players to agree on local and/or universal or global norms and rights that are between and not beyond the players. It is precisely this issue that gives rise to the question concerning privacy in the cyberworld insofar as this 'in-between' between the players seems to be within a separate, technologically enabled, digital sphere, the cyberworld, separated from selves and the world that enable it and that can give it a sense of being a specific materialization of the world and the self *as* seen from within the historically specific horizon of digital ontology. It is then not just a question of a multiplicity of contexts or "spheres", but of the idea of a cyberworld *itself* where the players *as* selves are merely digitally represented and therefore a priori apparently disconnected from their temporo-spatial existence. The question concerning contextual integrity appears then as enlarged or subverted by that concerning world integrity, which encompasses the temporo-spatial dimension in which free players can shape their lives as selves together in an ongoing interplay. The question concerning privacy is about the self and the world which build the basis for any kind of "contextual integrity". It is based on trust.

Nissenbaum's normative ethos-based contextual approach to privacy needs a deeper foundation in the experiential ethos of lived usages. But it is an important theoretical and pragmatic turn with regard to the traditional dichotomy between the private vs. public sphere as well as with regard to the concept of privacy as pertaining solely to personal data, which reduces the phenomenon of whoness to whatness. The question of trust is mostly seen on one side of the equation which means, in the case of the cyberworld, that it is located on the side of the owners and/or administrators of digital data about their 'subjects'. This paternalistic view of trust does not acknowledge the free and open interplay among selves in a shared world, but aims at substituting them in claiming that the cyberworld is the real world, where liberty now has its place rather than in any kind of individual privacy (which, in any case, is never an encapsulated, individualized privacy). This "knock-down" argument is paradoxically correct if and only if liberty is now conceived as located within the (cyber-)world as digitally materialized by computer technology with its apparently unlimited possibilities of control that would assuage free agents about any unforeseeable future.

This homogenous, linear space-time axis of the cyberworld shines back onto the conception of liberty, by freeing it of its abyssal dimensions that can be bridged only by trust within reciprocal interchanges. This is the highest imaginable danger for privacy since it turns self and world into uniform temporo-spatial and computational dimensions in which the ethical difference between who and what eventually disappears. Selves existing in a world then become subjects matched with objective data-packets that can be mined in order to precalculate individual and collective behaviour. The issue of privacy in the context of the cyberworld precipitated by digital technologies then turns into a key ethical challenge for the self and the world in learning to resist the digital temptation, not by looking for metaphysical security in normative "heavens", nor by taking a "moral time out", but by unmasking digital globality as driven by individuals and/or organizations that pretend to put their 'liberties' beyond those of all other players on the basis of their power over mega-digital resources. Nissenbaum provides selves with some kind of guerrilla tactics so as not to lose sight of what is at stake when the digital Leviathan raises its head in specific contexts.

The issue of personal privacy, however, concerns not just the flow of information from one context to another, as if it were a matter of preventing ubiquitous leaks. Rather, the fundamental phenomenon is the concealedness or disclosure of myriad evolving and dissolving, always temporally moving, situations in which I multifariously share my world with others, or perhaps only with myself. We become who we are only through interplay with one another in a shared historico-temporal world. We share world-situations with one another that change, evolve, dissolve, reconstitute themselves, etc., thus being constituted *as* we. The advent of digital technologies and the ongoing merging of the physical world with the cyberworld lead to the predicament of the possibility of the Big Bugging Operation enabled by powerful digital technologies that diligently record everything, so that even on a solitary walk in the woods, the trees have ears and eyes. The digital social media, in particular, open up (even liberating) potentials for sharing worlds and situations with one another in endless variations. They also open up the technological option for permanent eavesdropping into all kinds of situations, and that, indeed, presents a great danger to personal freedom. How is trust to be engendered in a cyberworld that enables self-determined world-sharing with selected others, when in the background service-providing masters of digital cybernetics loom?

3.8 Floridi's metaphysics of the threefold-encapsulated subject in a world conceived as infosphere[209]

There must be some kinda way outa here,
Said the joker to the thief.
Bob Dylan

3.8.1 The purported "informational nature of personal identity"

One probably must have spent a couple of years with Aristotle's *Metaphysics* to learn that traditional ontology is the investigation of "beings insofar as they are beings". Today, at the culmination of the scientific age, based tacitly on subjectivist metaphysics, the conception of ontology has shrivelled to the assertion, "The basic question of ontology is 'What exists?'"[210], where it is not asked what it means to "exist". Floridi does not represent any exception to this impoverished modern conception of ontology. In his article,[211] Floridi takes it upon himself "to explore the foundations of the construction of personal identities, by developing an informational analysis of the self. The broader thesis I shall defend is that ICTs are, among other things,

---

209 This and all subsequent sections of this chapter are the final authorial responsibility of Michael Eldred.

210 Chalmers 2009.

egopoietic technologies or technologies of self construction, significantly affecting who we are, who we think we are, who we might become, and who we think we might become". The question concerning "who we are" is hence front and centre of Floridi's endeavours, although not as an existential-ontological question concerning whoness, but as a matter of "technologies of self construction" which, of course, presupposes that selves are constructed. This conception of constructed personal identity must then perforce serve Floridi when approaching, in particular, the phenomenon of privacy (see below). In this section, however, a deeper-lying critique of Floridi's informational metaphysics will be offered.

The problem Floridi sets up starting from "Plato's famous metaphor of the chariot" in *Phaedrus* is that of the unity of the self and how this unity is maintained "at different times and through changes," whereby linear time is assumed as self-evident.[212] The problem of unity of the soul, which Floridi equates with the self, is how a tripartite, "multi-agent system" (MAS) consisting of a charioteer, one good horse and one bad horse, can constitute a unity, as if this "tripartite analogy" could provide the basis for a well-grounded philosophy of the self. This analysis of the unity of a metaphorical soul is to constitute a contribution to a problem of "egology", for which Plato's imagery for the soul is to be equated with the ego of the modern metaphysical subject, starting with Descartes, as if such a continuity could be assumed without further ado. "From Descartes onwards [...] the unity, identity, and continuity of the I, or self, as an entity become the subjects of an ontological investigation in their own right." This pretension to *ontology* is important in view of the merely *ontogenetic*, evolutionary *model* of self-constitution that, later in the article, Floridi will proceed to present without batting an eyelid. The question regarding "who we are" today is thus framed entirely within the modern metaphysics of the subject, and that in terms of third-person descriptions familiar already from Descartes, Leibniz, et

---

211 Luciano Floridi 2012. Unless otherwise specified, all quotations in this section are from the PDF-file for this article. I will go through the article in what I hope is not all too excruciating detail.

212 Cf. by contrast Eldred 2009/2011 § 5.7.

al. that proceed from a self-evident understanding of the subject as a certain kind of 'what' rather than a 'who' (even when Descartes speaks of "I" which turns out to be a res cogitans). Although he proceeds explicitly from an "analogy" or "metaphor" of Plato's, Floridi immediately asserts, "Plato quite literally interprets the self as a multiagent system (MAS)". The age-old traditional metaphysical distinction, however, is between 'metaphorical' and 'literal' (only metaphysical thinking has this distinction and this distinctive conception of language), so Floridi proceeds to contradict himself by shifting ground to the 'literal', as if this literal ground were solid. This move is necessary if he does not want to base his "egology" on a mere metaphor. But then, one way or the other, his starting-point is worthless, and it would be better to start from the simple phenomena themselves that are before our mind's eye. The "model" he presents later has an equally shaky basis in Plato's metaphor, for it is not phenomenally grounded.

By slipping in a theory of multi-agent systems underneath as his foundation, Floridi is able to regard the soul or self or ego as a "complex, engineered artefact", again a kind of what that can even be engineered, thus continuing, indeed, the long history of productionist metaphysics launched by Plato and Aristotle, according to which beings qua beings are somehow produced, like a carpenter produces a table. This move of Floridi's invites a "shift from a phenomenological or descriptive approach to the self to a constructionist or design-oriented approach", a quotation that reveals Floridi's understanding of phenomenology as mere ontic-factual description, as has become popular in the social sciences. That phenomenology could be the striving to bring what is most obvious and hence most hidden to light, namely, modes of being/presencing, does not occur to Floridi. In any case, the metaphysical tradition becomes a quarry for "selves-engineering techniques, as Plato already knew" in line with "the engineering of MAS" as "just AI translations of classic issues in the philosophy of the self" that extends even as far as "a design perspective [of] upbringing, training, education, social and political practices and norms". The question regarding "who we are" has thus been totally submerged beneath a constructive, engineering problematic of how a self as a somewhat is made. Shades of Aldous Huxley's *Brave New World.*

Following on from Plato, Floridi identifies two major problems in modern subjectivist metaphysics as "*diachronic* egology" which "concentrates on the problems arising from the *identification* of a self through time or possible worlds," and "*synchronic* egology," which "deals with the *individualisation* of a self in time or in a possible world", both being aspects of "an ontology of personal *identity*". Floridi concentrates in his article on the latter, making only brief comments on the former as a problem of how the self can be "modelled at a given level of abstraction" as a kind of "system" in which the main difficulty is to identify what is the same at different points of linear time. Such an ontology of the self is hence a theoretical construction supposed to "model" a certain "system", just like a scientist models reality with a theory on the basis of certain made-up hypotheses, interrogating reality with experiments to get the answers he needs to achieve an effective, successful intervention into this reality.

The problematic of self and other, famously approached in Plato's dialectical thinking in both *The Sophist* and *Parmenides*, plays no role whatever in Floridi's considerations. According to Plato, and Hegel coming after him,[213] the identity of a self, or the same (τὸ αὐτόν) is possible only through the identification with the other or with what is other (τὸ ἕτερον), a paradoxical subtlety that must be part of any ontology of the self.[214] Floridi considers only the well-known problem of how to identify a being, i.e. any being including "hospitals" and "Saul"/"Paul", as the same at different points of time, but this presupposes the subtle and deeper-lying phenomenological identification of *any* being *as* such-as-such, i.e. with its *other*, thus presupposing a *difference*. Identification is always identification with its or an other, which is what even the simplest of statements say: S is P, i.e. S shows

213 Cf. Hegel Plato's *Parmenides* — "the most famous masterpiece of Platonic dialectic" (dem berühmtesten Meisterstück der Platonischen Dialektik, VGPII 1971 W19:79).

214 Cf. Eldred 2008/2011 Section 3 iii) a) 'Dialectic of Self and Other'.

itself *as* P, e.g. "This is a glass." (identity) although, plainly, "this" is not "a glass" (difference).

Only implicitly is this subtle dialectic of the self with its other at play in Floridi's further account of the "synchronic individualisation" of the self that, he avers, precedes its identification. However, as already pointed out, identification as the same at different points along linear time (as opposed to three-dimensional, ecstatic time) presupposes anyway a dialectical identity and difference of self and other. Thus, Floridi introduces the "narrative" subjectivist conception of the self's identity via a quote from Proust, according to which "we 'identify' (provide identities) to each other," via the representations in consciousness we have of each other by matching these representations with "the sound of his voice," etc. "We compose in our minds those ideas" (Floridi citing Proust), so that *identity* of a certain self is conceived as a compositum, a narrative, of representations in the consciousnesses of others (who are *different*). Floridi then proceeds to confuse this question of self-identity with that of individualization of the self, so that one must ask why he introduced the distinction in the first place. Self-individualization concerns the problem of the self's unity which, Floridi claims, Locke (Locke 1690) discovered in the "unity of consciousness and the continuity of memories" and which the narrative approach finds in the unity of the narrative constructed through the representations inside others' consciousnesses. Thus, on the one hand, there is a unity of individual, first-person consciousness constituted by memory, i.e. an identification over linear time within an individual consciousness and, on the other, there is the supposed unity of a narrative existing inside the consciousnesses of others. Why this narrative is unified and how there could be unity of narrative constituted through a plurality of many different consciousnesses remain unasked questions.

Floridi then proceeds to claim that both approaches to the problem of individualization (or is it the problem of identification?) depend on "the right sort of informational skills" required to compose a unity of identity. So there is now a third approach to self-identity as informational unity, which is a problem that Floridi introduces with a long quote from Hume in which Hume proceeds from "all our particular perceptions", which Floridi glosses as "[bits or streams of information separate from each other]", and then becomes sceptically perplexed about "*the mind* [which] *never perceives any real connexion among distinct existences*". The dilemma for Hume is hence that the unity which is supposed to constitute "personal identity *arises* from consciousness; and consciousness is nothing but a reflected thought or perception", which Floridi glosses as "[information processing]". The problem for Hume is, apparently, that only sense perceptions are (posited to be) real, and reflected thoughts are (posited to be) unreal, merely ideal, residing somewhere inside an encapsulated consciousness.

In Floridi's terms, the problem is how all the different bits of information, based on 'real' sense-perception information-gathering, floating around as representations inside consciousness (one's own or those of others) are to be unified through some kind of information processing. Floridi then adduces Kant's solution for the unity of the information-processing subject that resides in the transcendental constitution of the subject in its unity prior to any experience of the world, i.e. prior to its information-gathering ways, but he is unsatisfied because Kant's transcendental argument (genuinely ontological within the constrictions of the metaphysics of subjectivity) does not explain ontogenetically "How such unity and coordination come to be there in the first place". Readers breathe a sigh of relief that finally they will be told a story. Why, however, should one demand ontogenetic explanations at all for an ontological problem of self-constitution? Would it not be more to the philosophical point to question Kant's subjectivist metaphysics itself and the ontological constitution of the self *within* subjective consciousness, cut off from the world in its objectivity, as Hegel and Heidegger have done? If one proceeds already from within subjectivist metaphysics that posits from the start an encapsulated consciousness that, if it is to maintain any connection at all to the world, must achieve it through streams of sense perceptions, i.e. bits of information, and presupposes that only these bits of information are really real, then one has a problem, namely, a pseudo-problem.

Floridi's problem is that of the constitution of the *informational* self as an information-processing unity rather than a unity of disparate perceptions or narrative bits and pieces. He proceeds to solve it by abandoning any ontological pretensions whatsoever and replacing them by an account of how the "informational unity of the self may be achieved, or at least described, through a three-phase development of the self," clearly an ontogenetic-explanatory task that Floridi tackles by proposing a "model" whose "goal is ultimately that of explaining in what sense ICTs are egopoietic technologies". If this is the goal, then Floridi's informational ontology of the self begs the question, for why should the self be made at all by any kind of technology, let alone by ICTs? If the self is made, it is conceived from the start as a kind of what, so any question regarding the phenomenality of 'who are we' is entirely obliterated. Moreover, it is also presupposed from the start that the self is a world-isolated subject facing the world's objectivity.

Floridi then proceeds to present his "model" of the self as a three-stage encapsulation by a series of three "membranes" through which an individual is "detached" from its environment and becomes thus capable of "internal auto-organization". The three membranes are "the corporeal, the cognitive and the consciousness or simply 3C [which] seem to be the main stations at which the train of evolution has called". Such an ontogenetic, evolutionary story presupposes that ultimately the human being is a conscious subject encapsulated threefold within itself against the world. Floridi asserts, "yet, there is nothing metaphorical in this, as anyone acquainted with the concept of the virtual machine in computer science can readily appreciate," which amounts to having constructed a model of the self already adapted to conceiving it as a kind of machine, viz. an information-processing machine, a Turing machine. Floridi proceeds from a conception of the world as infosphere in which, even prior to and independently of human life, "data might be flowing around, but there are no senders or receivers yet". Such data include "lights, noises, or magnetic fields". The corporeal membrane of the first evolutionary stage serves a "negentropic function" that allows a living organism to defy spilling out, thus dissipating in entropy. In this way, Floridi applies notions borrowed from modern physics, without any further examination, to a problematic of self-constitution, as if modern physics could tell us 'who we are'.

With the second, cognitive membrane, "which allows the encapsulation of data for processing and communication," "intelligent animals" arise. Finally, "the third phase is represented by the evolution of the consciousness membrane. We move from pre-conscious (aware) to post-conscious (self-aware) systems once data become repurposable information, including conventional meanings (e.g. sounds become a national anthem)". In line with this hypothesized model, an a priori affinity with the unquestioned metaphysical presuppositions of AI research and neuroscience is plain. A statement such as "the consciousness membrane is softwired (programmable)" must be welcome to today's AI scientists, since it updates the metaphysical 'old-speak' of a subject imbued with an intellect, and makes the problem of self-identity functionally operable. Floridi's model presents no obstacle to technological fantasies of one day engineering consciousness, and it works merely by the power of suggestion and the technological credulity rampant today. Or does it present an obstacle? Floridi writes, "a single human being needs to be embedded, at a very early stage of development, within a community, in order to grow as a healthy self-conscious mind: mere corporeal and cognitive bonds, in one-to-one interactions with the external environment, fail to give rise to, and keep together, a full self, for which language, culture and social interactions are indispensable". All three ontogenetic, evolutionary encapsulations of the I, "all the three membranes," are required, "— physical, cognitive, and semantic — that progressively generate the unity of the self".

The semantic membrane of consciousness in this narrative of the evolution of the I-self is brought into a connection with the ICTs that are said to be "the most powerful technologies to which selves have ever been exposed," leaving their mark on all three ontogenetically conceived membranes through "re-ontologisation". On all levels, the self is then *made* through technology, above all, through ICTs. An example of such re-ontologization through an ICT adduced by Floridi is the "invention of writing" already thematized by Plato, but how does this account for any asserted "unity of the self", which is the problem posed for the entire article? Writing as a purported ICT is a memory aid, as treated already by Plato, but in the context of questioning whether writing is a help or hindrance to genuine philosophical insight into the nature of being, which is what Plato's philosophy at its core is about. Writing as a memory aid already *presupposes* a unity of self that is extended also into the temporal dimension of the past which is, however, not past precisely because it can be retrieved by memory to a unified self that is able to experience what has been as its own biographical history. Writing may technologically enhance this ability to retrieve in an ontic-factual sense, but it presupposes already the self's unity in temporal space, its stretchedness toward its own past, and hence does not amount to any kind of re-ontologization.

So, when Floridi comes to treat today's digital information and communication technologies that push the possibilities of writing as a memory aid into hitherto unimaginable areas, because all sorts of happenings in the world can be recorded through various digital media apart from mere writing, it is unwarranted to claim any *ontological* significance for an *ontic-factual, historical occurrence*, to wit, "any technology, the primary goal of which is to manage records, is going to have an immense influence on how individuals develop and shape their own personal identities". The *temporal unity* of the self, at least toward the dimension of the past or been-ness (since it is not past and can be retrieved to presence, whilst *simultaneously* being refused presence) is already tacitly presupposed by any claim for how today's digital ICTs enhance or detract from individual selves' technologically empowered possibilities to "develop and shape their own personal identities". Floridi does not mention that the self is also always-already unified existentially-ontologically toward the temporal dimension of the future. The self as this temporally stretched, or temporally ec-static, unity is prior to any consideration of the effects of any particular ICT. This temporal unity of the self cannot be "made" by any technology at all, but is granted, given.

When Floridi remarks with regard to today's new digital ICTs, "the more memories we accumulate and externalise, the more narrative constraints we provide for the construction and development of personal identities," this may be true as an ontic-factual statement about our historical situation, but the observation itself presupposes ontologically that the self is already also, in an essential aspect, a shining-back from the world (cf. *1.2 Selfhood as an identification with reflections from the world*) in the sense of the narratives related about the self by others in the third person and the narratives each self tells itself in the first person about *who* it is. The whoness of the self is constituted also by a shining-back from the world through which it finds itself in, identifying selectively not only with the narrative related by the others, and also by itself, about itself, but above all with existential possibilities of myriad kinds such as the accent one adopts, the political convictions one comes to hold, sexual orientation, occupation, etc. etc. Such identification is the self's grasping of a *future-oriented* possibility of existing in the world as its own.

Such an existential-ontological insight is prior to and implicitly presupposed by Floridi's considerations of the impact of today's new digital ICTs on the scope for self-identification in a digitized world. Hence Floridi's technologically enhanced or restricted narrative self cannot be encapsulated within three purported membranes since the self's identity is always already out there in a temporally structured world as an identification with information about it floating out there in digital media. The self is an identification with the other-out-there. The "gaze", or today, specifically, the "digital gaze" of the others adduced by Floridi co-constitutes the self's identity, i.e. who it is in the world, so that it is impossible for selfhood to be conceived at all as an encapsulating membrane that detaches a subject from the world.

Floridi's "model" of a unified self encapsulated in a threefold membrane turns out to be an imagination, a fantasy constructed in line with modern subjectivist metaphysics but contradicted by the phenomena themselves such as the digital gaze which contributes to the narrative and existential options out there with which the self may or may not identify. "The self tries to see how others see itself, by relying on information technologies, which greatly facilitate the gazing experience. The self uses the digital imaginary concerning itself to construct a virtual identity through which it seeks to grasp its own personal identity." Since digital data and the narrative related by them about somewho are as real as one can get in the digitized world, there is no occasion to speak of a merely "virtual identity" constituted by the digital gaze. Through this digital third-person narrative available out there, the individual "seeks to grasp its own personal identity", i.e. it selects from this narrative shining-back from the world those masks of who-identity with which it identifies as its own and which therefore are a facet of its self in the sense of how it casts its self into a *future*, finite existence. A narrative out there told about somewho from the *third* person is only ever a *partial offer* of identity, i.e. a who-mask that may be repudiated; this offer must be grasped as one's own in the *first* person to become a facet of one's own self. Other facets of identity are not narrative at all.

To identify even narratively, however, the self must be already out there with those narrative data, and not encapsulated within a consciousness-membrane within whose sphere it constitutes itself as reflective self-consciousness which is thus conceived by Floridi's membrane model as the mirroring-back from the diaphanous consciousness bubble within which it is enclosed and captured. Rather, the self is always already ecstatically ex-sisting, i.e. out-standing, in the world, stretched out also temporally into three-dimensional time-space. From the shining-back from the world, the self grasps, or fails to grasp, its ownmost possibility of existing as its own, thus identifying its self freely with the other. The world as a whole, and not just the world of others, i.e. not just a so-called 'intersubjective world', offers a mirror through which to assume masks of identity. This mirror may be a third person narrative about somewho told by the others, or it may be simply the world in its openness for different existential castings (e.g. the shining-back of the forest inviting someone to become a forester), or it may be *you* in the *second* person who mirrors to me an ownmost possibility for existing. None of these considerations fits Floridi's informational model of the encapsulated self.

Floridi introduces in the final section of his article a concept from Aristotle's *Poetics*, namely, ἀνάγνωσις or 'recognition'. In Aristotle's thinking on tragedy, recognition is that phenomenon through which the character, such as Oedipus, tragically recognizes himself belatedly through the unfolding of events which, of course, in Floridi's informational metaphysics, amounts to a reinterpretation of one's third-person self-narrative on the basis of the receipt of new data packages from the infosphere. This adds a temporal dimension to self-identification with the other, already on the basis of a linear conception of time that distinguishes between Before and After and a point R (for recognition) on the time-line between A and B. "At point R, some information becomes available that does not make some information at point B (for before) false, but rather provides the right perspective from which to interpret it." The narrative information out there about oneself is thus reinterpreted, and so self-identity, i.e. the narrative out there with which the self identifies, changes over time. This presupposes, however, that the world out there is always already interpreted *as* such-and-such. Otherwise, it could not be reinterpreted.

Significantly, Floridi's adopted concept of recognition relates only to informational data packages telling a tale about the self's past. Even from the point-of-time after (A), the self is looking back in hindsight, not casting itself into future possibilities, although that is the point of Greek tragedy: the final downfall of the tragic character. What about the self's future? These data packages have not yet arrived, so how can they be taken into account? How can they be real for a realist model? This implies that the self has no future, because there exists no information from the future. Or, asked more cautiously, what is the ontological status, i.e. the mode of presencing, of futural "informational structures" (Floridi's preferred term for entities in his informational metaphysics of the infosphere)? Do they not yet exist? Do they exist only in fantasy, as the metaphysical tradition since Aristotle has supposed, or do they exist *as* futural scientific extrapolations of present scientific data? A similar, but not so pressing, question arises with regard to past informational structures. Floridi suggests they still exist only in memory, again a traditional metaphysical way of thinking, but is this memory cast as informational only by virtue of being stored in some sort of present-at-hand ICT medium such as writing, photos, film, magnetic tape, etc.? Or does it suffice that past informational structures still exist only in living or oral memory? Since Floridi does not break in the slightest with the traditional linear conception of time inherited from Aristotle, only that which exists *now* 'really' exists (as a *res*) at all. Since stored informational data of memory still exist *now* in some *real, physically present* medium, perhaps even a living human medium regarded *as* an informational structure counts as real, and Floridi may still have a plausible retort, but with respect to the future his cast of informational being looks highly implausible.

The threefold membrane model of the unified self is constructed to conform with the schema of subjectivist metaphysics cast already by Descartes and copied, with modifications, ubiquitously ever since. The early (ca. 1663) Leibniz's schema of the subject is instructive for its very graphicness.[215] Leibniz casts the subject as a series of four alternate pentagons and circles concentric upon the centre conceived as the invincibly free intellect. The self is hence conceived doubly fortified by two corporeal pentagons and two spiritual membranes, and the self's communication with the outside is mediated by sense data coming in and impulses of the intellect's will to act going out. There is already a problem here for subjectivist metaphysics, with which it has struggled from the outset (e.g. Locke), because it is a mystery how the sense data coming in, i.e. electrical impulses passing through the nerves to the brain, could be experienced in consciousness *as* a perception of a sensuous being *out there*. For instance, when someone steps on my toe in the elevator, I do not experience an electrical nerve impulse passing from my toe up to the brain which interprets it magically *as* someone stepping on my toe. Rather, I experience simply someone stepping on my toe (which, neuroscience tells me, is a quaint illusion). I am already out there in the world with beings, interpreting them *as* such-and-such; more strictly, it is not *my* achievement that I always already understand the world out there, but rather beings out there in the world already present themselves to me *as* such-and-such, e.g. as someone standing next to me in the elevator and — *pace* Floridi — not as an informational structure, which is a mere imagined 'model' that only distorts the view.

---

215 Cf. 1663/2003.

The same problem recurs with Floridi's informational model of the self encapsulated within three membranes, only now it is through informational data packets coming in that the self supposedly communicates with the world, picking and choosing its self from among third-person narrative data packets with which it will identify. Such data packets coming in from the world conceived as infosphere, however, must already be understood *as* information. How come the world presents itself *as* infosphere? Floridi simply asserts that it is, and maybe it is, but this is already an historical sending that has sent a casting of the being of beings *as* information, and *as* digital information in particular. Without this sending, no informational cast of being. This is not to be explained by any sort of ontogenetic explanation, but by looking back on the historical sendings of the cast of being received through the ages since Greek antiquity by thinkers.

Floridi seems to have received a message from presencing itself according to which the world is to be interpreted *as* an infosphere in which the basic entities are not you and me and useful things and natural things. Rather, Floridi views "the world as the totality of informational structures dynamically interacting with each other". In this infosphere-world, the ultimate informational structure is the threefold encapsulated self. "Selves are the ultimate negentropic technologies, through which information temporarily overcomes its own entropy, becomes conscious, and able to recount the story of its own emergence in terms of a progressive detachment from external reality." This says that selves are enclosed (i.e. negentropic, not leaking out entropically) data packages that i) are made ontogenetically by a technology and ii) are a bulwark against informational entropy by concentrating and encapsulating information within itself, i.e. within the consciousness membrane, in such a way as to finally kindle the fire of self-consciousness. Of course, this narrative of the self is also just an imagined fantasy with which we can choose freely to identify or not.

3.8.2 Floridi's purportedly "ontological interpretation of informational privacy"

What Floridi presents as 'The ontological interpretation of informational privacy'[216] is in truth a merely sociological discussion for acronym fondlers of issues around informational privacy, undertaken with many historical comparisons of the capabilities of various "information and communication technologies", or ICTs. It is instructive to look more closely and concentratedly at what Floridi understands by ontology, "ontological friction" and "re-ontologization". Given the philosophical-ontological pretensions of the article's title, its largely sociological, historical contents, with moral over- and undertones and dilemmas, can be left to sociologists and historians and analytic moral philosophers. The question raised by the article's title is, properly speaking, What is informational privacy?, which breaks into two questions: What is information? and What is privacy? To such questions, the sociologist or analytical philosopher is content to provide definitional answers that mark the phenomenon in question off successfully and clearly from other phenomena. Such a procedure is altogether different from asking what these phenomena are as modes of being, i.e. as ways in which beings show up and present themselves in the world, e.g. *as* (bits of) information, or the way in which privacy itself is to be understood as a mode of non-disclosive presencing of whos. Such questions have been addressed in previous chapters of this study (cf. esp. *1.4 The question concerning rights: personal privacy, trust and intimacy*). Here it is more a matter of looking briefly at what Floridi writes within the narrower umbra of these questions.

The aim of Floridi's article "is to argue in favour of a new ontological interpretation of informational privacy and of its moral value, on the basis of the conceptual frame provided by Information Ethics". He asks, "Why have digital ICTs made informational privacy one of the most obvious and pressing issues in computer ethics?" and asserts that new digital ICTs "have their roots in a radical and unprecedented

---

216 Floridi 2006a. Unless otherwise specified, all quotations in this section are from the PDF-file for this article.

transformation in the very nature (ontology) of the informational environment, of the informational agents embedded in it and of their interactions". Thus it becomes an issue to assess what Floridi understands by "ontology". As elsewhere, Floridi casts the world as the "model" of the "infosphere" as discussed in the preceding section. He introduces a central concept of his article: "'Ontological friction' refers here to the forces that oppose the information flow within (a region of) the infosphere, and hence (as a coefficient) to the amount of work required for a certain kind of agent to obtain information (also, but not only) about other agents in a given environment".

An *ontic-factual* blockage to the flow of information, modelled on classical mechanics, is supposed to be elevated to the status of an "ontological friction". It is also given a pseudo-scientific status borrowed from physics by employing a "coefficient" for "the amount of work" to overcome "forces". The concepts of 'force' and 'work' in classical mechanics belong to a scientific-mathematical conception that can be employed to grasp an ontic, physical friction, a hindrance to motion. They *presuppose* an ontology, namely a mathematico-productivist metaphysical casting of the physical world, but such an ontological presupposition remains hidden to Floridi as it does to physics itself. In short, the free flow of information in (a region of) the world cast *as* infosphere amounts to low informational friction, an easily comprehensible conception requiring no term as grand as "ontological friction". Floridi's approach to "informational privacy" thus amounts, in the first place, to assessing whether the new digital ICTs increase or decrease the friction in the flow of information about somewho or other according to an analogy with classical mechanics.

Floridi then discusses whether "throughout history, informational privacy has constantly decreased in relation to the invention and spreading of ever more powerful ICTs," asserting that "this would be a simplistic and mistaken inference". He adduces, for instance, the phenomenon of anonymity that arose with large cities as a privacy-enhancing factor rather than a privacy-eroding one. This is a sociologico-historical thesis having no ontological import, so it will be left to one side here. Floridi then proceeds to present digital ICTs themselves "as re-ontologizing technologies". What does this mean? Floridi breaks this down into five theses, but it can be said more succinctly as the digitization of information and its consequences. Since he casts the world itself as infosphere, for Floridi, the digitization of information amounts to a digitization of the world and, to an extent, its human inhabitants. It is the digital cast of being (a way of thinking that takes in how the world presents itself in the digital age), and not its materialization, "digital ICTs", that recasts the world in an ontological sense. "Digital ICTs" are made possible by the digital cast of being, not conversely, and the digital cast of being comes historically from a long way off, mediated through the co-casting performed by philosophical thinking from Pythagoras and Parmenides on that have co-cast the way the world shapes up and shows itself to human being. The historical event of the digital cast of being that is recasting today's world as the historical culmination of productionist metaphysical thinking cannot be gone into here.[217] Here it suffices to say that digitization of beings, their re-presentation *as* strings of bits, gives rise to a parallel digital world, the cyberworld, in which these digital beings can circulate freely with low informational-flow friction.

Secondly — and this point is basically Floridi's second thesis relating to "the homogenization of the processor and the processed" where he refers also to Turing — digital data (beings) can be automatically processed by executable code that is simply another digital string, i.e. a computing program. The Universal Turing Machine consists first of all of program code on the endless tape, followed by the digital data to be processed by the preceding program code. This does indeed amount to an ontological earthquake, because materially outsourced digital program code assumes a hitherto inconceivable autonomy vis-à-vis human beings in robots of all kinds that, supplied with electric power, *move on their own, steered by program code*, as if they were somehow alive. Human understanding of the world is thus outsourced to and embedded in an electromagnetic matrix where it becomes executable and does indeed bring forth movements/changes in both the digital and the

[217] Cf. Eldred 2009/2011, Capurro 2001, Capurro 2002.

physical world. Floridi's understanding of the digital cast of being, however, is much more superficial and reduced to merely ontic-factual description and explanation in terms of the historical ontogenesis of new digital ICTs. What Floridi understands by the "re-ontologized infosphere," is basically the digital parallel world in which digital beings (bit-strings) circulate, steered by cybernetic program code, which is also a bit-string. The bit-strings can be information of any conceivable kind, but also executable program code. The latter also gives human players in the digital cyberworld the ability to steer informational data in the sense of controlling and restricting its flow and dissemination, a phenomenon which Floridi books under the heading of "the protection of personal data", an instance of his misnamed "ontological friction".

After discussing various illustrations of friction in informational flow due to both old and new (digital) ICTs, Floridi turns to "assessing theories of privacy", of which he considers two: the "reductionist" (or consequentialist) and the "ownership-based" interpretations. The former focuses "on a variety of undesirable consequences that may be caused by its [information privacy's] breach", whereas the latter asserts that "a person is said to own his or her information" like other private property. Floridi points to inadequacies in these two theories and proposes instead his own so-called "ontological interpretation of informational privacy and its value" resulting from the advent in full force of digital ICTs. With this advent, what in this study is called the digital cast of being becomes a reality as a parallel digital cyberworld. In this brave new cyberworld, Floridi offers a reinterpretation of information privacy "by considering each person as constituted by his or her information, and hence by understanding a breach of one's informational privacy as a form of aggression towards one's personal identity". Informational privacy becomes "a fundamental and inalienable right" akin to the right to life and liberty. The person is thus not simply identified with its informational data as its other, but, for Floridi, simply *is* its informational data.

On this recasting, the human being becomes equated ontologically to an informational data package existing in the world cast *as* infosphere. I have already discussed in the previous section the severe shortcomings of casting the self's identity as an identification with data out there floating around in the infosphere, and the same flawed gesture of thinking is repeated here by Floridi. Apart from totalizing information to an informational cast of being in which beings are 'nothing other than' what he terms "informational structures", his interpretation of informational privacy overlooks that personal identity is always an identification with an *other* and therefore cannot be *equated* with the informational data reflected back from the parallel digital cyberworld. Rather, the self freely selects which identity on offer shone back from the world it identifies with, and casts its self accordingly, not as an information package, but into a possibility of existing that it identifies with as its very own. Only by misunderstanding the Platonic and Hegelian dialectic of the identification of self and other, and its existential-ontological reinterpretation,[218] and by collapsing the identification into an equation can Floridi assert, "looking at the nature of a person as being constituted by that person's information allows one to understand the right to informational privacy as a right to personal immunity from unknown, undesired or unintentional changes in one's own identity as an informational entity...". And further, "the ontological interpretation suggests that there is no difference between one's informational sphere and one's personal identity. 'You are your information'". However — *pace* Floridi — any identity presupposes and preserves difference, and vice versa. In this instance, it is the living, breathing human being, existing as an open temporal clearing for the presencing and absencing of beings in the world that identifies with possible castings for its own existence as mirrored back from the world, which is always more than mere 'information'.

All subsequent discussion by Floridi of the consequences of equating (rather than identifying) a person with his or her digital information is therefore otiose, for it is based on a skew-whiff ontological conception of the person. For instance, "the sharing of private information with someone" on the basis of confidentiality does not result in a "super-agent", and intimate trust between persons has to be conceived

[218] Cf. Eldred 2008/2011 Section 3 iii) a) 'Dialectic of self and other'.

ontologically rather as the fragile interplay between you-and-me.[219] The issue of personal privacy has to be approached as the non-disclosure by an individual as who he is in his personal life-world, as treated in other chapters of this study (cf. *1.4 The question concerning rights: personal privacy, trust and intimacy*). Personal privacy is the *privatio* of self-disclosure *as* who one is to the world.

3.9 On Charles Ess' appraisal of Floridi's information ethics

Ess' 2009 article[220] sets out "to evaluate Floridi's philosophy of information (PI) and correlative information ethics (IE) as potential frameworks for a *global* information and computing ethics (ICE)". He claims for Floridi, "Indeed, subsequent history may judge that his PI and IE stand among a handful of prominent developments of the first six decades of Western ICE (if we begin with Norbert Wiener, 1948)." Here I will concentrate on the foundations of Floridi's theories, viz. "PI as an ontology" which Ess, in the fourth section of his article, cursorily puts into relation to "the Heideggerian components of Rafael Capurro's intercultural information ethics". Ess' appraisal of "Floridi's treatment of privacy and the closely related matter of what counts as personal data" also deserves attention here. Ess is particularly interested in extending and making more robust Floridi's PI and IE in a *global* context by moving in the direction of a "new, post-Cartesian conception of the self and ethical imperatives" that makes it possible to encompass non-Western thinking such as Buddhism and Confucianism. Does Floridi's ontology really represent a move beyond Cartesianism? Preceding sections have already shown that it does not, but let us examine Ess' presentation.

---

219 Cf. Eldred 1997/2010.

220 All quotations from Ess in this and the following subsections are from Ess 2009, unless otherwise stated.

3.9.1 Informational ontology

As Ess cites, Floridi opens his ontology by postulating "'to be is to be an informational entity' (Floridi, 2008 p. 199)." which, Ess claims, is a "radical turn". Given Floridi's commitment to subjectivist metaphysics (cf. *3.8 Floridi's metaphysics of the threefold-encapsulated subject in a world conceived as infosphere*), this is questionable. With regard to Floridi's basic, all-encompassing, ontological postulate, the question is immediately posed: Does Floridi clarify the very meaning of being? No, he doesn't. And neither does Ess. Furthermore, the very term 'information' is drenched in the Western metaphysical tradition, as shown in detail by Capurro, starting with Aristotle's μορφή. and Plato's εἶδος, standardly rendered in English precisely as 'form'. In Ess' eyes, taking information as a foundational ontological category is supposed to enable an encompassing of ethical traditions beyond a merely Western horizon by shifting from the emphasis on the "(human) moral agent as primarily a 'psychic atom'—i.e., the *individual*". Information as non-human seems to provide an alternative to Western 'humanism'. But who is it, if not the human being, who is or could be open to beings *as* beings, including to beings *as* information? Isn't Floridi's casting of the being of beings *as* information only possible at the consummation of a long historical trajectory in Western metaphysical thinking when information technologies have 'invaded' and decisively shape our now globalized world? By postulating informational entities as fundamental, Floridi opens the way to conceiving artificial agents such as robots, too, as moral agents, which represents a further step on the way to the historical destruction of human being itself. As we shall see below, Floridi hedges his bets as to whether his informational ontology is indeed fundamental.

Furthermore "*individual*" is no innocent term, being not tied solely to the Cartesian subject of mathematized knowledge, since it is associated primarily with the modern individual who has only become historically possible in the last four hundred years through the coming to hegemony of a *reified* mode of sociating commonly, but misleadingly, referred to as 'capitalism based on private property' (cf. *1.6 The private individual and private property as a mode of reified sociation: the gainful game (classical political economy, Marx)*). Modern political philosophy to the present day continues in misconceiving the individual as an "atom", whereas in truth, the individual is itself a relatively late historical mode of *dissociated* human beings *associating* with one another through the mediation of privately owned things. (The individual 'atom' is always already sociated into a social 'molecule' via reified value.) This modern individual is the socio-political counterpart to the modern, encapsulated, conscious subject whose blue-print was first drafted by Descartes. As shown in preceding sections, Floridi is still captive to the metaphysics of the encapsulated subject. Floridi's notion of "distributed morality" does not break with the metaphysics of encapsulated subjectivity but is precisely compatible with it — as a mode of *intersubjectivity*. Intersubjectivity, however, does not amount to the ontological insight that subjects are always already in the world.

Ess discusses next an *ethical* implication of Floridi's informational ontology, namely, that it postulates "reality qua information as intrinsically valuable". This, Ess claims, enables Floridi to overcome a "modernist emphasis on the distinction between *things* and *value*" that arises from the Cartesian dualism between the conscious subject (which, purportedly, alone is valuable) and material things that are surrendered to mastery and exploitation by the modern subject. Ess overlooks thereby that the discourse on the value of things themselves has also a long history in modern political and moral philosophy that gave rise to political economy and economics. The thought that things are valuable has a long pedigree in Western philosophy going back to Aristotle, who is the originator of the distinction between use-value and exchange-value[221] that was to play such a pivotal role two millennia later in classical political economy and Marx's critique thereof. The use-value of things *is* only within the usages of human living itself in an historical world, which of course invites the misguided accusation of 'anthropocentrism', but there *are* valuable things *as such* only for

[221] Aristotle *Pol.* I iii 1257a10,14; Eldred 2008/2011 Chaps. 4 and 5.

human being itself that is open to beings qua beings, which includes beings qua valuable.

Such valuableness of things can extend to the appreciation of the *natural environment* itself as valuable for human dwelling on the Earth when human beings themselves, as they are doing today, come to an appreciation of the destructiveness of human productive activities for the environment on a global scale. It is only humans who historically can learn to care for and thus value the environment. Things, including Floridi's informational entities, are not "intrinsically" valuable, but only within a world inhabited by human beings. If we humans weren't here, there would be no question regarding value at all. To postulate intrinsic value of "reality qua information" is to indulge in a fantasy about things in themselves in the absence of any human being at all (not simply human *beings*, but the way of human presencing as the beings who are open to being, i.e. to the temporal play of presencing and absencing). This criticism of a purported intrinsic value of things as information obviates Ess' point that Floridi allows gradations of intrinsic value in his *model* via so-called "levels of abstraction". Such so-called LoAs amount to representations (models) constructed in (Floridi's) subjective consciousness that are interposed between the conscious subject and the world to make it shape up and make sense for that consciousness. The sense the world makes is thus constructed through models, rather than the world's meaning being received within a human openness to the phenomena as they present themselves of themselves.

That informational entities are (postulated as) intrinsically valuable leads on to Floridi's postulation of the "flourishing" of all entities *as* information. Ess defends this notion of flourishing by citing Floridi's "insistence on the goodness of being" with its Augustinian resonances. Since, in Floridi's ontology, all entities show themselves *as* information, this amounts to an informational casting of the being of beings in toto, whilst leaving the question as to the meaning of being itself unasked. Moreover, Floridi's informational ontology, which in its own founding postulation (see above) is *totalizing*, implies that Wiener's conception of flourishing as "human values (life, health, freedom, knowledge, happiness), and fulfilling 'the great principles of justice' drawn from

Western philosophical and religious traditions" can been seen from casting all these diverse things *as* information. Otherwise, the "convergence between Floridi and Wiener" conjured by Ess is hollow. How, for instance, is freedom or happiness or justice to be understood *as* information? Ess does not notice this antinomy in Floridi's ontology and ethics, and does not attempt to even hint how such fundamental questions concerning the totalization *explicit* in Floridi's informational ontology could be approached.

For Floridi, the opposite of flourishing is "entropy", which "is increased when Being, interpreted informationally, is annihilated or degraded. (Floridi 2008, p. 200)". This mention of "Being" confuses being itself with beings *as* beings, since Floridi's ontology only cast all *beings* as information. For him, therefore, entropy can only mean the annihilation or degradation of information. There must be, therefore, different grades of beings *as* information in a certain hierarchy, and one could discuss ethically the priorities that should be given to one grade of information over another when information is destroyed. One is then confronted, for instance, with the ethical dilemma of grading a cow *as* information vis-à-vis a carrot *as* information, which presupposes that, first of all, it must be said what a cow and a carrot are *as* information and how this information can be graded.

3.9.2 Informational privacy

When Ess turns to evaluate what Floridi's informational ontology and its associated ethics of informational flourishing and annihilation have to do with informational ethics and privacy, it is noticeable that, under the impact of Tavani's critical assessment of Floridi's theory of informational privacy (cf. previous sections), Floridi himself indulges in some back-peddling. He writes in response to Tavani, "informational ontology may help us to understand an individual as constituted by her information [and] is meant to contribute and be complementary to other approaches to e.g. physical or mental/psychological privacy"[222]. In view of the ontological postulate, "to be is to be an informational entity", this

[222] Floridi 2008 p. 199 cited in Ess 2009 p. 163.

amounts to a big climb-down. Floridi's ontology becomes a mere framework model complementary to, and *alongside* other models, thus admitting a pluralism of approaches.

We have already discussed Floridi's equating a person's personal information with their personal identity (*3.8.2 Floridi's purportedly "ontological interpretation of informational privacy"*) which opens the way to equating personal privacy with informational privacy. If, now, holes appear in Floridi's informational ontology, and it is degraded to the status of a partial framework model alongside other 'models', this implies that Floridi's conception of informational personal privacy is only piecemeal and subject to as many qualifications as there are alternative approaches, such as physical, psychological, mental, Confucian, Buddhist, etc. The consequence is a theoretical arbitrariness and disorientation consonant with an incoherent pluralism in which the issues that call for clarification are set adrift on an apparently tranquil sea of toleration for mutually incompatible approaches to the same phenomena. Fundamental ontological questions are left unasked and, above all, it is not seen that Floridi's informational ontology is a specific historical casting of the being of beings that is unaware of its captiveness to the long Western metaphysical tradition of successive metaphysical castings of the being of beings.

Ess does not see things this way at all, but instead, in his concluding section, praises Floridi for providing, on the basis of his "'lite' form of information ontology" an information ethics that is "one minimalist framework among others". But how can a basic casting of entities as informational be pluralistic? In connection with this 'liteness', Ess then cites Floridi (Floridi 2006), who claims for his information ontology that it provides "a more neutral ontology of entities modelled informationally. By referring to such a 'lite' ontological grounding of informational privacy, the theory allows the adaptation of the former to various conceptions of the latter, working as a potential cross-cultural platform." Accordingly, entities are "modelled informationally", which does not mean that they are seen adequately phenomenologically in their very being, i.e. their *modes* of presencing in the world, which are indeed plural, but not in the common sense of pluralism. The use of "neutral" in the quotation above is also unclear, since it could be understood as 'abstract', which would imply that an abstract, foundational informational ontology could be further concretized, say, within different cultural settings. But this interpretation of the term is excluded by the fact that Floridi has conceded ground to a mere parallel pluralism of various approaches.

The above quote also prejudices the approach to the phenomenon of privacy itself by presupposing that it is "informational privacy". As we have seen in Chapter 1, however — which throws light on privacy as the concealment of personal life-worlds, on the one hand, and the privacy of private property, on the other — such a conception of privacy is severely truncated. Ess' praise of Floridi's 'lite' ontology and associated ethics, to the effect that it provides a framework for approaching non-Western cultures, is therefore also misplaced, because it assumes that privacy in these cultures can be understood as informational, whereas in truth it has to do with the interplay of revealing to and concealing from each other *who* one is.[223] The issue of interculturality will be taken up again below in Chapter 4.

---

[223] In the lengthy abstract to Ess 2012, Ess speaks of "moves in 'the West' *away* from modernist notions of individual-exclusive *privacy* towards more group-based notions of privacy, if not the elimination of any sort of public/private boundary altogether" as well as claiming, "[b]y contrast, 'Eastern' attitudes are demonstrably shifting in the opposite direction – i.e., away from earlier emphases on privacy and property as *collective* and *inclusive*, towards ever greater emphases on individual privacy and property rights as positive goods". The result is then asserted to be an observable tendency toward "a *hybridization* in both 'Western' and 'Eastern' traditions – one that conjoins both modernist notions of individual selfhood with earlier notions (in both East and West) of relational selfhood". Whatever the merits of this empirical observation may be, it leaves open the philosophical question concerning the encompassing dimension of human being itself, viz. *whoness*, within which such shifts can occur and within which there are individually exclusive or collectively inclusive, culturally cultivated modes of associating with one another in *power plays* of *mutually estimating and esteeming* who one is and also of *revealing and concealing* who one is in different situations in various cultures (cf. Chap. 4). Furthermore, the very privacy of the private individual, whether in the West

3.9.3 Getting over the subject-object split

Ess also praises Floridi for being "among a growing array of philosophers enjoining us to move beyond the Cartesian mind-body split", but overlooks that Floridi's ontology of the encapsulated subject of consciousness (see preceding sections) does not overcome the Cartesian subject-object split, which is more fundamental. In fact, since in Cartesian subject-object dualism, it is precisely the bodily senses that mediate between the subject and the world of objects, it is questionable whether a "mind-body split" in Cartesian metaphysics is the crucial issue at all, but rather the Cartesian dualism between res cogito and res extensa. Ess confuses what today is meant by cognition as the activity of thinking with the breadth of the Cartesian cogito, which encompasses all that is represented in consciousness, including feelings. So Ess' plea for taking notice of embodied feelings and proceeding beyond "a purely Cartesian emphasis on the self qua disembodied mind" in a "move closer to both pre-modern Western and non-Western conceptions" is a misconception. The Cartesian mind already *is* embodied and *has* feelings.

The problem is rather that in all subjectivist metaphysics, including Floridi's, feelings are encapsulated within the embodied subject rather than being moods out there in the world to which human beings find themselves attuned (in German: sich befinden in einer Befindlichkeit), and *can* find themselves attuned, because human being itself is an ecstatic, ex-sistential (literally out-standing), quivering openness to the world (and not just to objects in the world). So long as thinking is captive to the subject-object split, the sharing of feelings has to be conceived as a kind of intersubjective communication, of one subject's empathetic ability to project itself into another's feelings, etc.

---

or the East, is socio-ontologically tied to the privacy of private property that enables in the first place a sociation of dissociated private property-owners as individual income-earners (cf. *1.6 The private individual and private property as a mode of reified sociation: the gainful game (classical political economy, Marx)*). Ess does not attempt any such socio-ontological grounding of whoness, nor does he phenomenologically unfold the privacy of private property.

encapsulated in its consciousness The phenomenological insight into human being itself as an existentially resonating 'standing-out' in the world is a more auspicious starting-point for engaging with other cultures than any variant of subjectivist metaphysics, including Floridi's, could ever be. Likewise, a phenomenology of whoness offers a way of getting over what Ess calls "androcentrism", thus taking up feminist concerns. How so? Because whoness is the phenomenon of showing off to each other who one is in a striving to be estimated and esteemed highly (cf. Chapter 1). The phenomenology of whoness still awaits its reception in the ongoing debate over information ethics.

3.10 Beavers' response to an objection by Floridi to AI by reverting to Husserlian subjectivist phenomenology

Beavers (Beavers 2002) takes up an objection by Floridi that "because computers, or computer programs, are locked in microworlds and human beings are not, AI research cannot approximate human intelligence, which is open-ended and able to deal with a broad range of contingencies."[224] which he proposes to overcome by showing the appropriateness precisely of microworld phenomenologies. Beavers starts by restricting legitimate, pertinent phenomenology to the Husserlian kind, to the exclusion of both Hegelian and Heideggerian phenomenology. Kant gains a place beside Husserl because both think within the problematic of the constitution of objectivity from within subjectivity. He wants to keep things encapsulated within a subject's consciousness to make them amenable to cognitive science and AI. From the outset the focus is on *causal explanation* and *effectiveness* in line with the demands of "science", "cognitive science" in this case.

"Let us define as 'ontological enveloping' the process of adapting the environment to the agent in order to enhance the latter's capacities of interaction. (Floridi 1999 p. 214)" This "ontological enveloping" in Floridi's sense is merely ontic-factual adaptation to the features of a restricted segment of the world. In Floridi's own words, it is "the

224 Beavers 2002 with reference to Floridi 1999.

process of adapting the environment to the agent in order to enhance the latter's capacities of interactions", in other words, the refinement of a model.

Beavers puts his finger on the weakness in Floridi's schematic-subjectivist ontology by pointing to the superiority of Kant's and Husserl's ontologies of transcendental subjective world-constitution, although in doing so, he truncates Kant to mirroring "the fundamental laws of science", thus keeping things 'under control' for the sake of control. Floridi's critique of AI "that human experience is open-ended and therefore not reducible to a microworld" overlooks the fundamental, genuinely ontological point (within the limits of Kantian and Husserlian subjectivist ontology) that computers do not and cannot constitute within their processors even a microworld. I.e. it is not a matter of pointing out that human consciousness is open to a wider world than a computer, but that a computer can never have a world at all, not even a microworld, first of all, because a computer is not exposed to three-dimensional, ecstatic time-space.[225]

Beavers fails to see this, thus levelling human being with computer being. Instead he focuses on the possibility of the (ultimately practical) usefulness of a Kantian/Husserlian microworld phenomenology. He wants philosophy to provide a template for a computer-programming task, thus slotting philosophy into the productive will to power. Thus he interprets Kantian/Husserlian phenomenology of world-constitution as a kind of processing akin to what a computer could be programmed to do: "For phenomenologists, the phenomenal world is just such a summation, a spatial and temporal objectification of the flux of sense data into a stable and knowable world according to a set of processes or procedures.[...] [T]here are discoverable rules that govern the process whereby consciousness transforms the flux of sense data into a world of possible objects of experience." Voilà: a parallelism between consciousness's cognitive processing and digital processing. "The import of this observation for AI should be clear; where we find rules, we find the possibility of algorithms." Hence philosophy proves itself

225 Eldred 2012a.

useful for AI. Subjective consciousness provides "the intellectual architecture that ontologically envelops such a world," through the "phenomenological reduction or epoché". The proof this pudding's truth is to be ultimately AI's productive effectiveness.

The phenomenological fallacy here is that it is assumed (empiricistically, thus misunderstanding both Kant and Husserl) that only sense data are given to consciousness, and that these sense data are processed into the representation of an object. But what is given to the mind by the world is not merely a constant flow of sense data, but the world itself and the beings in it that present themselves, first of all, AS SOMETHING. The category of something must be understood and taken for granted a priori to even see anything out there in the world and take in sense data about it. The computer screen presents itself, first and foremost, AS SOMETHING prior to being specified even AS a computer screen, and prior to the sequence of what can be seen on the screen in a succession of moments. The sense data always already shape up AS something or other. Beavers overlooks this crucial insight into the hermeneutic *as* that structures how a world shapes up and shows itself *as* a world. However, for subjectivist metaphysics, that something is out there in the world is, in turn, an a priori (transcendental in the Kantian sense, i.e. prior to experience) projection from the mind that constructs within itself some such thing as an object — the objects out there in the world AS objects are projections of subjective consciousness onto the Ding an sich. The "phenomenological representation [within consciousness ME] *is* the extra-mental world *as we take it to be*". The world does not present itself to us, but rather, *as we take it to be*. Hence, strictly speaking, objects exist only within subjective consciousness, and any objects out there in the world are only the projections of imagination. This would make science, too, a projection of subjective consciousness's imagination, construing a world of objects out there that are interrelated causally: "the natural world of science is ontologically enveloped [...] in advance by consciousness as a precondition for being able to frame cognitive claims about it." This "in advance" implies a priori ontological constitution, but Beavers equivocates on this a priori status, as we shall see.

Through his line of thinking, Beavers paints himself into the corner of the realist/idealist dilemma: Is the world really out there? To rely on Kant is to adopt a subjective idealism, but Beavers must try to elude this fate. This requires a leap of faith: "For it could well be the case that the phenomenological world, the transcendence in immanence constituted out of sense data by mental processes, maps adequately onto the world of things in themselves. Just maybe we get things right." This is akin to Leibniz' leap of faith into the "pre-established harmony" between the monad-subject and the world, which is necessary because the Leibnizian monad "has no windows". Once one has been cut off from the world through the subject/object split, there is no way out because — *pace* Beavers — it cannot be the case that "the 'world for us' is wrenched out of the data stream". No sense data could ever be received AS sense data without the beings out there in the world always already presenting themselves (a priori, transcendentally) AS SOMETHING acting on the senses, 'something' being the simplest of categories, the simplest 'look' (eidos) that a being presents of itself.

The subject/object split, however, is essential for the applicability, in any form, of phenomenology to cognitive science and AI in order to have an encapsulated, constructible starting-point whence to interact with things in a restricted microworld.. If the human mind were not thus encapsulated, but rather always already out there in the world among beings of all kinds,[226] there would be no toehold for cognitive science to make itself effectively, productively useful. Against the phenomenological evidence, cognition is posited 'realistically' and 'materialistically' to take place in "processes [that] are instantiated in the brain" locatable and enveloped within the body, and these brain processes then can be modelled and programmed as digital algorithms processed in a digital processor. Thus, American pragmatism aims to cut through the turgid prose of Husserl and German subjective idealism to wrench out what is effectively useful to realist, materialist, cognitive science. Insofar, what Beavers offers is only a slightly more

[226] Cf. Eldred 2012.

sophisticated subjectivist ontology than Floridi's crude, schematic one (see preceding sections).[227]

[227] Addendum by Rafael Capurro: Beavers thinks that phenomenology has to do with the first-person perspective and science with the third-person perspective. In this he is both right and wrong. He is right insofar as the phenomenologist tries to gather (λέγειν) and express what shows itself to him as 'his own'. But he is wrong insofar as he believes that that amounts to mere descriptive subjectivism or esoteric Wesensschau (contemplation of the ideas) from within a subject, since I put that which I take in and perceive (or more precisely: what I perceive already together with others) at their disposal and ask: Do you see that the same way as I do? The phenomenological contemplation of essence is anything but esoteric because it wants to express, as precisely as possible, what the (exoteric) phenomena show of themselves, apart from preconceptions or any kind of interposed theoretical schema or model. A table is a table, and not primarily a heap of physical data that I take in through sense organs and 'process' into the representation of a table in my consciousness. And a table is never merely just a table, but always already woven into an interconnection with other things, together with which the table has its determination *as* being-good-for this or that and so 'is' in the world. Of course, such determinations are not eternal, and they change in their ontic-factual detail, but within a world things are simply what they are. With regard to the modern scientific standpoint of objectivity, this standpoint cannot be separated from the 'subjective' standpoint in the sense just adumbrated, since science, too, is done by individual human beings. However, in this scientific context, the 'intersubjective' examination is subjected to other methodological yardsticks and boundary conditions, especially of a quantitative kind, which also are not eternal. Otherwise, we could never have any scientific revolutions that fundamentally change the paradigm. Beavers neglects these aspects, among others, and instead speaks of a schematic subject/object split that from the outset falsifies the phenomena at hand that are of concern, thus falsifying also phenomenology and science, and that leads nowhere except, perhaps, to a manipulation of the world through computers programmed with so-called AI.

4 Intercultural aspects of digitally mediated whoness, privacy and freedom

Rafael Capurro[228]

4.1 Privacy and publicness from an intercultural viewpoint

Recent research in information ethics shows that the notion and practices of privacy vary in different cultural traditions, thus having an impact also on digitally mediated whoness and freedom.[229] This intercultural discussion is still in its initial stages with regard to the 'Far East'[230] and also African and Latin American cultures, just as it is in comparative studies between, for instance, Europe and the United States as addressed, say, by Helen Nissenbaum (cf. *3.7 An appraisal of Nissenbaum's Privacy in Context*) and Beate Rössler (cf. *1.10 Privacy as protection of individual autonomy — On Rössler's* The Value of Privacy). How and as whom we reveal and conceal ourselves and our selves is not just an abstract conceptual matter, but is always concretized and rooted in cultural traditions. What is common and what is different shines forth from different perspectives that in some cases appear to be incompatible, although not necessarily contradictory. But even in these cases, as we shall see in the following analyses, various options for

---

228 All sections of this chapter are the final authorial responsibility of Rafael Capurro.

229 Ess 2010, Capurro 2008, Ess 2008, Brey 2007, Capurro et al. 2007, Hongladarom & Ess 2007, Ess 2006, Ess 2005.

230 The term 'Far East' goes back to European colonial history. The French sinologist and philosopher, François Jullien, has proposed the symmetrical code "Far East – Far West" ("Extrême Orient – Extrême Occident") to make clear the one-sided European perspective (Jullien 1995, 2008).

common practices and regulations are possible. The emphasis on the latter should not overlook, however, the deeper cultural layers as well as the foundational narratives on privacy and publicness. Such narratives, notions and practices are not just an accidental matter, but form the very historical soil of personal and social whoness. Who we are as a society takes place in a process in which also cultures mutually influence each other and hybridize. This is particularly so in a digitally globalized world in which such processes are not only accelerated but also subject to new forms of self-revealing and -concealing that bring the cultural layers underlying them to manifestation.

We are still far from a global digital culture of mutual respect, validation and appreciation based on trust with regard to such cultural differences. Trust is engendered by an understanding of the otherness of the other self/selves, enabling new forms of interplay between personal and socio-cultural whoness and opening new spaces of freedom to show ourselves and our selves off and also withdraw from such self-display in both the cyberworld and the physical world.

The following overview of implicit and/or explicit notions of privacy, particularly in the cyberworld context, in the Far East, Africa and Latin America, is a first attempt limited not only in the choice of cultures but also in the treatment of their inner complexity. There is no intent to simplify by using geographical markers. The few examples of differing narratives on privacy and publicness should be understood as illustrations of different ways of living the intertwining of personal and socio-cultural whoness according to changing rules of play for concealing and revealing who we are, mirroring our selves in and to each other. My self is always my self with other selves in a shared world.

We start with what can be regarded as a privative mode of whoness, namely the 'denial of self' in Buddhist and community-oriented cultures. In a second step, mostly implicit views on publicness and privacy in Latin America will be discussed, whose numerous and rich indigenous cultures, along with various forms of hybridization with European modernity, in particular in the way privacy in the cyberworld is played out, remain still largely a matter for future analysis. Finally, we take a look at African traditions, particularly the concept of *ubuntu*.

4.2 The Far East

4.2.1 Japan

In their seminal paper 'Japanese conceptions of privacy: An intercultural perspective', Nakada and Tamura write, "Japan is a complicated country — even for Japanese people themselves. Indeed, their lives are full of contradictory matters, including the problems related to privacy. People want to be free and pay attention to a 'right to control one's personal information,' but at the same time they want to get 'true' friends by sharing their secret information concerning their private, personal experience".[231] This can be said, of course, of any culture, but what is paramount is to analyze such "complicated matters" that shape lives in their uniqueness and, in particular, to see how selves understand themselves through digitally mediated whoness.

Before addressing the key issue of 'denial of self' (*Musi*), Nakada and Tamura analyze the framework that enables a proper understanding of the Japanese self or "Japanese minds", and of the view of privacy and publicness from this Japanese perspective. They start by explaining "a dichotomy between *Seken* and *Shakai* in Japanese minds".[232] *Shakai* means the principles and values adopted from the 'Far West', i.e. from Western modernity, while *Seken* means the traditional Japanese customs as shaped by Shinto, Buddhism and Confucianism. At the same time, they point to another layer of "Japanese minds", namely *Ikai*, which is "the aspect of the world from which evils, disasters, crimes, and impurity" emerge,[233] where '*i*' means 'different' and '*kai*' means 'world'. But *Ikai* means also "the world in which people can find certain kinds of hidden mental bodily energy as well as freedom".[234]

231 Nakada & Tamura 2005 p. 27. See also Capurro 2005, Nakada 2007, Capurro & Nakada 2009, Mizutani et al. 2004.

232 Nakada & Tamura 2005 p. 27.

233 Nakada & Tamura 2005 p. 27.

234 Nakada & Tamura 2005 p. 29.

Taking as an example a homicide, they show how private details about the victim's family were reported in the newspapers that contradict partly Western or *Shakai* standards of privacy protection, while a survey among students showed that they approved of publishing such news because it can help to find out the 'truth' of the matter and "share certain aspects of the meaning of this tragedy".[235] Nakada and Tamura interpret the students' reaction as coming from *Seken* and *Ikai*. If this interpretation of "Japanese minds" (which amounts to the specifically Japanese way of being-in-the-world) is correct, then it can be inferred that Japanese selves and world are shaped by the trichotomy of *Seken*, *Shakai* and *Ikai*. Another important aspect of Japanese being-in-the-world concerns the notions of *Aida* or 'in-between' and *Musi* or 'denial of self' as analyzed, for instance, by the Japanese psychiatrist and scholar, Bin Kimura.[236] They explain the relation between the two notions as follows: "In an objective way, 'between' or 'in-between' is nothing, but for dwellers of *Seken* or *Ikai*, 'between' or *Mu* is an ontological way to get to the sources of hidden power or 'true' subjectivity. In addition, 'between' seems to be related to certain types of shared or intersubjective meanings, especially 'common senses' — including the range of normal or expected behaviours in Japanese culture and settings."[237] Although this explanation is based partly on and biased by Western notions of subjectivity, it clearly points to what constitutes the Japanese self, namely, the negation of such a notion of an isolated and worldless subjectivity or, in Japanese terms, of a self addressing herself as divorced from *Aida* or 'in-between', i.e. from the openness of a shared world. They write, "*Mu* means 'nothing' or 'denial' and *si* means 'self' or 'subjectivity'. So *Musi* means 'denial of (surface) subjectivity'. In our culture it is often said that *Musi*, denial of subjectivity, is the best — but 'hidden' and difficult — way to learn fine arts, martial arts and so on".[238]

---

235 Nakada & Tamura 2005 p. 28.

236 Kimura 1972.

237 Nakada & Tamura 2005 p. 29.

238 Nakada & Tamura 2005 p. 29.

From the perspective of whoness, *Musi* amounts to questioning the Western standard view of subjectivity, whose autonomy is supposed to be protected by privacy. At the same time, the trichotomy of *Seken*, *Shakai* and *Ikai* as which "Japanese minds" shape their selves in their interplay with the world makes apparent the problem with the Western notion of privacy, namely, that it is limited to *Shakai*. The authors write, "But one thing is clear: privacy is not something like an 'intrinsic good' — to use a term by Deborah Johnson — for us. For example, expressing or sharing (parts of) one's privacy seems to be a popular and traditional way to get good personal friends in Japan".[239] Following the Buddhist tradition of "self-purification" developed by Shinran in the Kamakura era (1192-1333), giving up one's 'private minds' "is to view oneself from the point of view of Buddha".[240] News of the homicide whose revelation contradicts the standard privacy rules of *Shakai* would be acceptable and even desirable within *Seken*. Some evils would be interpreted as coming from *Ikai*. In any case, privacy conceived as the protection of a 'substantial' and autonomous subject is a problematic notion and value. Nakada and Tamura summarize the Japanese ethical stance as follows: "In the traditional and original views and perspectives of Japanese culture, *harmony* between people, along with trusted human relationships, seem to have been the most valuable virtues. In contrast, privacy or individualism still remain outside the lists of the most important values for Japanese."[241]

The difference between notions of privacy in the 'Far West' and the culturally fashioned Japanese way of being who in the world is further developed with regard to the notions of *Ohyake* and *Watakusi*, which are the standard translations of 'public' and 'private'. *Ohyake* means originally 'big house' and refers to the imperial court and government, whereas *Watakusi* or 'not *Ohyake*' means "partial, secret and selfish".[242] *Watakusi* is related to *Musi* or 'denial of self', *si* in both cases meaning 'I' or 'private' or 'oneself' with negative connotations, as already noted.

239 Nakada & Tamura 2005 p. 30.
240 Nakada & Tamura 2005 p. 30.
241 Nakada & Tamura 2005 p. 31.
242 Nakada & Tamura 2005 p. 32.

Nakada and Tamura point to the long history of more than a thousand years underlying these notions. *Ohyake* had mostly a positive value until in the 1970s public enterprises started to appear dangerous or useless to citizens.

For the Western notion of privacy a borrowed word, namely *puraibashii*, was created as a legal term in 1964 and counterposed to *Ohyake* but having a different meaning from that related to *Watakusi*. This shows once again the complexity of "Japanese minds", i.e. the ways in which Japanese exist as who in their world. Nakada and Tamura write, "We have a hypothesis that there are in fact two 'axes' defining 'public' and 'private' issues currently in Japan. One is the 'public' and 'private' axis (i.e. as anchored in the loan word *puraibashii*) and the other is the *Ohyake / Watakusi* axis. They are intermixed."[243] On the new axis, privacy as *puraibashii* meant the right to disallow interference from others and changed its meaning, after the development of information technology, to 'the right to control one's personal information'. But, in contrast to the Western concept of privacy, in Japan "privacy is discussed as a 'crisis of privacy issue' and not as the basis for democratic concern as it has been discussed in Western information ethics. In this way, Japanese society may have introduced one aspect of the concept of privacy as used in the West — but not the whole of it."[244] Hence, for the Japanese self living on the *Ohyake / Watakushi* axis, there is no privacy problem related to, for instance, open web diaries, where Japanese can conceal and disclose their selves differently from how they do face-to-face in their daily lives that are ruled by *Seken* or its synonymous *Ukiyo*, meaning 'this transient world'. "This means", the authors conclude, "that if communication on the Internet is nothing but another version of *Watakusi*-activity for the majority of Internet users in Japan, the Internet is at least partly a continuation of *Seken* (*Ukiyo*) event at this present time. And in fact, this

243 Nakada & Tamura 2005 p. 33.

244 Nakada & Tamura 2005 p. 33.

continuation has been confirmed in our research in a number of ways."[245]

An alternative analysis of the Japanese self has been proposed by Andrew Adams, Kiyoshi Murata and Yohko Orito.[246] They consider information privacy as rooted in various ways in which a self shows herself off or withdraws from view, taking into account the complex history of Japanese culture, that give the discussion on privacy a unique flavour with echoes in both Western and non-Western cultures.[247] The authors remark that, "despite being a collective-oriented society [...] the Japanese do develop a significant sense of selfhood, albeit one which is tempered by awareness of the position of that self within a group dynamic more so than at the other end of the spectrum in the individual-oriented society of, for example, the USA."[248] Self-formation is oriented toward "the drive to be like others, to remove or reduce the difference" along with a strong awareness of contexts of *uchi* (inside) and *soto* (outside), a separation that is not fixed, but relative to the social distance between people,[249] the primary general social reference being, as Nakada and Tamura also remark, *Seken*.

Focusing on "information privacy" as distinct from privacy in physical spaces and the privacy of the physical body, Adams et al. highlight the importance of the difference between *soto* or "regularly encountered external people" and *tanin* or "the outsider rarely or never directly encountered", a difference that has changed with the advent of information technology. They write, "Unlike other societies where such concepts of the other exist, to the Japanese such *tanin* may receive significant private information, due to the lack of continuing contact depriving such revelations of their danger. [...] The advent of networked information processing has caused a re-evaluation by Japanese people of the safety of such revelations to *tanin*."[250] Although there are strong

245 Nakada & Tamura 2005 p. 34.
246 Adams et al. 2009.
247 For a comparison between Japan and Korea see Orito et al. 2011.
248 Adams et al. 2009 p. 330.
249 Adams et al. 2009 p. 330.
250 Adams et al. 2009 p. 331.

reasons in Japan and in the West to keep certain information private, they vary according to differences in cultural whoness. The authors have analyzed similarities and dissimilarities between Japanese and UK students using SNS (Social Network Services) with regard to digital identity-awareness. In contrast to UK students, Japanese students refuse, for instance, to use their real names but in both cases most students had SNS connections only with those whom they knew in real life.[251]

In my opinion, the anatomy of the Japanese self proposed by Nakada and Tamura offers a more comprehensive view of the cultural layers that make up the Japanese self than that put forward by Adams et al. Their account is considered to be based on what Nakada and Tamura call *Shakai*. The notions of 'inside' and 'outside' as well as that of Japanese whoness are better understood if the phenomena of *Aida* and *Musi* are taken into account. On the question regarding collectivism and individualism in "Japanese minds", Nakada and Capurro confirm the findings of Adams et al. but they remark, "[…] when we examine this equilibrium between collectivism and individualism in a more detailed way (through factor analysis), we get two different types of 'collectivism' along with a set of 'individualism'. […] This means that in Japan 'collectivism' consists of more complicated or broader meanings than might be generally imagined."[252] The limits and traps of using subjectivist categories when analyzing the phenomenon of the self in Japan as well as in other cultures are manifest. This applies also to the separation of information privacy from physical and bodily privacy, which implies a dichotomy between body and self, world-openness being reduced to physical spaces in the present.

4.2.2 Thailand[253]

Soraj Hongladarom and other Thai ethicists have discussed privacy issues particularly in the context of the introduction of a national digital personal identity card in a country with no specific law protecting

---

[251] Adams et al. 2011 p. 3.

[252] Capurro & Nakada 2009 p. 342.

[253] The following analysis reproduces the findings in Capurro 2008 pp. 654-656.

personal information.[254] The threat of political abuse raises the issue of the nature of privacy and its justification. Hongladarom explores this question from the perspective of two famous Buddhist sages, namely Nagarjuna (c. 150-250 AD), founder of the Mahahāyāna Buddhism, and Nagasena (c. 150 BC). He writes, "The reason I believe the Buddhist perspective is important in this area is that Buddhism has a very interesting claim to make about the self and the individual on whose concept the whole idea of privacy depends".[255]

In Hongladarom's view, the fact that Buddhism rejects the individual self does not mean that it rejects privacy. To elucidate this counter-intuitive argument, he distinguishes between the absolute and conventional level of assertion. From an absolute standpoint, there is no distinction between subject and object. If there is no inherently existing self, then privacy is grounded in the conventional idea that it is necessary for democracy, which means that privacy has an instrumental status rather than being an intrinsic or core value. Hongladarom claims, however, the distinction between intrinsic and instrumental values has an insecure foundation since all values rest on our attachment to them. In Nagasena's thinking, the conventional self exists in conventional reality and is shown to be a mere illusion after analysis in terms of the "ultimate truth". Hongladarom parallels Nagarjuna's distinction between "conventional truth" and "ultimate truth" with Kant's distinction between a "phenomenal" and a "noumenal" realm. But in contrast to Kant there is no "I" providing a transcendental unity of apperception.

Privacy as practised in everyday life is not denied in Buddhism. It is in fact justified as an instrument for the end of living harmoniously in line with democratic ideals. But "from the ultimate perspective of a Buddha, privacy just makes no sense whatsoever".[256] Violations of privacy are based on the three "mental defilements" (*kleshas*), namely greed, anger and delusion, the antidote being to cultivate love and compassion. He writes, "Compassion naturally arises from this

---

254 Hongladarom 2007, Ramasota 2007, Kitiyadisai 2005.

255 Hongladarom 2007 p. 109.

256 Hongladarom 2007 p. 120.

realization when one realizes that other beings are no different from oneself. All want to get rid of suffering, and all want happiness. The benefit of this realization for information ethics is that compassion is the key that determines the value of an action."[257] Compassion is the basic mood of Buddhist experience of the uniqueness of the world and our existence that we have to care for.

Pirongrong Ramasoota examines information privacy in Thai society. Classical Buddhist teaching may not necessarily reflect the behaviour of relatively secularized Buddhists in contemporary Thai society. Ramasoota presents an overview of privacy and data protection in Thai legislation. The Thai public is aware of the importance of control over the circulation of one's personal information, particularly on the internet, to limit state surveillance. Pattarasinee Bhattarakosol points out that there are various aspects related to the development of IT ethics in Thailand, a major one being family background.

Krisana Kitiyadisai explores changes in the concept of privacy in Thai culture, which is based on consensual collectivism and non-confrontation. In traditional Thailand, 'being in private' applies to the space shared by family members. The lack of a Thai word for privacy, Kitiyadisai says, is due to the feudal heritage of Thai society with its system of hierarchical ranking, politeness protocols and patronage. Strong relationships are based on the principle of non-confrontation to avoid the disastrous results of 'losing face' (*siar-na*) in favour of saving face (*koo-na*). Phenomenologically speaking, saving and losing face is a matter of how well the faces (masks, personae) which one puts on display to the world as who-masks are regarded and estimated by others. A culture that emphasizes the crucial importance of saving face is one in which *being* a self is highly dependent on having one's appropriate who-status, whether high or low, mirrored back affirmatively by others. Kitiyadisai maintains, "the combination of privacy as 'private affairs' (*rueng-suan-tua*) and the right of 'non-interference' works in support of 'saving face'".[258] These values are similar to Confucian values of

---

257 Hongladarom 2007 p. 120.

258 Kitiyadisai 2005 p. 18.

"ancestor reverence, respect for 'face', responsibility, loyalty, modesty and humility".[259] In Buddhism, human rights are not intrinsic to human individuals but are necessary for conducting a virtuous human existence. Kitiyadisai provides an overview of the data-protection legislation in Thailand. She stresses the ongoing tensions between "imported liberal democratic values" and "traditional Thai values".

4.2.3 China

The Chinese ethicist, Lü Yao-Huai, writes, "In the Chinese cultural tradition, ethicists pay special attention to the concept of 'Shen Du'. [...] 'Shen Du' means that 'a superior man' must be watchful over himself when he is alone."[260] He illustrates this with the following quote from *The Great Learning*, one of the *Four Books* of Chinese classic texts selected by the neo-Confucian scholar, Zhu Xi (1130-1200): "There is no evil to which the mean man, dwelling retired, will not proceed, but when he sees a superior man, he instantly tries to disguise himself, concealing his evil, and displaying what is good. The other beholds him, as if he saw his heart and veins; — of what use is his disguise? This is an instance of the saying — 'What truly is within will be manifested without'. Therefore, the superior man must be watchful over himself when he is alone."[261] According to Lü, *Shen Du* is a key notion when dealing with the question of the self, particularly within the context of the cyberworld, since it addresses the question of reducing "proactively [...] the number of online activities that violate legal frameworks."[262]

Lü focuses on the self in his relations to himself and to others — the masculine might be a bias in Zhu Xi and, indirectly, also in Lü — based on the possibility of concealing and revealing who they are as selves. He critically addresses this issue with regard to the predominance of English on the internet in a paper presented to the first international symposium on intercultural information ethics held in Karlsruhe, Germany in

259 Kitiyadisai 2005 p. 24.
260 Lü 2007 p. 70.
261 Lü 2007 pp. 70-71. Quote from *Chinese/English Four Books* 1992 p. 9.
262 Lü 2007 p. 71.

2004.[263] He writes, "The preferred scenario is, of course, multi-directional intercultural dialogues and channels. [...] in order to avoid being assimilated by English, the non-English-speaking people, especially in developing countries, must preserve the cultural characteristics of their homelands when they develop information technologies and information societies. [...] The local cultures of their homelands are the actual intellectual content embodied in the right to communicate for people from different countries."[264] Although in the meantime things have changed with regard to the predominance of English on the internet, the issue of whoness addressed from a Confucian perspective remains as crucial as it was in 2004.

Lü criticizes the historical analyses of the Chinese notion of privacy by McDougall and Hansson[265] as referring "primarily to studies of Chinese elites, focusing on the gentry and/or rulers" instead of giving an account of today's views on privacy, particularly among ordinary people. Lü maintains there is an ongoing transformation of contemporary Chinese "consciousness" of privacy — which means a transformation of the Chinese self — starting with economic and political reforms since 1980.[266] This change comprises three main aspects:

1) "[...] individuals gradually expand their self-consciousness of a right to privacy. Earlier, Chinese in conversation, especially between friends, would usually feel free to talk about anything (with the exception of some sensitive political topic). But now, if someone's

---

[263] The symposium Localizing the Internet. Ethical Issues in Intercultural Perspective was sponsored by the Volkswagen Foundation (see http://icie.zkm.de/congress2004). The proceedings were published in Capurro et al. 2007. See also Capurro 2009a. On 28-29 October 2010 the International Conference on China Information Ethics was held at Renmin University in Beijing. Issues of privacy and data protection were discussed in group meetings based on short presentations. See Capurro 2010/2011 and www.capurro.de/home-cn.html

[264] Lü 2007 p. 73.

[265] McDougall & Hansson 2002.

[266] Lü 2005 p. 7.

question to a conversation partner deals with matters that the partner does not want to make public — the conversation partner usually declines to answer the question, on the plea that 'this is my privacy'."[267]

2) "[…] many Chinese today are no longer inclined to interfere with what they perceive to be the privacy of others: indeed, to some extent, they now show respect for others' privacy."[268]

3) The common Chinese concept of privacy *Yinsi* ('shameful secret') has been expanded to include "all personal information (i.e. whether shameful or not) that people do not want others to know".[269]

With the rise of the internet in the 1990s, the question of data privacy emerged in China. In his review of three recent (2003-2004) Chinese articles on privacy, Lü points to the influence of Western individual-oriented thinking on privacy with regard to respect and informed consent, while at the same time the right to privacy from a traditional Chinese perspective is conceived as being based on social requirements (security of society, stability of the social order). He writes, "They all affirm both the value of the protection of the right to privacy to the individual to some extent, and place special emphasis on the interests of nation and society. This mode of thinking is in accordance with the larger variety of ethics in contemporary China".[270] Lü questions the view that privacy remains a foreign concept for normal Chinese people, although in rural areas, following the tradition of collectivism, "people are more interested in other people's private matters than are people in cities".[271] Although many Chinese still think that there is no right to privacy within the family, a survey among the younger generation shows the opposite interest. Lü foresees a strong influence of Western views on privacy in Chinese culture, implying that Chinese whoness might become, or is already, hybridized, in particular regarding the notion and practices of privacy on the internet.

267 Lü 2005 p. 8.
268 Lü 2005 p. 8.
269 Lü 2005 p. 8.
270 Lü 2005 p. 12.
271 Lü 2005 p. 12.

A basic issue common to Far East cultures involves the practice of indirect speech, i.e. of the self concealing and *at the same time* revealing herself through language or, more precisely, through silence.[272] The Daoist tradition developed a *dao*-centred self, indirect speech being the adequate way to be part of a permanent process of becoming since it leaves open future possibilities of being. According to Chuang Tzu (370-301 BC), self-awareness consists in learning to breathe as a medium between the world, the '*dao*' and the self.[273] The leitmotif of the *dao*-centred self is 'don't block!' which can be interpreted as a translation of the famous Daoist notion of *wuwei* or 'non-action'.[274] Instead of a global information morality governing privacy and publicness on the internet from a fixed perspective, the Daoist sage would look at keeping it moving within a never-ending creative process. From this perspective, privacy as a practice of indirect speech is at the core of different views of the self and, implicitly, of privacy in the Far East.

4.3 Latin America

Latin American cultures came about through the violent encounter of indigenous traditions with nascent European modernity. Indigenous collectivism faced pre-modern, particularly scholastic thinking, that praised the individual as a person no less than liberal traditions do, which are based on the idea(l)s of work, private property, competition and technology.[275] As the Argentinian philosopher, Rodolfo Kusch, writes, "The ways of life of the Indian and the well-off city dweller are impermeable to each other. On the one hand, the Indian retains the

[272] Capurro 2010/2011.

[273] See Jullien 2008 pp. 71-75.

[274] Wohlfart 2002.

[275] See von Barloewen 1992 p. 132. On Latin American cultures from a philosophical perspective see Kusch 1962 and 2010. There are several studies on the history of private life in Latin American countries such as Argentina (Cicerchia 1998, Devoto and Madero 1999), Brazil (Novais & Schwarcz 1997), Chile (Sagredo and Gazmuri 2005) México (Gonzalbo 2004) and Uruguay (Barrán et al.1996).

structure of an ancient form of thinking, a thousand years old, and on the other, the city dweller renews his way of thinking every ten years".[276] This "ancient form of thinking" can be grasped with regard to the concept of 'reciprocity'. Indigenous people were not properly remunerated for their work, "because everything was taken by the cacique (or *mallkus*) [...] the indigenous worker is only repaid with food".[277] The equivalent of "reciprocity" in Aymara is *ayni*, "which means 'the one obligated to work for another who worked for him'".[278] If the indigenous worker was obliged to give everything he produced to the Inca, but not to the Spaniards, there was nevertheless a reciprocity from the side of the Inca, namely the obligation "to refrain from interfering with the stockroom of the domestic sphere".[279]

This dichotomy between the public and the private sphere in Inca culture has a parallel in the Greek dichotomy between *agora* and *oikos*. The 'domestic sphere' of the Inca worker was no less important for his self than the obligation to give his powers and the products of his work to the *mallku*, or chief. The system underlying this 'reciprocity' was not contractual, but based on the *pacha* or mother earth as something prior to the separation of a 'subject' from an 'outside, objectified' world. Kusch writes, "*Pacha*, instead, refers to a concept more properly related to what we call a subject, and it is located in a terrain prior to that of the perception of things. Here we have a subjectified, private space and time that refers to a vital habitat where *our* time and *our* space melt into the pure fact of living here and now when this involves the time of *my* life, *my* family, and in this place, the place of *my* community. All of this implies naturally an indiscriminate vision of external reality."[280] Although Kusch is employing the modern European notion of subject, he describes the phenomenon of self of the indigenous Inca which implies not only an original plurality of selves forming a community, but also an original relation of the community to nature.

---

[276] Kusch 2010 p. 2.
[277] Kusch 2010 p. 91.
[278] Kusch 2010 pp. 92-93.
[279] Kusch 2010 p. 93.
[280] Kusch 2010 p. 94.

The violent encounter between indigenous and European *conquistadores* led to a history of oppression and underdevelopment with tensions between collectivism and individualism.[281] The result was cultural hybridization and what Kusch calls *pueblo*. He writes, "Besides, there is no doubt that the concepts of modern or indigenous man are no more than abstractions, and thus, in the case of América, one should actually speak of someone real who is neither totally modern nor totally indigenous. This is what is vaguely called *pueblo*, but it alludes to an average type in which both the middle class and the peasant are present."[282] One might consider that this cultural hybridization affects also the notion of privacy when coming from indigenous traditions hybridized with modern European notions of autonomy, work, property, competition and money, and leading perhaps to a kind of *mestizo* privacy in the cyberworld based on communal life rather than on contract.

The Latin American 'who' is just as much an indigenous person as an urban inhabitant. Kusch writes, "If the urban dweller were to ask himself at this point, 'Who am I?', he would see himself reduced to a 'just living,' carrying his absolute on his back and a *who* that is lost in mystery. This nebulous *who* is the sum of what one achieves through this path. But it is a lot."[283] At this point, Kusch's analysis of Latin American indigenous whoness intersects with the Buddhist experience of the simple 'being there' ("estar ahí") of a person.[284] "They start, in short, from the only truly philosophical experience: the surprise of discovering the crossroads that obtain within mere estar, bearing the sense of the absolute, even if through negation. It is all that man, in the

---

281 On ethics and development in Latin America see Sen & Kliksberg 2005.

282 Kusch 2010 p. 138.

283 Kusch 2010 p. 171.

284 Kusch analyzes the difference between the Spanish verbs for 'to be', namely 'ser' and 'estar'. "[…] 'estar' comes from the Latin *stare*, 'to stand up', which implies restlessness, *Ser*, on the other hand, comes from *sedere*, 'to be sitting down, which connotes a foundation from which springs the possibility of definition'." (Kusch 2010 p. 160), 'Estar' is closely related to the indigenous *pacha*, the experience of 'just living', Latin America being a culture of 'estar'.

end, can think about himself. That is why it can also be found in the urban dweller. And that is why not to accept it is to fall into an infantile seminality."[285] And, we may add, it can be found in the urban or indigenous or *mestizo* dweller of the cyberworld, assuming that he can think about himself instead of giving up his self, i.e. his privacy on the internet, contractually to someone else, thus falling into individual or socially infantile digitality.

The debate over intercultural information ethics in Latin America has only just begun.[286] There is a lack of philosophical and empirical ethical analysis on privacy,[287] particularly from an intercultural perspective and in relation to the internet.[288] One of the pioneers in the field of information ethics in Latin America is Daniel Pimienta, who created the virtual community MISTICA that produced in 2002 the document 'Working the Internet with a Social Vision'.[289] Although it does not deal explicitly with the question of privacy, it can be seen as an expression of Latin American collective thinking striving for common values of more

---

285 Kusch 2010 p. 171.

286 The first paper on intercultural information ethics from a Brazilian perspective is probably that by Dürmaier 2008. See Capurro 2009. The first Brazilian conference on Information Ethics took place in March 2010 at the Federal University of Paraiba (João Pessoa): http://dci.ccsa.ufpb.br/editais/SBEI.pdf See proceedings Freire 2010. See also Capurro 2010.

287 For an overview on privacy in Latin America from the perspective of Western philosophy, dealing particularly with legal aspects of 'sensitive data', see Pfeiffer 2008. On Latin American cultures see Kusch 1962 and von Barloewen 1992.

288 See the portals RELEI (*Red Latinoamericana de ética de la información*) http://redeticainformacion.ning.com and *Red Universitaria de ética en el ciberespacio* http://www.redciberetica.org. See also the international seminar on privacy and data protection at the *First Brazilian Internet Forum* São Paulo, 13-14 October 2011. http://forumdainternet.cgi.br

289 MISTICA (*Metodología e Impacto Social de las Tecnologías de Información y Comunicación en América* – Methodology and Social Impact of Information and Communication Technologies in America) 2002 at http://www.funredes.org/mistica/english/project/ The following quotes are from this document at http://www.itu.int/wsis/docs/pc2/misc/mistica.doc . For a history of MISTICA see Pimienta 2007.

equitable, less discriminating societies. In the final section, No. 13 "Reflexions on the social appropriation of the Internet in our actions and projects", the authors make a plea for a "sensible use" of the internet in order to promote "the transformation of existing economic, political and social relations" as well as "social appropriation" of this technology by giving "the Internet a proper, autochthonous and genuine meaning", leading to "more equal and more sustainable societies". Point 5 of Section 13 poses the following questions with regard to "the defense of protected spaces on the Internet and the dissemination" of local knowledge:

"a. How do the actions that are promoted boost the production of local contents?

b. What level of participation do the people with whom we work have in the development of local contents?

c. To what extent do actions which are promoted allow to disseminate and promote local contents?

d. In what way is the Internet promoted as a space of expression for the less favored and for popular cultures?"

All these questions deal with privacy issues, not only with regard to the protection of locally produced knowledge, but especially protection of the communities or selves that produce such knowledge as being a genuine expression of their cultural identity. This is also underscored by the next point (6) "On the social change produced by the Internet" addressing the following issues:

"a. In what way do the actions which are promoted for the development of the Internet prompt elements such as development of personal and collective self-esteem, community organization, improvement of educational standards, capacities of interaction between people, empowerment, or development of the capacity to make proposals from the people with whom the work is done?

b. In what way are actions for the development of the Internet transforming the daily lives of the peoples, from an individual, occupational, interpersonal or citizen viewpoint?

c. What level of probability is there that the transformations produced by the actions that are carried out have a follow-up in the future?"

It is evident — at least from the concept of privacy developed within the present study — that issues around the "development of personal and collective self-esteem" are genuine privacy issues, even if they are not addressed as such. It is also apparent that privacy issues as issues of the self cannot be resolved on an abstract level, but must be addressed by individuals and societies within the specific framework of their historical, and particularly indigenous, roots, experiences, aspirations and opportunities that stakes out how they play their who-games.

An example of this kind of nascent intercultural reflection on privacy in Latin America is the work by Francisco Mannuzza dealing with indigenous cultures of Venezuela being confronted with the cyberworld.[290] Mannuzza emphasizes that in order to recognize the other *as* other, it is important to pay attention not so much to the "digital divide" but to the "cultural difference."[291] This paper was presented at the First Regional Conference on Infoethics in Cyberspace for Latin America and the Caribbean held in Santo Domingo in 2008 under the patronage of UNESCO. At the same conference, Anabella Giracca remarked that "most Latin American countries are the product of a history that put obstacles in the way to understanding a plural reality, based on proposals as varied as mestization, homogenization, assimilation and integration of the various populations under a 'Western' or 'modernized' vision".[292] How to speak about information ethics — or privacy — in Latin America, she asks, without an intercultural evaluation of digital language with its codes and symbols "which are not common to all cultures (especially indigenous cultures)"?[293]

290 Mannuzza 2008.

291 Mannuzza 2008 p. 231 (my translation, RC).

292 Giracca 2008 p. 82 (my translation, RC).

293 Giracca 2008 p. 86 (my translation, RC).

4.4 Africa[294]

The African philosopher, Mogobe Ramose, maintains that *ubuntu* is "the central concept of social and political organization in African philosophy, particularly among the Bantu-speaking peoples. It consists of the principles of sharing and caring for one another".[295] Ramose interprets two maxims "to be found in almost all indigenous African languages," namely: "*Motho ke motho ka batho*" and "*Feta kgomo tschware motho*". The first maxim means that "to be human is to affirm one's humanity by recognizing the humanity of others and, on that basis, to establish humane respectful relations with them. Accordingly, it is *ubuntu* which constitutes the core meaning of the aphorism." The second maxim signifies, "that if and when one is faced with a decisive choice between wealth and the preservation of life of another human being, then one should opt for the preservation of life".[296]

A detailed analysis of the relationship between *ubuntu* and privacy was provided by Olinger et al. at the Sixth International Conference on Computer Ethics: Philosophical Enquiry in 2005. They write, "The African worldview driving much of African values and social thinking is 'Ubuntu'" (Broodryk 2002). The Ubuntu worldview has been recognized as the primary reason that South Africa has managed to successfully transfer power from a white minority government to a majority-rule government without bloodshed (Murithi 2000). The South African government will attempt to draft a Data Privacy Bill and strike an appropriate balance within the context of African values and an African worldview."[297] According to Broodryk, *ubuntu* is an African worldview "based on values of intense humaneness, caring, respect,

---

294 The following analysis reproduces some of the ideas and findings in Capurro 2007. For an overview of past, present and future actitivies in the field of information ethics in Africa, see Capurro 2010a.

295 Ramose 2002 p. 643.

296 Ramose 2002 p. 644.

297 Olinger et al. 2005 p. 292.

compassion, and associated values ensuring a happy and qualitative human community life in a spirit of family".[298]

In a comparative study of ethical theories in different cultures, Michael Brannigan addresses African ethics under the heading "To Be is to Belong."[299] Olinger et al. write, "Human beings are recognised as being all equal, sharing a common basic brotherhood, having the right to life and finding their ultimate meaning and purpose within communities. The last attribute is in stark contrast to the extreme individualism and self-centredness of Western cultures."[300] African whoness, at least from the *ubuntu* perspective, is rooted in community and not based on isolated, worldlessly encapsulated individuals. The *ubuntu* core values are communalism and interdependence. They are the basis for humaneness, caring, sharing, respect and compassion.[301]

The authors state that, "during the extensive literature review privacy was not explicitly mentioned anywhere among the Ubuntu writings".[302] This is easy to understand if privacy is conceived as pertaining to an isolated individual in which case, "[...] personal privacy would rather be interpreted as 'secrecy'". This "secrecy would not be seen as something good because it would indirectly imply that the Ubuntu individual is trying to hide something instead of protecting something — namely his personhood".[303] Clearly, the protection of *ubuntu*-personhood is not understood as privacy protection, nor is *ubuntu* culture itself oriented toward openness and transparency of an originary being-together in a common world according to the saying, "*Umunto ungumuntu ngabanye abantu*" (Nguni languages of Zulu and Xhosa), which means "A person

---

298 Broodryk 2002. On "African communalism" see the study of the Nigerian philosopher Simeon Eboh (Eboh 2004).

299 Brannigan 2005.

300 Olinger et al. 2005 p. 294.

301 As presented in Section 1.6, and on a more abstract plane of sociation, even the reified gainful game of capitalism is open to a re-interpretation, and hence an alternative lived ethos, if reification itself is seen through and 'taken back', and earning a living itself is seen to be originarily — in the open clearing of a shared world — a mutual valuing of and caring for one another.

302 Olinger et al. 2005 p. 296.

is a person through other persons."[304] Individual privacy conceived as persons having "their own unique thoughts, ideas, characteristics and accomplishments" or "the private possessions of an individual" is also "enjoyed in Ubuntu communities", although it is seen as "secondary" with regard to community values.[305] Olinger et al. remark that the population of southern Africa has yet to rediscover *ubuntu* because many have not experienced it, due to many living in two different cultures, practising *ubuntu* in rural environments and Western values in urban milieus.

The issue of privacy and data protection in Africa was discussed at the workshop on Africa Information Ethics and e-Government held on 23-27 February 2009 in Mount Grace — Magaliesburg, South Africa, sponsored by the South African government and under the patronage of UNESCO.[306] Africa is culturally a complex continent. The issue of privacy in Africa from an ethical and intercultural perspective is only now being put on the agenda.[307] This applies especially to the Arab countries in North Africa.

4.5 Conclusion

Homi Bhabha, director of the Humanities Center at Harvard University, has proposed a "global ethics that extends 'hospitality' to all those who lost their place where they belong due to an historical trauma, injustice, genocide or death".[308] Privacy understood from the

---

303 Olinger et al. 2005 p. 296.

304 Olinger et al. 2005 p. 293.

305 Olinger et al. 2005 p. 296.

306 The workshop was organized by the University of Wisconsin-Milwaukee (USA), the International Center for Information Ethics (ICIE) and the Universiy of Pretoria. See the web-site of the workshop at the Africa Network for Information Ethics http://www.africainfoethics.org/conferences_2009.html as well as the report of Group 3 with country reports from Botswana, Eritrea, Swaziland and South Africa http://www.africainfoethics.org/pdf/2009/-Group%203%20breakaway.pdf

307 See Capurro 2012.

308 Bhabha 2007 p. 44 (my translation, RC). On the Humanities Center at Harvard University see http://www.fas.harvard.edu/~humcentr/about/homi.shtml

perspective of whoness in the digitized cyberworld calls for an ethics of reciprocal hospitality, not only with regard to diverse ethical norms and principles, but also with regard to those who are marginalized in a global society in which digital technology has a dominating presence. Intercultural information ethics adopts a critical stance toward all kinds of destruction of the human habitat in the world, particularly such ways of thinking and life-practices that exclude others from their use or impose on them a particular way of playing out the interplay of whoness, thus thwarting their becoming free selves.

The thoughtful and practically oriented search for common values and principles should not overlook or 'forget' the complexity and variety of human cultures that are a genuine expression of humaneness, and not something to be overcome. This concerns, in particular, the notion of privacy conceived as what is proper to human self-understanding in being able to withdraw from others' gaze and lead one's own life shared with certain freely chosen others. An intercultural view of privacy must pay attention also to what is in-between cultures, allowing the individually and socially moulded self to transform and enrich its identity through the cultural interplay both within and between cultures. Phenomena of cultural exclusion are a sign that a specific cultural ethos has lost contact with the common source, i.e. with the shared world-openness within which all cultures define themselves in an open exchange and mutual recognition and estimation of ways of life. At times this may include also rivalry, contestation and conflict. Sight must not be lost of the character of intercultural interplay also as a *power* play in which, in the first instance, the powers and abilities of different peoples in their respective peculiar, unique historico-cultural shaping and configuration enter into an interplay of mutual estimation. Nationalism and chauvinism are negative modes of playing out this interplay that lead inevitably to conflict.

Respect for intercultural privacy implies respect for this diversity in the ways different cultures play out the game of displaying and concealing who one is. The ethical criterion is then not 'anything goes' but 'anything goes if it does not lead to mutual blockage'. Clearly, this maxim of care cannot foresee potential ambivalent situations in which privacy customs in one culture collide with privacy customs in another. In such situations, a pragmatic and/or technical solution is necessary, but not sufficient, to overcome misunderstandings and enhance or regain mutual trust. Patient intercultural research into this issue with a long-term orientation is necessary, for which the above examples provide only a rough and very limited selection of the work currently available to us. Intercultural information ethics does not deal primarily with ethical declarations that codify in an abstract way norms and values, since their interpretation and application require an ongoing analysis of their cultural presuppositions. Its practical outcome is to foster trust through better understanding differences and commonalities when dealing, for instance, with privacy issues in the ever-growing cyberworld, where a shared transcultural ethos is in the making that remains open to future technological challenges.

5 Cyberworld, privacy and the EU

Daniel Nagel

5.1 European integration, freedom, economics

Freedom has always been a central principle in modern Western democracies. Based on this legacy, European integration, which was initiated by traditionally Western states, was naturally centred thereon. This can be seen from the fact that when the European states set out for the first time to define basic common fundamental principles, all of them related to an area within the broad gamut of freedom. The free movement of persons, goods, services and capital was defined as the core of European co-operation.

Arguably, this freedom does not mirror the classical understanding of freedom as delineated, for instance, in the U.S. Bill of Rights. The latter rights were established against a considerably different background. In 1789 the First U.S. Congress assembled and discussed for the first time the recently enacted Constitution, which in turn was written at a time when the states' independence was still in its infancy. The Bill of Rights thus addressed issues the representatives thought were of utmost importance and should be taken into consideration: after having established general guiding principles for the new order, the common desire was to protect individuals from an abuse of power by the newly created government.[309] The Bill of Rights thus had the objective of securing fundamental freedoms of the citizens of an independent

[309] Cf. Preamble to the Bill of Rights dated 4 March 1789: "The Conventions of a number of the States, having at the time of their adopting the Constitution, expressed a desire, in order to prevent misconstruction or abuse of its powers, that further declaratory and restrictive clauses should be added: And as extending the ground of public confidence in the Government, will best ensure the beneficent ends of its institution."

state.[310] Thus, the first amendment to be accepted stated that Congress shall make no law respecting an establishment of religion, or prohibiting the free exercise thereof; or abridging the freedom of speech, or of the press; or the right of the people peaceably to assemble, and to petition the Government for a redress of grievances.[311] Hence, the Congress clearly intended to safeguard from interference the unfolding and exercise of the recently gained liberty. Thus, it explicitly listed the freedom of selves to determine their religious beliefs, to express their opinions in oral and written form and to interact with other selves.

The First Amendment consequently is a collection bin of ethical core values (cf. *1.3 Values, ethos, ethics*) that are deemed necessary for a free democratic society from a traditionally Western point of view. The principles therefore can be seen as the basic foundation that needs to be present before secondary aspects such as the free movement of goods can be addressed. However, since these fundamental preconditions had already been present within the national legislations of the European member states who were to agree on co-operation, such aspects were not at the centre of attention but were covered up by needs and challenges which had arisen in respect to cross-border transactions. Thus, European co-operation manifests predominantly an economic drift. This phenomenon can further be explained if the historical background of the European member states is taken into account, above all the World Wars, when neighbouring states seemed to have turned into irreconcilable enemies. Following the atrocities and deep wounds inflicted, it was far easier for the member states to find economic compromises first, since they shared common economic needs which could be addressed without opening up old wounds. Despite the fact that the states involved were located on the same continent and had many similarities in their roots and traditions, an assimilation of fundamental policy principles proved to take much longer — and required outside factors to be catalyzed.

310 Interestingly, the only two amendments that were rejected by the First Congress were amendments of a mere procedural nature: the redistribution of constituents.

311 Cf. Amendment 1 of the Bill of Rights dated 4 March 1789.

Consequently, from the very beginning, European integration was promoted from an economic perspective. When France, Italy, Germany, Belgium, the Netherlands and Luxembourg signed the ECSC Treaty in 1951, the main objective was to establish a common market in coal and steel. Thus, the focus was on the protection of economic interests in both public supply and — to some extent — the protection of private property, since mainly big steel and coal companies profited (and propelled) the politics of the early days. The latter, however, were a mere spin-off of economic co-operation and not a result of a clear intention to protect private property of all individuals; rather it was driven by the need to secure a sufficient supply of energy.

A year later, the European Defence Community was created to counter emerging tensions between East and West. The sword of Damocles of a potential new World War forced western European states to overcome differences and mistrust, and also boosted the existing will to co-operate. If it had not been for a French veto in 1954, the member states would have agreed on very close political co-operation at a very early stage which would have shifted the focus from mere economic issues to finding political consensus in many fields, including law and politics.

As a consequence, the continuing integration efforts, such as the Euratom Treaty and the EEC Treaty in 1957 reverted to a purely economic focus. The following years manifested a steady decline in successful co-operation and harmonization efforts, mainly due to the so-called empty chair policy of France which paralyzed European integration.[312] Nevertheless, the member states tried to also align politics. In 1966 the Luxembourg Compromise was reached. This compromise weakened the ability of the Community to act but at the same time freed the pursuit of common objectives from lethargy.[313] The

312 Which was due mainly to France's fear of a loss of sovereignty and power — cf. the politics of grandeur and the founding of the Fifth Republic by Charles de Gaulle.

313 Qualified majority voting was introduced, but at the same time both the sphere of co-operation was limited and the Commission weakened. Cf. the Final Communiqué of the extraordinary session of the Council, Bulletin of the European Communities, March 1966 pp. 5 – 11.

objective of closer political co-operation was reintroduced — albeit important decisions were barred as long as they could be considered as being of vital national interest.

In the 1970s the Davignon Report was released. It provided for quarterly meetings of foreign ministers and the establishment of a permanent political secretariat. However, driven by the historical events of that time, the focus still lay on finding a common approach to tackle the challenges of foreign policy. Moreover, foreign policy was aligned with the NATO and thus did not merely reflect a purely European viewpoint.

The initial enlargement of the European Community in the late seventies and eighties led to a rebirth of the quest for common European aims. Nevertheless, not until the Iron Curtain was about to fall and more member states joined the Community (which was renamed at that very time), the focus finally shifted from foreign politics and the striving to guarantee the best possible level of military security to internal objectives, and finally to citizens. The quest to shield the Community from danger could be said to entail also considerable benefits for its inhabitants, but the trigger for protection was clearly the threat of war. So it does not come as a surprise that the very first cross-border agreement on guaranteeing fundamental freedoms and privacy was not headed by the European Union but by another European player who had always focused on the interests and protection of individuals. It was not an association focused on ending the division of the European continent and on the need to create firm bases for the construction of a future Europe,[314] but founded to develop common and democratic principles throughout Europe based on the European Convention on Human Rights and other reference treaties on the protection of individuals,[315] viz. the Council of Europe.

---

314 Cf. the Preamble of the EEC treaty.

315 Cf. the objectives of the Council of Europe laid out in the Treaty of London (Statute of the Council of Europe) dated 5 May 1949.

5.2 The European Convention for the Protection of Human Rights and Fundamental Freedoms

In 1950 the European Convention for the Protection of Human Rights and Fundamental Freedoms laid down clear standards for what was considered worthy of protection.[316] This convention was tailored to the needs of people in a century of wars, persecution and oppression. It focused on the victims of these catastrophes, the people. The founding fathers set out to create a binding scheme for a common and conclusive protection of individuals.[317] Consequently, the Preamble stresses the joint ethical values that united and led the parties to the Convention to agree on a joint document by highlighting that the provisions would represent the common traditions and ideals of the signatories to the Convention. With regard to the founding fathers, these traditions were clearly of a western European nature, albeit the Convention later proved to be also acceptable for states that do not share the traditional Western background.[318] The core of these values is composed of the protection of fundamental human rights such as the right to life, the prohibition of torture, slavery and liberty as well as additional fundamental freedoms.

The European Convention for the Protection of Human Rights and Fundamental Freedoms for the first time contained a safeguard for its implementation in practice. It both provided for a Commission that administrated complaints and — more notably — a Court to oversee the adherence of member states to the Convention. Finally, the rights set out by the Convention are not only a set of passive rights that can be invoked when an infringement is made, but also a positive obligation on

---

316 European Convention on Human Rights, Rome 4 November 1950.

317 At that time the Convention was established by the governments of the Kingdom of Belgium, the Kingdom of Denmark, the French Republic, the Irish Republic, the Italian Republic, the Grand Duchy of Luxembourg, the Kingdom of the Netherlands, the Kingdom of Norway, the Kingdom of Sweden and the United Kingdom of Great Britain and Northern Ireland.

318 Cf. e.g. the ratification of the Convention by Russia in 1998 and Azerbaijan in 2002.

member states to guarantee an automatic minimum level of protection.[319]

These basic rights mirrored the quest to end years of atrocities and war crimes and to clearly demonstrate the intent to treat and protect individuals, irrespectively of their nationality, race or ethnicity. The European Convention for the Protection of Human Rights and Fundamental Freedoms not only introduced these very basic principles, but also established a scheme to safeguard additional freedoms centring on the self, its free development and the potential to freely interact with other selves.

Notably, the right to demand respect for private and family life is the first right that is mentioned which does not refer to bodily integrity and liberty, but to the freedom of the self to choose how and when to interact with other selves in a shared world. Article 8 states that "(e)veryone has the right to respect for his private and family life, his home and his correspondence". Thus, not only the private sphere in a personal, spatial sense but also in respect to the interplay with other selves is regarded as a fundamental value of human rights. Section two of this Article delineates a major safeguard in this respect, but also an erosion of that very right, namely, that "there shall be no interference by a public authority with the exercise of this right except such as is in accordance with the law and is necessary in a democratic society in the interests of national security, public safety or the economic well-being of the country, for the prevention of disorder or crime, for the protection of health or morals, or for the protection of the rights and freedoms of others".

The limitation of the self's freedom to choose when, how and what to conceal and reveal is thus made subject to and qualified by security interests of the state. This arguably entails the danger of undermining the right to determine the spectrum of what to reveal or conceal depending on the context in which the self finds itself situated, since it leaves a back door open to invoke security issues in many contexts as a pretence

---

319 Cf. e.g. McCann and others vs. United Kingdom, Eur. Ct. HR (1995) 21 EHRR 97.

to curtail this right to privacy. Nevertheless, at the same time, the wording is chosen to expressly address the state by making any interference subject to the rule of law. If the Preamble is also taken into account, which presupposes a free democratic society as the best possible breeding ground for a flourishing of fundamental liberties, it is clear that the fathers of the Convention did not aim at creating deliberate loopholes in order to be able to deprive selves of the very rights just proclaimed. Nevertheless, it leaves room to doubt the Convention's effectiveness. After all, the expression "such as is in accordance with the law" also leaves room for deviation. Who is to condemn a limitation on the basis of a legal background which itself might allow for such limitations? How is a distinction to be made and secured in the 'rule of law' between the protection of human freedom and the merely formal enactment of law by a democratic legislature?

When the following Articles are examined, it can be seen how the notion of privacy was further understood. Articles 9 and 10 of the European Convention for the Protection of Human Rights and Fundamental Freedoms guarantee the freedom of thought and expression. This is the basis of a free interplay among self-determined selves because only the ability to freely express oneself allows also for free interaction. As long as a self is guaranteed the freedom to deliver its thoughts to other selves without restrictions on content or form s/he is able not only to develop and shape its character, but also to foster a viable, fluid society through free interplay with others. Only such pluralistic interplay, in turn, is capable of bolstering the precondition mentioned in the Preamble, namely, a free democratic state. Both freedom of thought and freedom of expression, however, are also qualified; both are subject "to such limitations as are prescribed by law and are necessary in a democratic society in the interests of public safety, for the protection of public order, health or morals, or for the protection of the rights and freedoms of others".

While a basic limitation can be seen as generally necessary to be able to guarantee equal protection of all selves, thus supporting a free interplay which neither allows for an imbalance nor for a certain stage-direction to be followed, this exception also manifests a dilution of the proclaimed freedoms. This becomes apparent when the interpretation of vague terms such as public safety and public order is left open. Repressive states, too, uphold a certain kind of public order and employ means to ensure public safety; nevertheless these will hardly be in line with what the founding fathers intended to express when inserting these exceptions. Nevertheless, such uncertainty cannot be attributed to negligence or even the intention of individual parties to the Convention to reserve the right to deviate from the agreement. Rather, this is the result of an attempt to find a common approach to issues which may have traditionally or historically been treated differently on a regional or national level. Hence the strength of an international compromise, namely, the fact that national political borders do not restrict it, at the same time constitutes its main challenge. The quest for uniformity does not end with the creation of a common document but needs continuous efforts not to avert one's eyes from developments within other member states.[320] International uniformity can only be attained if viewed from an international perspective.[321]

The freedom of thought and expression is rounded off by a guarantee of the freedom of assembly in Article 11. This freedom is a basic requirement to enable a free interplay among selves and to prevent a focus on an individual, encapsulated self without regard to the shared world (cf. *1.4 The question concerning rights: personal privacy, trust and intimacy*). Naturally, this freedom is subject to the same limitations as its aforementioned counterparts, thus leaving room for discrepancy and endangering uniformity.

In conclusion, the 1950 European Convention for the Protection of Human Rights and Fundamental Freedoms already painted a clear picture with respect to the ethical values of living underlying European policy as regards privacy: the core to be protected is a self who shall be free to determine its interaction or non-interaction with others.

---

320 A prominent current example might be the imprisonment of the former Ukrainian president — Ukraine ratified the European Convention for the Protection of Human Rights and Fundamental Freedoms in 1997.

321 Cf. Del Duca et al. 2008 pp. 51-65.

5.3 The International Covenant on Civil and Political Rights

In 1966 the United Nations furthered international legislative measures to secure the fundamental freedoms of persons by drafting the International Covenant on Civil and Political Rights.[322] It came into force on 23 March 1976. This Covenant had a slightly different weighting. While the main emphasis of the European Convention for the Protection of Human Rights and Fundamental Freedoms clearly was on the protection of individuals against interference from governments, the Covenant on Civil and Political Rights stressed personal freedom of the self:[323] Article 1 provides that all peoples have the right to self-determination. It further proclaims that "by virtue of that right they freely determine their political status and freely pursue their economic, social and cultural development". This attempt to enshrine free self-determination on an international basis can be seen as remarkable at a time when equality still was a newly introduced term in many states that were considered to be progressive.[324] Article 1 mirrors a broad understanding of the notion of self-determination. On the one hand, it shows that self-determination involves both the ability to freely determine of one's own volition without influence or interference by third parties or authorities, and the ability to decide about one's self-world casting. The latter can be seen from the explicit exemplary listing of the embodiment of this very right. The right comprises the ability to

---

322 Adopted and opened for signature, ratification and accession by General Assembly resolution 2200A (XXI) dated 16 December 1966, available at: http://www2.ohchr.org/english/law/ccpr.htm. The Covenant has been signed or ratified by 74 states up to the present day including most European states, the U.S., China and Russia.

323 The right to life, the protection from torture and slavery, liberty and equality before the law follow in Part III of the Covenant.

324 Cf. e.g. the end of segregation in the U.S. which is often linked to the case Brown vs. Board of Education of Topeka, (347 U.S. 483 (1954)) in the mid-fifties, or the fact that many European states (e.g. France, Italy, Belgium) only introduced the right for women to vote in the late forties, Switzerland not until 1971.

determine one's own political status and pursue a self-chosen economic, cultural and social life. This is all the more apparent when section two of Article 1 is examined. It provides that "All peoples may, for their own ends, freely dispose of their natural wealth and resources without prejudice to any obligations arising out of international economic co-operation, based upon the principle of mutual benefit, and international law". Thus, the right to free self-determination addresses the self both as the freedom-exercising subject and the object (requiring protection) of the right. However, an interpretation of this right cannot (and should not) end at a mere assessment of an encapsulated individual case. This can already be seen from the Covenant itself.

The Covenant on Civil and Political Rights does not proclaim an unqualified right, but allows also for limitations under certain circumstances. Article 4 of the Covenant provides for exceptional cases in which states might deviate from the guaranteed right to free self-determination: Nevertheless, it is explicitly stated that such deviation is admissible only if it does not constitute a discriminatory measure.

The wording of the limitation can be seen as remarkable if the international context — and the signatories to this Covenant[325] — are considered. The reproach that it impairs its effectiveness is countered by limitations on the limitations. It is not sufficient that there be some opaque national security interest or a law which would allow for a deviation.[326] The Covenant demands that any deviation be "strictly required by the exigencies of the situation". In addition, such a situation also cannot freely be assumed by the respective player, but has to be consistent "with their other obligations under international law" and shall not involve "discrimination solely on the ground of race, colour, sex, language, religion or social origin".

Arguably, the Covenant on Civil and Political Rights can still be seen as a watchdog with soft, wiggly teeth since enforcement is dependent on the willingness of sovereign states to oblige themselves to really keep to

---

325 Who include states whose forms of government are still considered as non-democratic.

326 Which, by contrast, is regarded as sufficient in Article 10 (2) of the European Convention for the Protection of Human Rights and Fundamental Freedoms.

a strict interpretation close to the wording. Nevertheless, there is not only a negative aspect to the limitation. It also shows an embodiment of the fact that the right to self-determination cannot be seen solely as the right of an isolated subject alienated from the outside world. As the introduction of the right clearly states, such right shall be conferred on "all persons". Every self is entitled to exercise this right and is only able to exercise the right in an interplay with others in a shared world. In particular, the explicitly mentioned social and cultural self-determination presupposes a social and cultural environment. Thus, free self-determination can always only be seen if put in a broader context, namely, the plurality of selves in interplay who are free to determine their own moves in the interplay. To put it differently, the "ethical quest for authenticity is not only a process through which we become different by mutually recognizing our differences. It means, more radically, to be interpellated by the other."[327]

5.4 The Council of Europe Resolution on the protection of the privacy of individuals vis-à-vis electronic data banks in the private and public sectors

The Committee of Ministers of the Council of Europe started in the seventies to shift the focus from a general appreciation of the protection of individual free self-determination and privacy to a more specific protection in certain circumstances. It issued two Resolutions for this purpose, the Resolution on the protection of the privacy of individuals vis-à-vis electronic data banks in the private sector[328] and the Resolution on the protection of the privacy of individuals vis-à-vis electronic data

327 Cf. Capurro 2005a.

328 Resolution (73) 22 of the Council of Europe, adopted by the Committee of Ministers on 26 September 1973 at the 224th meeting of the Ministers' Deputies.

banks in the public sector.[329] Both Resolutions stress the need for prevention of abuses in storing, processing and dissemination of personal information by means of electronic data banks as well as the importance of finding a joint international approach. In addition, both resolutions are more directed at data controllers than at the individual data-subject. Consequently, they serve as additional armoury for the fundamental principles set out by the European Convention for the Protection of Human Rights and Fundamental Freedoms in a changed world, where data storage no longer refers only to dusty filing cabinets but comprises the transformation of information into electronic bit-strings that render both the filing specialist and index cards superfluous.

The Resolution on the protection of the privacy of individuals vis-à-vis electronic data banks in the private sector defines the framework within which collection and storage of data in electronic data banks is admissible. It already sets out clear boundaries for such collection and storage as well as defining basic principles such as, in particular, the principle of data quality: Article 1 of the Annex to the Resolution provides that data should be accurate, kept up to date and not recorded or disseminated if this might lead to unfair discrimination. In addition, it also introduced the collection and use-limitation principle,[330] the purpose-specification principle[331] as well as making cautious attempts at security, accountability and even transparency.[332] These principles can

[329] Resolution (74) 29 of the Council of Europe Adopted by the Committee of Ministers on 20 September 1974 at the 236th meeting of the Ministers' Deputies.

[330] Article 2 provides that "the information should be appropriate and relevant with regard to the purpose for which it has been stored."

[331] Cf. Article 5 "Without appropriate authorisation, information should not be used for purposes other than those for which it has been stored, nor communicated to third parties".

[332] Cf. Article 6 a general rule, the person concerned should have the right to know the information stored about him, the purpose for which it has been recorded, and particulars of each release of this information.

be found in many subsequent legislative approaches to the protection of data and privacy.[333]

This wickerwork of rules can be seen as a good first shot against the abuse of the right to determine what to conceal and reveal of a personal world, which is endangered by the automatic means of data-collection which easily eludes the control of the self-determining self. Nevertheless, any security net cast out can only be regarded as a successful elaboration of the right to privacy if the self is in charge of the fishing boat's rudder. The mere right to access information stored without the power to redress and, moreover, without effective sanctions, can hardly prevent loss of control due to automation. Nonetheless, the Resolution demonstrates awareness on the part of the Council of Europe that a mere right to privacy chiselled in stone cannot suffice to counter challenges in a globalized, modern world if there are "unjustified divergencies between the laws".[334]

The Resolution on the protection of the privacy of individuals vis-à-vis electronic data banks in the public sector, in turn, strengthens the defence against intrusion and infringement of personal privacy by the state. It is drafted against the backdrop of the recognition that the use of electronic data banks by public authorities has given rise to increasing concern about the protection of the privacy of individuals. However, the intent also is — as in respect to the Resolution on the protection of the privacy of individuals vis-à-vis electronic data banks in the private sector - to meet the challenges of securing a basis for a comprehensive protection of the right to privacy in a modern world. A major objective thus is to keep individuals informed. Article 1 stipulates that "[a]s a general rule the public should be kept regularly informed about the establishment, operation and development of electronic data banks in the public sector". In addition, also the principles laid out for the private sector are seen as important for the public sector. Moreover, there also is

---

333 Cf. e.g. Article 6 of the Directive (EC) 95/46 of the European Parliament and of the Council of 24 October 1995 on the protection of individuals with regard to the processing of personal data and on the free movement of such data [1995] OJ L281/31.

334 Cf. introductory remarks to Resolution (74) 29.

a strong tendency visible to subject any collection or storage of data by the state to the principle of lawfulness. The state has to lay out clear and unambiguous laws that legitimate such collection. In addition, there are already some basic safeguards as regards the possibility to deviate from such rules. In particular, Article 8 calls for a code of conduct, thus strengthening the rights of the individual. Nevertheless, this approach also lacks the means to restore control to the self because neither sanctions nor a proposal for an effective redress system are integrated into the Resolution.

A major additional flaw is the fact that these Resolutions represent mere recommendations and do not provide for a binding commitment. Notwithstanding this, the principles outlined have met with the approval of many multinational and international instruments in that basic principles were mirrored by the OECD and the European Union. Moreover, they were also used as a foundation for future instruments of the Council of Europe.

5.5 The Convention for the Protection of Individuals with regard to Automatic Processing of Personal Data and the OECD Guidelines on the Protection of Privacy and Transborder Flows of Personal Data

In 1981 the Council of Europe laid out the Convention for the Protection of Individuals with regard to Automatic Processing of Personal Data.[335] According to its Preamble, this convention aims at creating greater unity in the dissemination of the rule of law, human rights and fundamental freedoms as well as fostering unity among member states. This reference clearly addresses loopholes left by the European Convention for the Protection of Human Rights and Fundamental Freedoms and developments which had eventuated since it came into force. Hence, the Convention for the Protection of Individuals with regard to Automatic Processing of Personal Data was not intended as another broad compromise on fundamental principles. It neither

335 Convention No. 108 dated 28 January 1981 (http://conventions.coe.int/-treaty/en/treaties/html/108.htm).

ventured to lay down new rights; rather, it was drafted to address new challenges to the existing protection of individuals and their privacy which arose during the course of an increase in surveillance, identity-recognition, distribution and storage systems by virtue of a rapid development of the technical means employed.

While traditionally threats to privacy could be located in the immediate surroundings of a self and could thus be controlled by the self and its governments, through conscious decisions about carrying out and protecting the play of concealing and revealing information, these threats were taken to a next level by digitization. Information and acts that relate to a self and were considered private in the sense of belonging to a personal world where the self should be free to determine whether they should be disclosed or kept secret, started to be economically valuable and roused the desires of more and more third parties. It also became easier to access and collect such data thanks to the dawn of the electronic information age. Finally, emerging globalization also took its stake in the economic striving for gain. Hence the Convention can be seen as an attempt at defining basic rules and principles with respect to issues relating to the collection, storage, use and transferral or, more generally, the concealment and disclosure of personal data.

The drafting process of this Convention involved close co-operation with the masterminds behind the OECD Guidelines on the Protection of Privacy and Transborder Flows of Personal Data which were published a year earlier.[336] The OECD set-up — while establishing comparable general rules — differed slightly from the Council Convention by putting the main emphasis on trans-border flows and automated treatment of data. The OECD deemed a general framework necessary since cross-border data-flows increased and at that time only half of OECD members had started to establish regimes for the protection of personal data, and these were not capable of effectively and, especially,

336 OECD Guidelines on the Protection of Privacy and Transborder Flows of Personal Data dated 23 September 1980 (http://www.oecd.org/document/18/-0,3343,en_2649_34255_1815186_1_1_1_1,00.html).

universally addressing challenges posed by ever more powerful and ubiquitous means of processing data easily and quickly.[337]

The Convention for the Protection of Individuals with regard to Automatic Processing of Personal Data states that its objective is to secure "for every individual […] respect for his rights and fundamental freedoms, and in particular his right to privacy". Thus first and foremost, the self is to be protected. If compared to the Council Resolutions (see 5.4 above), there is a shift from being the mere object of protection to being the starting-point for any consideration of what is worthy of protection. This shift has to be applauded since privacy should be understood not only as a merely defensive right, as in the case of the right to be left alone.[338] Privacy is more than that and, in particular, since European tradition harks back to the Greeks, the notion of privacy has to include also *epimeleia heautou* (ἐπιμέλεια ἑαυτοῦ; taking care of one's self) in the Socratic sense,[339] and thus does not constitute a mere regulation of background conditions, but the establishment of surroundings within which a self-determining self is free to choose what to disclose to whom, how and when. However, it must be borne in mind that privacy cannot be decreed. It is hardly possible to legally regulate any potential aspect without creating an impediment to the freedom of the self or that of others. Privacy needs to be established with a fine balance between the free self-determination of selves, their interplay in a shared world and the need for external stimuli. These stimuli thus need to provide solely a practise-ground for becoming who you are if the self is to be respected as autonomous, since any imbalanced increase in

337 Only Austria, Canada, Denmark, France, Germany, Luxembourg, Norway, Sweden and the United States had enacted privacy laws, and Belgium, Iceland, the Netherlands, Spain and Switzerland had prepared draft bills at that time. Cf. the Preface to the OECD Guidelines.

338 Cf. for instance the dissenting opinion of Justice Brandeis in *Olmstead v. United States*, 277 U.S. 438 (1928), who delineated the scope of this right as "every unjustifiable intrusion by the Government upon the privacy of the individual, whatever the means employed, must be deemed a violation of the Fourth Amendment".

339 Cf. also Foucault 1988.

protection by the state without regard to free self-determination could amount to a shove along the slippery slope toward a nanny state and thus might ultimately even curtail fundamental rights.[340]

The Convention already contains several provisions which can be regarded as providing such a fertile soil. It includes both a definition of what is to be considered as personal data and an enumeration of basic principles which need to be respected.[341] It also contains a first attempt at securing these principles by defining a subject who is responsible for handling the data.[342] The basic principles set out represent a remarkable multi-faceted nutshell approach or, in Greenleaf's words, these principles "while stated briefly, do contain versions of most of the elements we now recognise as core data privacy principles".[343]

The main principle laid down by the Convention concerns the quality of data.[344] This principle sets out the requirements for fair and lawful processing on the basis of specified, legitimate purposes with regard to adequacy and relevance for the respective purpose, as well as accuracy and a limitation of the storage-period to the necessary minimum. Hence, any collection or processing of personal data is subject to a variety of considerations intended to restrict data controllers as far as possible and thus attempt to put the free self back in charge of the process. The collection and storage of information about a self should only be effected as an *ultima ratio*, namely, when such information is compelling for the fulfilment of legitimate purposes. Arguably, this

340 Cf. Nagel 2011.

341 Personal data are specified as "any information relating to an identified or identifiable individual". This definition can be found also in the first part of the OECD Guidelines on the Protection of Privacy and Transborder Flows of Personal Data dated 23 September 1980.

342 Cf. Article 2: "controller of the file" means "the natural or legal person, public authority, agency or any other body who is competent according to the national law to decide what should be the purpose of the automated data file, which categories of personal data should be stored and which operations should be applied to them".

343 Greenleaf 2012.

344 Cf. Article 5 of the Convention.

leaves room for interpretation since both the notions of legitimate purpose and 'adequacy and relevance' are rather nebulous.

This holds true especially if the international character of the Convention is taken into account.[345] This situation is exacerbated by Article 9 which provides that a derogation of the data quality principle shall be allowed "when such derogation is provided for by the law of the Party and constitutes a necessary measure in a democratic society". This is even further eroded by the fact that Article 9 subjects this very measure to the interest of "protecting State security, public safety, the monetary interests of the State or the suppression of criminal offences". As even a financial, taxation interest of the state can form the basis for severely exceeding the limitation for data collection and storage to a minimum, it might be asked whether the Convention is a well-intentioned but toothless tiger. To put it differently, this exception entails the danger that the mere economic value of data is more highly appreciated than the who from whom such data originate.

Nevertheless, the Convention contains a further fundamental milestone: Article 6 defines a basis for qualifying data.[346] Certain categories of data, most notably data ascribable to the sphere of a very traditional understanding of privacy — in the sense of information a self usually does not readily and voluntarily reveal in any context, but solely in a very limited way, often under the pressure of need, such as information about personal health and well-being disclosed to a surgeon, — are qualified as sensitive and hence are subject to a higher level of protection. Article 6, however, is also subject to potential derogation as stipulated in Article 9. Nevertheless, even though it might be

345 Cf. in this respect the never-ending disputes over vague terms within international instruments such as e.g. "reasonable" within Article 39 CISG (Cf. Baasch-Andersen 2011 p. 33; Laimer & Nagel 2012 p. 44).

346 Article 6 reads "Personal data revealing racial origin, political opinions or religious or other beliefs, as well as personal data concerning health or sexual life, may not be processed automatically unless domestic law provides appropriate safeguards. The same shall apply to personal data relating to criminal convictions."

circumvented by individual states, it points the way forward to a multilayered approach toward dealing with privacy protection.

Notwithstanding the unfortunate back door which might endanger the intended scope of protection, the Convention for the Protection of Individuals with regard to Automatic Processing of Personal Data can still be seen as a regulatory success. It has been ratified by forty-four member states of the Council of Europe so far, all of which have privacy laws and thus, at least, have acknowledged that privacy is a core value for living that is worthy of protection.

5.6 Directive 95/46/EC[347]

Directive 95/46/EC of the European Parliament and of the Council dated 24 October 1995 on the protection of individuals with regard to the processing of personal data and on the free movement of such data represented a landmark in legislative European measures aimed at the protection of personal privacy. It enshrines the principles laid out in past decades, and can be seen as representing perhaps the best possible consensus among European member states on a common minimum level of protection for their citizens' privacy.

Directive 95/46/EC focuses on personal data as "any information relating to an identified or identifiable natural person". The latter is defined within the directive as "a person [...] who can be identified, directly or indirectly, in particular by reference to an identification number or to one or more factors specific to his physical, physiological, mental, economic, cultural or social identity."[348] Thus, the EU for the first time ventured to clearly define aspects of privacy which it considered worthy of protection; a difficult task as such, since firstly, the interests of various stakeholders have to be considered and respected because otherwise a consensus and, especially, broad acceptance cannot

---

347 Directive 95/46/EC of the European Parliament and of the Council dated 24 October 1995 on the protection of individuals with regard to the processing of personal data and on the free movement of such data, Official Journal No. L 281/31 dated 23 November 1995.

348 Cf. Article 2 of Directive 95/46/EC.

be achieved. Secondly, any definition which might be tailored to present conditions might be outdated shortly after its drafting since — particularly in the fields of ICT — developments and innovation cannot be surely predicted.[349] Nevertheless the definition within Directive 95/46/EC proved to be a stronghold of protection for the years to come. If the broad scope of this definition is also taken into account — since not only information relating directly to a self, but also any information which can be indirectly linked to that very self is safeguarded — it might be argued that this Directive finally offered a breakthrough as regards adequately safeguarding personal privacy.

This is all the more remarkable if regard is had to the fluid field privacy may encompass. Any rigid definition is usually doomed to failure since privacy is dependent on a vast variety of factors influencing a free interplay among selves, which is in constant change from both a temporal and context-related perspective. The German Constitutional Court once depicted this by using as a metaphor different layers of privacy within which a free development of personality is possible and requiring different levels of protection.[350] While the inner core of the self's privacy is sacred, outer boundaries are seen as less sensitive and may even be limited insofar as the interests of other stakeholders are valued as equally important or even more so. The definition within the Directive takes a less sophisticated but equally effective approach. For the purpose of effectively protecting personal data, applicability shall cover a very broad range, or — in the image used by the German Constitutional Court — applicability shall generally reach the outer layers of privacy because even information that can be indirectly linked to a self is characterized as personal data and is thus prima facie equally worthy of protection as information with a direct link, such as name and date of birth. To show that a grading is nevertheless possible and important, after simply putting all personal data behind the moat for a basic level of protection, Directive 95/46/EC establishes a second

349 Cf. e.g. the option to automatically collect and store biometric data which was not long in coming after the Directive had been implemented.

350 Cf. BVerfGE 6, 36 in respect to the free development of personality, the so-called "Kernberichstheorie", Article 2 (1) of the German Constitution.

fortification for sensitive data: the preamble provides that "(w)hereas data which are capable by their nature of infringing fundamental freedoms or privacy should not be processed unless the data subject gives his explicit consent".[351]

Article 8 of Directive 95/46/EC furthers this train of thought by providing that "Member States shall prohibit the processing of personal data revealing racial or ethnic origin, political opinions, religious or philosophical beliefs, trade-union membership, and the processing of data concerning health or sex life".[352] Thus, there is a clear catalogue of information considered worthy of an additional level of protection. It is interesting in this respect that the catalogue, in particular, mirrors the self's freedom regarding how to partake in the interplay with other selves, whereas master data which cannot be influenced, such as date of birth — with the exception of health data — are categorized as secondary with respect to level of protection. This can be seen as a consequence of the underlying objective of a comprehensive protection of freedom. Every self is more than the sum of its physical and biological preconditions since it is capable to freely choose how to develop its personality. This very choice needs a special degree of protection if the fundamental principles of freedom to which all of the member states of the European Community and the Community itself have committed themselves are to be effectively safeguarded. By listing important aspects of these fundamental principles, the Directive manages to fortify and protect these values.

In addition, the scope of the basic level of protection granted to personal data not listed in Article 8 of Directive 95/46/EC can also be qualified as remarkable. The wording of the definition of personal data (which is often criticized as too vague (since there is neither a definition for what is to be understood by the term "information", nor whether an indirect link has to be present for everybody or just for some third party[353]) allows for a context-related interpretation rendering the 'rigid

[351] Cf. Recital 33 of Directive 95/46/EC.

[352] Cf. Article 8 of Directive 95/46/EC.

[353] Cf. in this respect the doctrine of the relativity of information that indirectly allows a data-subject to be identified with respect to IPv4-addresses, where

rule' more flexible.[354] As a consequence, Directive 95/46/EC is finely meshed and extensive at the same time: extensive, since the scope — subject to a particular interpretation — is unlimited, and finely meshed, since it casts a net capable of catching all constellations of the interplay of revealing and concealing one's self and personal world.

Moreover, the Directive clearly confirms the idea that when considering privacy protection, the freedom of selves regarding what to reveal and conceal should be put at the centre of any decision, be it in an economic, technical or political respect. Even though the Directive's harmonization efforts are explicitly linked to the economic benefit of future use of ICT data-processing systems (the Preamble states that "(w)hereas the difference in levels of protection of the rights and freedoms of individuals, notably the right to privacy, with regard to the processing of personal data afforded in the Member States may prevent the transmission of such data from the territory of one Member State to that of another Member State"[355]), the preamble to the Directive also provides that "data-processing systems are designed to serve man", wherefore "(...) they must, whatever the nationality or residence of natural persons, respect their fundamental rights and freedoms, notably the right to privacy, and contribute to economic and social progress,

---

many scholars argue that the mere possibility of a single internet service provider of linking the IP-address to an internet connection and thus to a physical address and, above all, a name, cannot be seen as sufficient to consider such information as personal data. In particular, if it is taken into account that without a court order nobody is allowed to carry out this identification process. Nevertheless, it has also to be taken into account that the mere existence of the possibility of identifying might suffice for the classification as personal data since there is no guarantee that no such identification will be carried out, e.g. via an abuse of the very possibility (Cf. in this respect Nagel & Weimann 2011). Thus, it does not come as a surprise that the European Court of Justice declared IP-addresses to be generally considered as personal data in the sense of Directive 95/46/EC (ECJ, Scarlet Extended vs. Société belge des auteurs, compositeurs et éditeurs SCRL (SABAM), judgement of 24 November 2011, Cf. Nagel & Weimann 2011a).

354 Or 'watered-down' as critics may argue.

355 Cf. Recital 7 of Directive 95/46/EC.

trade expansion and the well-being of individuals".[356] Hence, despite the traditionally purely economic objective of the European Union (cf. *5.1 European integration, freedom, economics*), the fundamental freedoms of selves are kept at the core of any consideration, and any economic boost facilitated by the rapid development of ICTs is subordinate to these.

The Directive was also clearly intended not only to create an extrinsic layer of protection, but also to put control back into the hands of free, self-determining selves. This can be seen from the fact that the consent of selves was declared as pivotal to any use of data on each self,[357] thus creating a barrier to deliberate intrusions into the privacy of selves and equipping them with a means of redress. This can already be derived from the Preamble that states "[...] in order to be lawful, the processing of personal data must in addition be carried out with the consent of the data subject".[358] Arguably, this Recital also names the exceptions to this principle, namely, that consent is not necessary if the processing is "necessary for the conclusion or performance of a contract binding on the data subject, or as a legal requirement, or for the performance of a task carried out in the public interest or in the exercise of official authority, or in the legitimate interests of a natural or legal person". However all these exceptions are subject to the condition "that the interests or the rights and freedoms of the data subject are not overriding". This is also highlighted by the definition of the term 'consent' within the Directive as "the data subject's consent' shall mean any freely given specific and informed indication of his wishes by which the data subject signifies his agreement to personal data relating to him being processed".[359] Thus, the self remains the starting-point for any assessment, since the self's freedom to freely choose what to reveal or conceal is established as a barrier to undue influence or abuse.

To safeguard fundamental rights of selves via the protection of personal data, Directive 95/46/EC lays down various principles on how

---

356 Cf. Recital 2 of Directive 95/46/EC.

357 Cf. Article 7

358 Cf. Recital 30 of Directive 95/46/EC.

359 Cf. Article 2 (h) of Directive 95/46/EC

to treat personal data. These principles can be found already in various predecessors; nevertheless, due to the strong political foundation of the Directive, the consequences vary considerably if compared, say, to the 1981 Council of Europe Convention for the Protection of Individuals with regard to Automatic Processing of Personal Data or even the Council of Europe Resolutions on the protection of individual privacy vis-à-vis electronic data banks in the public and private sector. The member states of the European Union are bound to effectively implement the principles down out in the Directive,[360] especially since it clearly sets out the scope of its implementation.[361]

The fundamental principles are set out in Articles 6 and 7 of Directive 96/46/EC. Article 6 codifies the principles of fair and lawful processing of data, purpose-limitation,[362] collection-limitation,[363] data-quality,[364] and a time limit for lawful use.[365]

---

360 Article 32 of Directive 95/46/EC stipulates, "Member States shall bring into force the laws, regulations and administrative provisions necessary to comply with this Directive at the latest at the end of a period of three years from the date of its adoption".

361 Cf. Article 4 "Each Member State shall apply the national provisions it adopts pursuant to this Directive to the processing of personal data where:
(a) the processing is carried out in the context of the activities of an establishment of the controller on the territory of the Member State; when the same controller is established on the territory of several Member States, he must take the necessary measures to ensure that each of these establishments complies with the obligations laid down by the national law applicable;
(b) the controller is not established on the Member State's territory, but in a place where its national law applies by virtue of international public law;
(c) the controller is not established on Community territory and, for purposes of processing personal data makes use of equipment, automated or otherwise, situated on the territory of the said Member State, unless such equipment is used only for purposes of transit through the territory of the Community."

362 Cf. Article 6 (1) (b): collected for specified, explicit and legitimate purposes and not further processed in a way incompatible with those purposes. Further processing of data for historical, statistical or scientific purposes shall not be considered as incompatible provided that Member States provide appropriate safeguards.

Article 7 of the Directive reinforces the principle of consent by listing the only exceptions to it.[366] Thus, a clear guiding framework is created which both limits the use of data to a necessary minimum and establishes the necessity of justifying any use of personal data.

As a consequence, Directive 95/46/EC established for the first time a uniform approach in addressing the issue of movement of data that could no longer be kept within national boundaries due to technological developments such as, in particular, the potential to communicate and transfer information electronically. In addition, Directive 95/46/EC is more than just another European Directive: it is directed at a pivotal objective, since the protection of individuals with regard to processing

---

363 Cf. Article 6 (1)(c): adequate, relevant and not excessive in relation to the purposes for which they are collected and/or further processed.

364 Cf. Article 6 (1) (d) accurate and, where necessary, kept up to date; every reasonable step must be taken to ensure that data which are inaccurate or incomplete, having regard to the purposes for which they were collected or for which they are further processed, are erased or rectified.

365 Cf. Article 6 (1) (e) kept in a form which permits identification of data subjects for no longer than is necessary for the purposes for which the data were collected or for which they are further processed. Member States shall lay down appropriate safeguards for personal data stored for longer periods for historical, statistical or scientific use.

366 Cf. the exceptions within Article 7 of Directive 95/46/EC: processing is admissible if it

"- is necessary for the performance of a contract to which the data subject is party or in order to take steps at the request of the data subject prior to entering into a contract; or
- is necessary for compliance with a legal obligation to which the controller is subject; or
- is necessary in order to protect the vital interests of the data subject; or
- is necessary for the performance of a task carried out in the public interest or in the exercise of official authority vested in the controller or in a third party to whom the data are disclosed; or
- is necessary for the purposes of the legitimate interests pursued by the controller or by the third party or parties to whom the data are disclosed, except where such interests are overridden by the interests for fundamental rights and freedoms of the data subject which require protection under Article 1 (1)."

personal data safeguards also a crucial aspect of individual freedom. To uphold this freedom, any processing should not be subject to deliberate or random influences. The development of the cyberworld vividly shows that the self is no longer capable of preventing all of these influences itself, since times when it was sufficient to employ guards, dig a moat and build a wall to create a private realm have long passed. The freedom of the self thus is dependent on additional, extrinsic protection. Nevertheless, the latter also needs to strike a balance between safeguarding and curtailment, since a comprehensive guarantee of freedom means that it is ultimately for the self to decide whether information which is directly or indirectly linked to him/herself is reproduced, transferred and disseminated in the form of personalized bit-strings of data from the haven of concealment to a place where the access restrictions are at the mercy of each recipient processor. Directive 95/46/EC can be seen as a successful first attempt at providing such protection by specifying and confirming the rights of the self without taking away control. The ubiquitous principle of consent enshrined within Directive 95/46/EC may be regarded as the best possible compromise between nannyish protection and a fully unimpeded freedom of choice, namely the freedom to determine the personal scope of privacy.

Of course, Directive 95/46/EC cannot be viewed as the magic potion for all privacy issues. This is prevented by several factors. Firstly, the scope of Directive 95/46 is clearly and exclusively directed at the processing of personal data and the free movement of such data. Thus, not all aspects of privacy are covered (cf. *1.4 The question concerning rights: personal privacy, trust and intimacy*), but only a small — albeit important — detail of the privacy picture. In addition, even with respect to the processing of personal data, Directive 95/46/EC is capable only of providing a limited scope of protection since, notwithstanding the rights to access or correct or even claim deletion of data, there is only a weak assortment of second-level rights.[367] Due to technical potentials of the cyberworld, any attempt to undo the disclosure of personal data outside

367 Which now forms the basis for discussion on the ambivalent "right to forget".

the sphere of the self's control resembles a quixotic quest: the most comprehensive right is not worth the paper it is written on if it remains uncertain how and against whom it can be enforced. The latter unfortunately holds true in several respects: The long arm of the law does not reach beyond the political borders of the European Union unless the third-party state concerned either recognizes the European standards or provides a comparable standard of data protection. If it is taken into account that (including all of the European states individually) only 89 states globally have adopted some sort of data protection law so far,[368] the impediment is obvious. Furthermore, even within the political borders of the European Union, enforcement might be hindered. Due to a slightly different interpretation among member states of certain terms, such as the term 'controller', it is not inconceivable that the legal implementation of the Directive in one member state might qualify an entity seated in another member state as the controller of data, whereas under the laws of the latter this quality is denied, so that no claim can be effectively directed against this entity. Moreover, the current framework presupposes a separate enforcement of claims against any third party who might have stored the disclosed personal data. Thus, any attempt to undo the disclosure of data resembles the race between the hare and the hedgehog:[369] as soon as one claim is effectively enforced a claim against another party is needed because the data are "already there".[370]

In addition, Directive 95/46/EC is often criticized as being ineffective on the grounds that the European Union refrained from enacting a Regulation. A Regulation would have had immediate and direct effect in all member states. A Directive, by contrast, leaves room for play within

---

368 Cf. Greenleaf 2012. many among them have "European laws" — 27 EU member states and Iceland, Liechtenstein, Norway, Albania; Andorra; Azerbaijan; Bosnia & Herzegovina; Croatia; Faroe Islands; FYROM (Macedonia); Gibraltar; Guernsey; Isle of Man; Jersey; Montenegro; Moldova; Monaco; Russia; San Marino; Serbia; Switzerland; and Ukraine.

369 Cf. Grimm's fairy-tale 'The Hare and the Hedgehog' Grimm 1857 no. 187.

370 The hedgehog positioned his wife at the end of the race track, who shouted "I am already here" as soon as the hare was approaching. Upon the suggestion to the hare to run back again, the hedgehog himself repeated his wife's words.

the necessary implementation by the member states.[371] This entails not only a threat to uniformity, but also the threat of creating areas of legal uncertainty since the data may be treated differently, depending on the players involved and the location where they are collected, stored or used. The right of access established by Directive 95/46/EC is a striking example of this. Article 12 of Directive 95/46/EC provides that member states shall guarantee every data-subject the right to obtain from the controller "without constraint at reasonable intervals and without excessive delay or expense confirmation as to whether or not data relating to him are being processed and information at least as to the purposes of the processing, the categories of data concerned, and the recipients or categories of recipients to whom the data are disclosed, communication to him in an intelligible form of the data undergoing processing and of any available information as to their source, knowledge of the logic involved in any automatic processing of data concerning him at least in the case of the automated decisions (…)". The use of the vague term "without excessive delay" already sufficed to provoke a wide variety of national regulations. While some states use no specification[372] or only a vague term,[373] others request that such

---

371 Cf. e.g. the stipulation in Article 4 95/46/EC, which states that "Each Member State shall apply the national provisions it adopts pursuant to this Directive to the processing of personal data where:

(a) the processing is carried out in the context of the activities of an establishment of the controller on the territory of the Member State; when the same controller is established on the territory of several Member States, he must take the necessary measures to ensure that each of these establishments complies with the obligations laid down by the national law applicable;

(b) the controller is not established on the Member State's territory, but in a place where its national law applies by virtue of international public law;

(c) the controller is not established on Community territory and, for purposes of processing personal data makes use of equipment, automated or otherwise, situated on the territory of the said Member State, unless such equipment is used only for purposes of transit through the territory of the Community."

372 E.g. Germany, § 34 BDSG (German Data Protection Act) solely provides that "Data subjects may request information about recorded data relating to them, including information relating to the source of the data, the recipients or

information shall be provided within 8 business days,[374] 15 days,[375] 30 days,[376] a month,[377] 40 days,[378] within two months,[379] eight weeks,[380] or even more sophisticated systems[381] or exceptions.[382] Since even non-

---

categories of recipients to which the data are transferred, and the purpose of recording the data.
Data subjects should specify the type of personal data on which information is to be given. If the personal data are commercially recorded for the purpose of transfer, data subjects may request information about the source and recipients only if there is no overriding interest in protecting trade secrets. In this case, data subjects shall be given information about the source and recipients even if this information was not recorded".

373 Norway or Finland ("without undue delay", cf. e.g. Finnish Data Protection Act, Sect. 28), or Italy ("without delay" Combination between Sections 7 and 8 of the Italian Personal Data Protection Code (Legislative Decree No. 196, dated June 30, 2003).

374 Cf. Slovakia, which allows 15 days in case of an answer in Braille type.

375 E.g. Romania.

376 Cf. Denmark (Persondataloven of 2 June 2000 § 30, stk. 2 sml. Stk. 1), Hungary, Art. 15 Act CXII of 2011 or Poland (cf. Polish Act on Personal Data Protection from 29 August 1997).

377 Cf. Netherlands (Artikel 36 Wet bescherming persoonsgegevens).

378 Cf. the UK Data Protection Act 1998 which specifies that the information has to be transmitted "Promptly but in any event within 40 days" or Ireland ("as soon as may be, in any event not more than 40 days, cf. Sect. 4 Irish Data Protection Act 1988 & 2003).

379 France, Art. 94 Décret n°2005-1309 du 20 octobre 2005 pris pour l'application de la loi n° 78-17 du 6 janvier 1978 relative à l'informatique, aux fichiers et aux libertés.

380 Cf. Austria, § 26 Abs. 4 Datenschutzgesetz.

381 Cf. Spain, where there is a period of one month for acceptance and notification of access options to the data subject and another ten-day period following the data-subject's choice.

382 Cf. Sweden, where the period is one month § 26 Personuppgiftslag, SFS 1998:204; however, the deadline for a response may be extended by up to 4 months from date of application if special reasons so require.

European states started to accept similar approaches[383] a common definition would have been desirable.

Furthermore, the Directive also contains actual loopholes. For instance, it does not differentiate between adults and minors. The same level of protection is applied irrespective of the age or capacity of the self to understand the consequences of a disclosure of personal data and thus to declare informed consent. The challenges thereby posed are addressed in most member states via the regulation on the capacity to contract. Apart from that, the law does not allow for a two-tiered approach, even though Directive 95/46/EC employs a double standard in other respects by acknowledging that sensitive data call for special protection.[384]

In addition, the so-called Safe-Harbour agreement between the U.S. and the EU,[385] which was designed to facilitate the safe transfer of data proved to be a Trojan horse. Since Directive 95/46/EC prevents the transfer of personal data to non-European Union states that do not meet the European Union adequacy standard, the U.S. Department of Commerce and the European Commission developed a safe-harbour framework, which enables companies based in the U.S. to carry out a self-certifying compliance process. The latter is unfortunately open to abuse, since the certification process is no real obstacle to non-compliance with EU-standards, in particular, when it is taken into account that enforcement within the U.S. is first of all subject to "U.S. law and will be carried out primarily by the private sector" as well as that "Private sector self-regulation and enforcement will be backed up as needed by government enforcement of the federal and state unfair and deceptive statutes".[386]

---

383 Cf. Article 13 of the draft Data Protection Act in Turkey, which provides for 15 days or Art. 1 (4) Verordnung zum Bundesgsetz über den Datenschutz in Switzerland which fixes a period of 30 days.

384 Cf. Nagel 2011.

385 http://export.gov/safeharbor/eu/eg_main_018365.asp.

386 Cf. U.S. Dept. of Commerce, Safe Harbor Enforcement Overview. Federal and State "Unfair and Deceptive Practices" Authority and Privacy, July 14, 2000.

Furthermore — apart from the safe-harbour agreement — since the European Union tends to be very critical when it comes to assessing the privacy standard of non-European states, only very few states are recognized as having an adequate standard of data protection.[387] While this has to be applauded in terms of preventing a transfer of data to states where the data might be abused, it has to be noted that this also shows the comparably small area within which personal data enjoy at least an adequate standard of protection, thus leaving much room for public or private entities to operate from a non-compliant base to prevent any control.[388] Thus, even with Directive 95/46/EC in place, data-outsourcing remains problematic in many cases since data gathered in one country but stored in another are subject to different legal regimes which in turn might hinder enforcement, or lead to a — as one U.S. District Court prominently showed[389] — complete ignorance of the regulations of the other state involved.

Finally, the developments in digital technologies made incredible leaps at the turn of the millennium. This has led to the circumstance that, while the terms of Directive 95/46/EC could still be applied to the new status quo, the concepts and lines of thought of its founding fathers were soon outdated.

5.7 Directive 2002/58/EC

These problems fortunately did not go unnoticed. In 2002, the European Union amended Directive 95/46/EC with Directive 2002/58/EC of the European Parliament and the Council dated 12 July 2002 concerning the processing of personal data and the protection of

---

387 Andorra, Argentina, Canada, Switzerland, Faroe Islands, Guernsey, Israel, Isle of Man and Jersey; pending: Uruguay and New Zealand.

388 Unless the company is big enough to be tracked down within the EU as Google recently had to experience (again) when being faced with a fine from several Data Protection Authorities, such as from Norway in August 2012.

389 See AccessData Corp. vs. Alste Techn. Gmbh, 2010 WL 318477 (D. Utah Jan. 21, 2010) where the Court held that it was empowered to compel the production of the data even if it would require a violation of the Data Protection Act of the other country.

privacy in the electronic communications sector (Directive on privacy and electronic communications). This Directive was intended "to respect the fundamental rights and (observe) the principles recognised in particular by the Charter of fundamental rights of the European Union".[390] In addition, the Directive addressed the fact that Directive 95/46/EC could no longer be regarded as sufficient since "(n)ew advanced digital technologies are currently being introduced in public communications networks in the Community, which give rise to specific requirements concerning the protection of personal data and privacy of the user."[391] Thus, the clear aim was to find ways to counter ubiquitous data collection, which was facilitated by the introduction of Web 2.0 and the development of new electronic communication platforms. In particular, the new technical means of tacit or hidden data collection were seen as a threat since, due to a lack of transparency and awareness, individual selves were in danger of losing control in these situations.[392]

The European Union thus saw the need to extend the extrinsic protection created by Directive 95/46/EC: "In the case of public communications networks, specific legal, regulatory and technical provisions should be made in order to protect fundamental rights and freedoms of natural persons and legitimate interests of legal persons, in particular with regard to the increasing capacity for automated storage and processing of data relating to subscribers and users."[393]

However, despite this noble objective, the actual regulatory body of Directive 2002/58/EC was rather limited. Only very few stipulations can be regarded as real progress if it is taken into account that ultimately the freedom of the self is at stake. The most important reform is the reinforcement of the control by the individual self by introducing the principle of informed consent with respect to data that do not necessarily qualify as personal data in the sense of Directive 95/48/EC.[394] In

390 Cf. Recital 2 of Directive 2002/58/EC.

391 Cf. Recital 5 of Directive 2002/58/EC.

392 This is why Directive 2002/58/EC is also labeled "cookie Directive".

393 Cf. Recital 7 of Directive 2002/58/EC.

394 Cf. Article 5 (3) of Directive 2002/58/EC: "Member States shall ensure that the use of electronic communications networks to store information or to gain

addition, Directive 2002/58/EC addresses the use of traffic data[395] and location data.[396] Apart from that, the Directive contains only minor adjustments in respect o technical developments,[397] but no real solution to the problems, which persisted after Directive 95/46/EC and its respective national implementations came into force. Moreover, Directive 2002/58/EC clearly shows the limits of the authority of the European Union since it provides that it "does not alter the existing balance between the individual's right to privacy and the possibility for Member States to take the measures referred to in Article 15(1) of this Directive, necessary for the protection of public security, defence, State security (including the economic well-being of the State when the activities relate to State security matters) and the enforcement of criminal law. Consequently, this Directive does not affect the ability of Member States to carry out lawful interception of electronic communications, or take other measures, if necessary for any of these purposes and in accordance with the European Convention for the Protection of Human Rights and Fundamental Freedoms, as interpreted by the rulings of the European Court of Human Rights."[398] Thus, national variations are explicitly permitted.[399] This can be understood

access to information stored in the terminal equipment of a subscriber or user is only allowed on condition that the subscriber or user concerned is provided with clear and comprehensive information in accordance with Directive 95/46/EC, inter alia about the purposes of the processing, and is offered the right to refuse such processing by the data controller. This shall not prevent any technical storage or access for the sole purpose of carrying out or facilitating the transmission of a communication over an electronic communications network, or as strictly necessary in order to provide an information society service explicitly requested by the subscriber or user."

395 Cf. Article 6 of Directive 2002/58/EC.

396 Cf. Article 9 of Directive 2002/58/EC.

397 Cf. the regulation on directories of subscribers (Article 12), unsolicited communication, presentation and restriction of calling and connected line identification (Article 8) and Itemised billing (Article 7).

398 Cf. Recital 11 of Directive 2002/58/EC.

399 In addition to the fact that as Directive 2002/58/EC was passed in the form of a Directive, slight deviations in the transposition are possible anyway.

from the perspective of member states' fearing to lose sovereignty, but at the same time represents a setback for the freedom of the self since the hands of the very body who ventured to protect this freedom on a multinational basis are tied by national interests. Nevertheless, Directive 2002/58/EC at least outlines the type of measures member states may undertake that it deems admissible, thus creating a mental barrier to deliberate use or abuse of the possibility to deviate from the Directive's principles: "Such measures must be appropriate, strictly proportionate to the intended purpose and necessary within a democratic society and should be subject to adequate safeguards in accordance with the European Convention for the Protection of Human Rights and Fundamental Freedoms."[400]

Notwithstanding its rather limited introduction of changes, Directive 2002/58/EC faced many challenges in the aftermath to its decreeing. Since the Directive not only imposes additional requirements on tracking tools, but also allows for exceptions, Internet Service Providers have been fast in finding ways to circumvent the unpleasant provisions which hinder a deliberate use of — in particular — cookies and other tracking mechanisms by interpreting the exceptions very broadly. In the meantime this has been countered by Article 29 Data Protection Working Party,[401] which provides clear guidance on how the exception should and, above all, should not be read.[402] The provision still leaves room for debate and — at the latest when new tracking means are developed — will stir up more dust in the future. In addition, several

400 Cf. Recital 11 of Directive 2002/58/EC.

401 Which was set up by Directive 95/46/EC to "provide expert opinion from member state level to the Commission on questions of data protection, to promote the uniform application of the general principles of the Directives in all Member States through co-operation between data protection supervisory authorities and to advise the Commission on any Community measures affecting the rights and freedoms of natural persons with regard to the processing of personal data and privacy." Cf. Articles 29 and 30 of Directive 95/46/EC

402 Cf. Article 29 Data Protection Working Party Opinion 04/2012 on Cookie Consent Exemption

states have failed to implement the Directive within the prescribed time limit,[403] which impedes the explicit aim of harmonization.[404]

Consequently, while establishing and confirming important principles, Directive 2002/58/EC has not succeeded in overcoming major difficulties which persisted after Directive 95/46/EC had been implemented.

5.8 Communication (2010) 609

Calls for amendments to or improvements of Directive 95/46/EC have continued. The most prominent example is perhaps the call to establish *habeas data* by the European Group on Ethics,[405] which probably represents the best possible paraphrase of the importance of the protection of personal data with respect to the freedom of the self.[406] The European Union has not gone as far, but nevertheless again has acknowledged the need to further improve the European data protection framework. In 2010, the Commission, the European Parliament, the Council, the Economic and Social Committee and the Committee of the regions issued the Communication "A comprehensive approach on personal data protection in the European Union".[407] This sweeping but — unfortunately — non-binding statement contained a vast range of suggestions to counter issues that were either not dealt with or not fully covered by the existing data protection framework.

---

403 Most prominently Germany, which failed to reach an agreement on the implementing law even a year after the elapse of the implementation period.

404 Cf. Recital 8 of Directive 2002/58/EC: "Legal, regulatory and technical provisions adopted by the Member States concerning the protection of personal data, privacy and the legitimate interest of legal persons, in the electronic communication sector, should be harmonised in order to avoid obstacles to the internal market for electronic communication...".

405 EGE 2005.

406 Cf. Rodotà in EGE Opinion no. 20; cf. on the origin of *habeas corpus* Charles II, 1679: 'An Act for the better secureing the Liberty of the Subject and for Prevention of Imprisonments beyond the Seas.' *Statutes of the Realm: volume 5: 1628-80* (1819), pp. 935-938, which enabled any prisoner to claim to be heard by a judge.

407 COM (2010) 609 final.

Nevertheless, like the preceding Directives, the Communication is deeply rooted in the foundations of the European Union and thus aimed at a twofold objective, namely, both to safeguard fundamental rights and to further the realization of the internal market. This two-pronged approach represents — as might be argued from a strictly human rights-centered perspective — the European Union's main dilemma: the European Union devoted itself to furthering the economic well-being of the Union; hence, it has to outweigh or balance purely economic interests with fundamental rights. This does not necessarily have to lead to a trade-off — after all, economic aims can be well aligned with fundamental rights since economic well-being is based ultimately on mutually estimating and esteeming of each other's fluid, living powers and abilities on a basis of mutual benefit (cf. *1.6 The private individual and private property as a mode of reified sociation: the gainful game (classical political economy, Marx)*). Nonetheless, conflicts of interest are possible. This holds true in particular if the enormous value of personal data is taken into account as well as the looming imbalance caused by the technical potentials of the cyberworld such as data-linkage, data-mining and hidden data-gathering. It is true that the latter means may lead to high profits; however, they can heavily impair the freedom and privacy of selves at the same time.[408]

This imbalance has not been overlooked by European law-makers since the Communication clearly states that there is "a need to clarify and specify the application of data protection principles to new technologies, in order to ensure that individuals' personal data are actually effectively protected, whatever the technology used to process their data, and that data controllers are fully aware of the implications of new technologies on data protection."[409]

---

408 Cf. the introduction to COM (2010) 609 final: "Today technology allows individuals to share information about their behaviour and preferences easily and make it publicly and globally available on an unprecedented scale. (…) At the same time, ways of collecting personal data have become increasingly elaborated and less easily detectable."

409 COM (2010) 609 final.

To tip the scales in favour of effectively protecting the self's freedom to control what should be revealed and what should be concealed on both a peer-group and international plane, the Communication lists many factors that should constitute the basis of a new European regulatory framework: Globalization should be taken into account, international data transfers improved, a stronger institutional arrangement for the effective enforcement of data protection rules should be provided, the coherence of the data protection legal framework should be improved and transparency for data subjects should be enhanced.[410]

The requirement that data-subjects should be clearly informed in a transparent way via information that is easily accessible and easy to understand is a clear assertion of the fact that, despite any economic benefits of data-processing, the self has to remain the core of any considerations. This is highlighted also by the fact that the Communication argues that this applies specifically to children thus, for the first time, taking into account that the capacity of selves is a pivotal factor when it comes to protecting the individual self's choice as to what to reveal and what to conceal. In addition, the clear intention to enhance not only the information to be given to a self, but also to reinstate the self's control via a reinforcement of the principle of data minimization,[411] and "the retention by data subjects of an effective control over their own data"[412] further reaffirms this approach.

Moreover, the Commission was not ostrich-like about another fact: privacy cannot be decreed. The best possible regulatory framework not only needs to support the self, but also leave enough room for free self-development in a free interplay within a shared world. Thus, any regulatory framework can never suffice on its own if overly restrictive consequences are to be avoided and if principles are to be safeguarded effectively. Hence, the free interplay also has to have the potential to develop rules by itself. The appreciation of this need is mirrored within

---

410 Ibid.

411 Which had already been introduced by Directive 95/48/EC.

412 COM (2010) 609 final.

the Communication insofar as the Commission "continues to consider that self-regulatory initiatives by data controllers can contribute to a better enforcement of data protection rules."[413]

Finally, the Communication also reflects on the strength of the fact that it represents a multinational approach which comprises different legal, historical and political backgrounds. As such it has served and can serve as a role-model for putting harmonization efforts on a global plane. Or in the words of the Communication: "The EU legal framework for data protection has often served as a benchmark for third countries when regulating data protection. Its effect and impact, within and outside the Union, have been of the utmost importance. The European Union must therefore remain a driving force behind the development and promotion of international legal and technical standards for the protection of personal data."[414]

5.9 Draft Regulation COM (2012) 11 final

Following this Communication and detailed criticism thereof,[415] on 25 January 2012 the European Parliament and the European Council published a Draft Regulation on the protection of individuals with regard to processing personal data and on the free movement of such data (General Data Protection Regulation).[416] If this Draft Regulation comes into force in its current version, it will represent the next major milestone in the quest for a common European regulatory framework for effective protection of the self's freedom to freely decide on what to reveal and conceal. The Draft once again affirms the fact that the fundamental rights of the self need to form the basis of any considerations, a fact which had also been repeatedly upheld by

413 Ibid.

414 Ibid.

415 Cf. Opinion of the European Data Protection Supervisor on the Communication from the Commission to the European Parliament, the Council, the Economic and Social Committee and the Committee of the Regions – A comprehensive approach on personal data protection in the European Union, Brussels 14 January 2011.

416 COM (2012) 11 final.

European Courts.[417] This objective is perfectly summarized by Recital 2 of the Draft Regulation which states that "The processing of personal data is designed to serve man; the principles and rules on the protection of individuals with regard to the processing of their personal data should, whatever the nationality or residence of natural persons, respect their fundamental rights and freedoms, notably their right to the protection of personal data."

Moreover, the Draft Regulation would also represent a landmark in the history of data protection due to several novelties that would be introduced were it to be enacted. First and foremost, the European Parliament and the Council decided to pass a Regulation and thus chose an instrument which would have immediate, direct effect in all of the member states and hence prevent any variations through national implementation. In addition, the Draft Regulation would constitute a huge step forward toward a more comprehensive approach to effective data protection, since many of the main points of criticism of Directive 95/48/EC would be resolved. Finally, the Draft Regulation would also stress the importance attached to the self's freedom to control what to reveal and conceal because reinforced rights would be paired with severe sanctions.

The Draft Regulation — like the Directives — provides for a very broad scope of applicability. Unfortunately, the very Article laying out this scope at the same time represents the main weakness of the Draft Regulation because it also allows for several, albeit enumerated, exceptions.[418] The most surprising exception among them probably is

---

417 Cf. e.g. Court of Justice of the EU, judgement dated 9.11.2010, Joined Cases C-92/09 and C-93/09 Volker und Markus Schecke and Eifert [2010] ECR I-0000.

418 Cf. Article 2 (2) "This Regulation does not apply to the processing of personal data:

(a) in the course of an activity which falls outside the scope of Union law, in particular concerning national security;

(b) by the Union institutions, bodies, offices and agencies;

(c) by the Member States when carrying out activities which fall within the scope of Chapter 2 of the Treaty on European Union;

the fact that while establishing strict rules, the European Union does not want to be bound by them itself. While the European Union cannot be regarded as the most dangerous data processor, this nevertheless qualifies the seriousness suggested by Article 1 of the Draft Regulation, namely to protect "the fundamental rights and freedoms of natural persons, and in particular their right to the protection of personal data". Such rights can only be seen as effective if they can be used as a defence against the law-maker as well.[419]

Nevertheless, the Draft Regulation still has to be applauded. Article 4 delineates an updated, finely tuned understanding of the term data-subject: "'data subject' means an identified natural person or a natural person who can be identified, directly or indirectly, by means reasonably likely to be used by the controller or by any other natural or legal person, in particular by reference to an identification number, location data, online identifier or to one or more factors specific to the physical, physiological, genetic, mental, economic, cultural or social identity of that person". Thus, in comparison to Directive 95/46/EC, the very technical developments and new means of collecting data and types of data collected which led to discussions over the past decade,[420] are considered and explicitly included.

In addition, the draft enshrines the very principles which have evolved since the first multinational approach to data protection was made which can be found in many regulatory bodies, most prominently the principle of fair and lawful processing, the principle of collection and purpose

---

(d) by a natural person without any gainful interest in the course of its own exclusively personal or household activity;
(e) by competent authorities for the purposes of prevention, investigation, detection or prosecution of criminal offences or the execution of criminal penalties."

419 Which arguably in this case does not have the power to impose severe or unjustified obligations on the subjects.

420 Cf. e.g. the discussion on whether IP addresses of the IPv4 protocol can be seen as personal data (cf. Nagel/Weimann March 2011). Online identifiers are now explicitly included.

limitation, the principle of data minimization as well as the principle of data quality, data security and accountability.[421]

Finally, the Draft Regulation contains a clarification of loopholes and amendments with respect to issues that have not been dealt with or not been as extensively provided for by its predecessors. Among them is the affirmation of the principle of consent,[422] the explicit enactment of a higher level of protection for children,[423] the principle of transparency and access,[424] a clarification of execution of a subject-access request,[425] the call for codes of conduct,[426] a clarification of secure and admissible

---

421 Cf. Article 5 of the Draft Regulation: "Personal data must be:

(a) processed lawfully, fairly and in a transparent manner in relation to the data subject;

(b) collected for specified, explicit and legitimate purposes and not further processed in a way incompatible with those purposes;

(c) adequate, relevant, and limited to the minimum necessary in relation to the purposes for which they are processed; they shall only be processed if, and as long as, the purposes could not be fulfilled by processing information that does not involve personal data;

(d) accurate and kept up to date; every reasonable step must be taken to ensure that personal data that are inaccurate, having regard to the purposes for which they are processed, are erased or rectified without delay;

(e) kept in a form which permits identification of data subjects for no longer than is necessary for the purposes for which the personal data are processed; personal data may be stored for longer periods insofar as the data will be processed solely for historical, statistical or scientific research purposes in accordance with the rules and conditions of Article 83 and if a periodic review is carried out to assess the necessity to continue the storage;

(f) processed under the responsibility and liability of the controller, who shall ensure and demonstrate for each processing operation the compliance with the provisions of this Regulation.

422 Cf. Article 7 of the Draft Regulation.

423 Cf. Article 8 of the Draft Regulation which provides that "the processing of personal data of a child below the age of 13 years shall only be lawful if and to the extent that consent is given or authorised by the child's parent or custodian".

424 Cf. Articles 11, 14 and 15 of the Draft Regulation.

425 With a uniform period of 1 month, cf. Article 12 of the Draft Regulation.

426 Cf. Article 38 in conjunction with 23, 30 and 33 of the Draft Regulation.

data transfer,[427] the extension of powers of supervisory authorities,[428] the setting up of a European Data Protection Board to ensure the consistent application of the Regulation,[429] severe sanctions for non-compliance[430] and the right to be forgotten.[431]

Despite the vast variety of rules, the Draft Regulation still can be seen as leaving sufficient space for selves to exercise their freedom of choice on what to reveal and to conceal by only marking out the area within which such choices are supported by legal buttresses and within which individual selves are given effective means of redress in case their freedom is unjustifiably violated by others. Consequently, if enacted, the Draft Regulation would represent a more elaborate basis for striking a balance between the freedom of the self and regulatory interferences and thus establish a more concise regulatory framework than any of its predecessors.

5.10 Conclusion — a watertight approach?

The European Convention for the Protection of Human Rights and Fundamental Freedoms, the International Covenant on Civil and Political Rights and the Council of Europe Resolutions on the protection of the privacy of individuals vis-à-vis electronic data banks in the private and public sector as well as the Convention for the Protection of

---

427 Cf. Articles 40 to 44 of the Draft Regulation.

428 Cf. Articles 46 et seq. of the Draft Regulation.

429 Cf. Articles 64 et seq. of the Draft Regulation.

430 Cf. Article 79 of the Draft Regulation.

431 Cf. Article 17 of the Draft Regulation, which, however, cannot live up to its ambivalent name (cf. the criticism by Javier Aparicio Salom, el derecho al olvido no existe ni debe existir, Expansión 6 June 2011, or Rosario G Goméz, 'Quiero que Internet se olvide de mì' *El País* 7 January 2011.) but nevertheless contains a remarkable approach since a controller is obliged upon request by a data-subject to "take all reasonable steps, including technical measures, in relation to data for the publication of which the controller is responsible, to inform third parties which are processing such data, that a data subject requests them to erase any links to, or copy or replication of those personal data. Where the controller has authorised a third party publication of personal data, the controller shall be considered responsible for that publication".

Individuals with regard to Automatic Processing of Personal Data all spread out a basic safety net for the self. Nevertheless, in particular, the exceptions woven in allowing for deviations and derogations show that not only the interests of the selves concerned (citizens living their private lives), but also strong economic interests as well as the interests of the contracting states to conserve power, including the power of taxation, were considered when the various principles were laid down. This can arguably be attributed also to the fact that all conventions and principles represent a compromise in the form of the lowest common denominator of sovereign states with different cultures, political interests, legal systems and history. Nevertheless, all of these states, especially the member states of the European Union, regard themselves as modern democracies based on the principle of freely self-determining citizens as the ultimate source of any legitimate state power.

When freedom is held to be a treasured, indispensable quality of social life, both individual freedom and the joint freedom of selves in interplay, irrespectively of viewing angle, need to be upheld and secured by legal instruments. Thus, a clear respect for free self-determination and not-unduly-influenced free decisions about what to reveal and what to conceal about one's personal, shared, private world need to be fostered and safeguarded.

The European Union has proclaimed such freedoms within its fundamental common principles of freedom, notably with respect to the free movement of goods, persons, services and capital.[432] The European Union further delineated this with respect to personal privacy in a landmark attempt to harmonize data protection, European Directive 95/46.[433] This directive (re)introduced another important principle, the so-called principle of consent.[434] If it had not been for several

432 Cf. the Treaty Establishing the European Community, Title I and Title III dated 25 March 1957.

433 Directive (EC) 95/46 of the European Parliament and of the Council dated 24 October 1995 on the protection of individuals with regard to the processing of personal data and on the free movement of such data [1995] OJ L281/31.

434 Cf. the Preamble "Whereas, in order to be lawful, the processing of personal data must in addition be carried out with the consent of the data subject" and

exceptions to this principle,[435] the focus finally would have shifted to the true starting-point for any protection, namely, people themselves, since any power to decide on privacy would have been vested in the hands of selves living their lives in mutual interplay. At least this directive no longer allows for justifying a limitation of privacy on the basis of vague rules, but clearly stipulates the only contexts within which a deviation is permissible. However, due to the indirect effect of a directive, it was only able to establish a very basic scheme and still contains major flaws,[436] in particular regarding a closer consideration of the self and the various contexts in which selves shape their own lives.[437]

In 2003 the European Union again showed its willingness to finally enshrine fundamental principles in a way that would have created inalienable fundamental rights for any citizen of the member states all over Europe by drafting a Charter of Fundamental Rights within a European Convention.[438] Unfortunately, the ratification of this

---

Article 7 "Member States shall provide that personal data may be processed only if: the data subject has unambiguously given his consent" of Directive (EC) 95/46.

435 Article 7 also allows for data collection in the case of necessity for the performance of a contract, for compliance with a legal obligations, to protect the vital interests of the data subject, for the performance of a task carried out in the public interest or in the exercise of official authority vested in the controller and also for the purposes of legitimate interests pursued by the controller or by a third party or parties, to whom the data are reasonably disclosed.

436 Cf. e.g. the leeway for individual member states to deviate from the principles laid out in Directive 95/46 and the problematic issue of an "equal level of protection" as a prerequisite for the transfer of data to non-EU states which, in conjunction with the Safe-Harbour Agreement, not only divided the world into good and bad from a data-protection perspective, but also received considerable criticism because a balanced realization of this conception proved to be extremely difficult.

437 Cf. Nagel 2011b.

438 Cf. in particular Chapter II of the Charter of Fundamental Rights (2000/C 364/01) which formulates the protection of individual freedoms as absolute rights without mentioning within the same Chapter any potential room to deviate.

Constitution also would have implied a loss of sovereign power for the individual members, wherefore in the end consensus proved to be impossible.

The 2009 Lisbon Treaty saved the Charter, albeit by giving it only the same status as the basic treaties, and not the legal force a Constitution would have had.[439] Nevertheless, the European quest to find the best way to protect the freedom and privacy of its citizens does not end here.[440] The Union tries to keep pace with technological developments, even if, due to continuing technological and other developments in the cyberworld, this might seem Sisyphean. The European Union still has to be encouraged and applauded — after all, it is the freedom of selves and thus our own freedom that is at stake.

---

[439] Cf. Article 6 of the Treaty of Lisbon amending the Treaty on European Union and the Treaty establishing the European Community, signed at Lisbon, 13 December 2007, 2007/C 306/01: "The Union recognises the rights, freedoms and principles set out in the Charter of Fundamental Rights of the European Union of 7 December 2000, as adapted at Strasbourg, on 12 December 2007, which shall have the same legal value as the Treaties."

[440] Cf. the draft of the Regulation of the European Parliament and of the Council on the protection of individuals with regard to the processing of personal data and on the free movement of such data (General Data Protection Regulation) of 25 January 2012, COM(2012) 11 final.

6 Brave new cyberworld

Michael Eldred

Brave new world,
That has such people in't!
Shakespeare *The Tempest* V. i.

6.1 What's coming

Our brave new cyberworld is still arriving historically, embellished and fitted with countless, still emerging digital technologies, each of which gives rise to new social phenomena, modified life-practices, new socio-political issues and contestations. The gamut of emerging digital technologies is bewildering and has long since outstripped the phenomenon, internet, be it 2.0 or a later version. The technologies include ubiquitous, ambient computing, artificial intelligence in robots and countless other devices, things implanted with chips embedding them in the cyberworld thus enabling constant signalling among devices, digital 'enhancements' for human beings via implanted chips, new varieties of online social networks[441] enabling all sorts of messaging, new ways of doing both wholesale and retail commerce, etc. etc. Even an entirely new arena for human warfare opens up in the cyberworld: cyber-warfare, and strategy planners are well under way considering how to attack and defend through the digitized medium of the cyberworld.

For instance, a well-known business magazine describes things settling in at home in the cyberworld as follows:

> Thanks to advances in sensor technology and data analytics, the world's basic systems are becoming intelligent. At any given time, 7 billion devices are communicating with one another worldwide, according to IDC. Sensors are

[441] Cf. the online social networks option document of the acatech project, *A Culture of Privacy and Trust for the Internet* 2011-2013.

embedded in roadways, power grids, irrigation systems, household appliances, and even clothes, feeding a flood of data that can help smooth traffic flow, conserve resources, and improve health care delivery, among others.[442]

Apart from any other issues, such as surveillance and control, each of these technologies is two-edged: each is promoted as a new convenience for living well, whilst at the same time wiring[443] each of us into the cyberworld, ensnaring us more and more in its ever-further-spun digital web that we can no longer do without.

It would be sheer folly to attempt to take up any of these issues in detail in the concluding chapter, each of which requires also detailed empirical data for an informed discussion.[444] Instead, here is the place to show why it has been profitable to have 'taken the long way round' in developing, step by step, a theoretical foundation for approaching the cyberworld in connection with the phenomena of privacy and freedom. As this study has underscored, discussions in information ethics hitherto have invariably skipped over the phenomenon of the world, and hence also that of the cyberworld. In so doing, presuppositions have crept in that distort the view of the phenomena in question, thus giving rise to spurious conceptions, issues and remedies. One such presupposition is to assume that the world is populated by autonomous subjects interacting more or less freely with each other. A more careful look at whoness aims at disabusing us of this prejudice (cf. Chapter 3).

To finish, here is a sketch of how to approach one option for existing that has emerged and is quickly developing and ramifying as the cyberworld grows: e-commerce. As an approach, this may allow further discussion on issues surrounding e-commerce, especially in relation to personal privacy and its latent conflict with the striving to earn profits by private enterprise, to be situated under a larger sky and with a compass taking its bearings from the most elementary, all-encompassing phenomena.

---

442 Fortune 2012

443 Zabala' 2012.

444 Cf. ETICA http://ethics.ccsr.cse.dmu.ac.uk/etica and ETHICOBTS http://ethicbots.na.infn.it/index.php

6.2 e-Commerce[445]

The *cyberworld*, which is more comprehensive than the internet and comprises all the electromagnetic media through which bit-strings circulate, is an artificial world that opens up a digitized space also for a worldwide agora, i.e. a global market-place. The ancient Greek agora, which was place of assembly, meeting-place and market-place, is thus transformed in today's era of the digital cast of being into a digitized parallel world (cf. *2.5 The parallel cyberworld that fits like a glove*) in sync with the wider world. *E-commerce* is the name adopted for the gainful exchange of goods and services in this technologically enabled, digitized market-place that manifests many, indeed most, phenomena analogous to the parallel physical world in which we human beings have lived hitherto, 'pre-Turing'. The digitized dimension of the cyberworld serves as an artificial place where 'merchandise meets', i.e. commercium is done. Who we are, our very identities, become bit-strings circulating through the cyberworld (cf. *3.1 Digital identity - a number?*) via whose mediation we can partake online in the gainful game of capitalism (cf. *1.6 The private individual and private property as a mode of reified sociation: the gainful game (classical political economy, Marx)*) and, in particular, in e-commerce. E-commerce in the narrower sense comprises only a segment of the *e-economy* embedded in the cyberworld, namely, all kinds of transactions with *end-consumers*. A globally connected, digitized market-place offers opportunities for players, large, medium and small, to engage in income-earning on a scale and with an easy accessibility and cheapness hitherto unknown. A worldwide arena is opened for economically engaged players to offer their powers and abilities to each other on a mutually beneficial basis. The interplay among players estimating, and thus *valuing*, each other's powers is digitally enabled on an extended, global plane.

In particular, as a powerful, immensely versatile technological product, the cyberworld provides entrepreneurial players, i.e. enterprises, with the opportunity for massive cost-reductions in all sorts

---

[445] Cf. the e-commerce option document of the acatech project, *A Culture of Privacy and Trust for the Internet* 2011-2013.

of ways, especially through automating production and circulation processes, and also for increasing the rate of turnover of capital, and thus profits. This is achieved especially by facilitating communications with employees, customers, suppliers, but also by unleashing productive potentials of all kinds of digital technologies that can be embedded in or linked to the cyberworld (e.g. telematics).

At the same time, all the dangers of conventional market-places 'naturally' find their cyberworld analogues such as *cybertheft* and *cyberfraud*, but also unfair market practices of all kinds, including in particular monopolistic and oligopolistic market-plays, which could be called *cybercheating*. Apart from that, the reified form of sociation (cf. *1.6 The private individual and private property as a mode of reified sociation: the gainful game (classical political economy, Marx)*) among market-players that characterizes any market economy assumes now the *digitally reified* guise of circulating bit-strings. Trading on the *global cybermarket* requires transactions to be conducted likewise via an exchange of bit-strings, so that money as means of payment itself becomes a bit-string that as a store of value must be jealously guarded by means of encryption techniques and digitized security measures. Because of the quantitative nature of money, digitized money and cyberbanks are quite a natural offspring of the cyberworld, and programmers have already been very inventive in developing safe and easy digitized payment methods. However, although money in its functions as means of payment and store of value has been digitized without resistance (in units of national, or supranational, currency), digitized money as a denationalized[446] measure of value and alternative to state fiat money runs up against the stiff opposition of (supra-)national state power.

Because the global cybermarket offers the opportunity of (both honest and dishonest, fair and unfair, including especially monopolistic and oligopolistic) gain, there has been a powerful, ineluctable incentive to

[446] Cf. e.g. Hayek 1976 and the European R&D project, SEMPER (Secure Electronic Marketplace for Europe), at http://www.semper.org/ accessed June 2012.

drive, with copious inventiveness, the development of e-commerce, as the consumer-oriented segment of e-economy, into every imaginable area of business-to-consumer and even consumer-to-consumer commercial interplay (say, on auction web-sites). Commodity products bought and sold on the cybermarket may be from the physical world, or they may themselves consist entirely of bit-strings. A peculiarity of digital products is that their reproduction is extremely cheap compared to any normal physical products; they can be easily 'ripped off'. As a commodity, a digital product is a *reified value* worth such-and-such in monetary terms on the market. Since the reproduction of a digital product is efficient and cheap, this increase in productivity expresses itself first of all in consumer-friendly, lower market-prices. Secondly, the cheap reproducibility of digital products means that the enterprises producing them have the strategy of scaling up production to maximum mass-market proportions. Thirdly, however, a massive problem of wrongful reproduction, and thus cybertheft, of digital products arises. Since all executable program code (software) represents an outsourcing of human intelligence, and furthermore many intellectual products such as text, music and film naturally put on a digital garb, cybertheft of intellectual property calls for modified conceptions of private property and legal measures to redefine and protect it, with some even proclaiming that digital intellectual property makes no sense.[447] In particular, since the cybermarket is global, but e-commerce is naturally often cross-border, this circumstance requires other kinds of legislation and international legal treaties and practices to ensure lawful cyber-trading and to fight commercial cybercrime.

With specific regard to *personal privacy* there is firstly the issue that digital data about private persons are a valuable source for firms' (targeted) advertising techniques and strategies, with all the attendant dangers of manipulating consumers and overstepping the line into individuals' private lives. For the sake of gain, many firms have an unhealthy interest in their customers' private circumstances, as reflected in personal digital data available somewhere in the cyberworld. The

[447] Cf. Coy 2007.

freedom of private selves to reveal or conceal who they are is threatened when digital data relating to them are gathered and cybernetically mined with an eye to gain. *Consumer trust* is thus undermined by e-businesses regarding private persons simply *as* e-consumers to whom as much as possible is to be sold. Moreover, the global, cross-border nature of e-commerce and the inventiveness of programmers open up opportunities for hoodwinking private consumers in hitherto unheard-of ways, so that companies have a further interest in *engendering trust* with consumers for them to be confident in being able to transact business safely online. *Corporate reputation* for trustworthiness and reliability become even more important for conducting consumer business via the cyberworld.

Moreover, the very digital technologies that enable increases in labour productivity, especially through digitized communication, also promote a tendency to encourage all players engaged in the gainful game to let themselves become the appendages of their digital devices. In order not to miss a business opportunity, a manager or executive may maintain digital contactability twenty-four hours a day. Or employees may find it very difficult to draw a line to their employers' demands outside contractual working hours. E-economy in this broad sense of playing the gainful game globally through the medium of the cyberworld thus has a tendency to erode freely determined private life-worlds in new, digital ways for the sake of commercial gain's Siren calls. The global e-economy practised via the cyberworld of circulating bit-strings encourages and furthers on an even greater scale than hitherto the augmentative movement of reified value as capital. Global flows of money-capital (investment capital as well as the money-capital phases of the movement of individual capitals) themselves are digitized, thus facilitating their frictionless movement. The acceleration of the movement and turnover of total global capital hits back at all the players engaged in the total global gainful game, accelerating their life-movements, too, and eroding their lives' privacy.

We are thus confronted with issues of human freedom that, at first glance in this strange, new, cleverly digitized world, are scarcely recognizable as such.

6.3 Forgetfulness

If this were one of Seneca's letters to Lucilius, there would now come an interjection from Lucilius to Seneca's train of thought, "Quod ergo?" — "So what?" For those committed to grappling with the 'real issues' arising from the internet age, 'taking the long way round' seems like a useless detour, antithetical to any pragmatic solutions. Why is it important to have in mind such things as the cyberworld embedded in the world, the three-dimensional temporal clearing in which all beings present and absent themselves, the distinction between whoness and whatness, the digital cast of being, the evaluating, estimating interplay among humans and things, privacy conceived as the interplay in which we reveal and conceal to each other who we are, etc.? What this study "really offers is a potentiality to be a match for the cyberworld, and that is only possible on the basis of a cast of being which does not exclude the digital cast of being, but shows up its limitations. And this, in turn, can only be achieved if the horizon of being, i.e. the question concerning the meaning of being, is kept open. The latter has always been and still is difficult because we human beings are always strongly oriented toward security — to the detriment of freedom".[448]

[448] Rafael Capurro, personal communication 02 August 2012, my translation.

7 Bibliography

Adams et al. 2009

Adams, Andrew, Kiyoshi Murata & Yohko Orito 'The Japanese Sense of Information Privacy' in *AI & Society* Vol. 24 2009 pp. 327-341. URL: http://www.springerlink.com/content/708886t6482g3v62/fulltext.pdf

Adams et al. 2011

Adams, Andrew, Kiyoshi Murata, Yohko Orito and Pat Parslow 'Emerging Social Norms in the UK and Japan on Privacy and Revelation in SNS' in *International Review of Information Ethics* Vol. 16 2011.

Altman 1975

Altman, Irwin *The Environment and Social Behavior: Privacy, Personal Space, Territory,· Crowding* Monterey Ca.: Brooks/Cole 1975.

Ariès & Duby 1985/1989

Ariès, Philippe & Georges Duby (eds.) *Geschichte des privaten Lebens* (ed.) Paul Veyne, translated by Holger Fliessbach 3rd ed. Hamburg: Fischer 1989 (original: *Histoire de la vie privée* Paris: Seuil 1985). I. Band *Vom Römischen Imperium zum Byzantinischen Reich.*

Aristotle *Met.*

Aristotle *Metaphysics* in *Works in Twenty-Three Volumes* Vols. XVII & XVIII Loeb Classical Library, London: Harvard U.P. and W. Heinemann 1938ff.

Aristotle *Eth. Nic.*

Aristotle *Nicomachean Ethics* in *Works* Vol. XIX.

Aristotle *Phys.*

Aristotle *Physics* in *Works* Vols. IV and V.

Aristotle *Pol.*

Aristotle *Politics* in *Works* Vol. XXI.

Arendt 1958/1998

Arendt, Hannah *The Human Condition* 2nd ed. with an introduction by Margaret Canovan, Chicago U.P. 1998, 1st ed. 1958.

Augustine Confessiones

Augustine *Confessiones*, many editions.

Baasch-Andersen 2011

Baasch-Andersen, Camilla 'Noblesse Oblige ...? Revisiting the Noble Month and the Expectations and Accomplishments it has prompted' *Festschrift for Ingeborg Schwenzer Private Law national — global — comparative* Bd. I & II, XXIII Bern: Stämpfli Verlag AG 2011.

Barrán et al. 1996
Barrán, José Pedro, Gerardo Caetano & Teresa Porzecanski (eds.) *Historias de la vida privada en el Uruguay* Montevideo: Taurus 1996ff.

Beavers 2002
Beavers, Anthony F. 'Phenomenology and Artificial Intelligence' in *CyberPhilosophy: The Intersection of Philosophy and Computing* James H. Moor and Terrell Ward Bynum (eds) Oxford: Blackwell 2002 pp. 66-77. Also in *Metaphilosophy* Vol. 33.1/2 2002 pp. 70-82.

Bernstein et al. 2009
Bernstein, Daniel J., Johannes Buchmann & Erik Dahmen (eds) *Post-Quantum Cryptography* Berlin/Heidelberg: Springer 2009.

Bhabha 2007
Bhabha, Homi K. 'Ética e Estética do Globalismo: Uma Perspectiva Pós-Colonial' in Fundaçao Calouste Bulbenkian and Fórum Cultural O Estado do Mundo (eds.) *A Urgência da Teoria* Lisboa: Ed. Tinta-da-china 2007 pp. 21-44.

Bien 1985
Bien, Günther *Die Grundlegung der politischen Philosophie bei Aristoteles* Freiburg: Karl Alber Verlag, 1985.

Borgmann 1999
Borgmann, A. *Holding On to Reality* Chicago/London: University of Chicago Press 1999.

Brannigan 2005
Brannigan, Michael C. *Ethics Accross Cultures with PowerWeb Ethics* New York: McGraw-Hill 2005.

Brey 2007
Brey, Philip 'Global Information Ethics and the Challenge of Cultural Relativism' in *European regional Conference on the ethical dimensions of the information society* 2007. URL: http://portal.unesco.org/ci/en/ev.php-URL_ID=25455&URL_DO=DO_TOPIC&URL_SECTION=201.html

Broodryk 2002
Broodryk, Johann *Ubuntu: Life lessons from Africa* Ubuntu School of Philosophy, Pretoria 2nd ed. 2002.

Capurro 1978
Capurro, Rafael *Information: Ein Beitrag zur etymologischen und ideengeschichtlichen Begründung des Informationsbegriffs* Munich: Saur 1978. URL: www.capurro.de/info.html

Capurro 1986
Capurro, Rafael *Hermeneutik der Fachinformation* Freiburg: Karl Alber Verlag 1986.

Capurro 1987
Capurro, Rafael 'Die Informatik und das hermeneutische Forschungsprogram' *Informatik Spektrum* Vol. 10 pp. 329-333 1987 URL: www.capurro.de/winograd.htm
Capurro 1992
Capurro, Rafael 'Informatics and Hermeneutics' in Christiane Floyd, Heinz Züllighoven, Reinhard Budde, Reinhard Keil-Slawik (eds.) *Software Development and Reality Construction* Berlin: Springer Verlag 1992 pp. 363-375. URL: www.capurro.de/floyd.htm
Capurro 1995
Capurro, Rafael *Leben im Informationszeitalter* Berlin: Akademie Verlag 1995.
Capurro 2001
Capurro, Rafael 'Beiträge zu einer digitalen Ontologie' 2001 URL: www.capurro.de
Capurro 2003
Capurro, Rafael 'Medien (R-)Evolutionen. Platon, Kant und der Cyberspace' in ibid. *Ethik im Netz* Stuttgart: Franz Steiner Verlag 2003 pp. 182-197. URL: www.capurro.de/leipzig.htm
Capurro 2005
Capurro, Rafael 'Privacy: An intercultural perspective' *Ethics and Information Technology* Vol. 7 2005 pp. 37-47. URL: www.capurro.de/privacy.html .
Capurro 2005a
Capurro, Rafael 'Passions of the internet' in Wolfgang Palaver and Petra Steinmair-Pösel (eds.) *Passions in Economy, Politics, and the Media. In Discussion with Christian Theology* Vienna: Lit Verlag 2005 pp. 331-343. URL: www.capurro.de/passions.html
Capurro 2006
Capurro, Rafael 'Hermeneutik revisited' in Pellegrini & Blumauer 2006 pp. 527-533.
Capurro 2007
Capurro, Rafael 'Information Ethics for and from Africa' in *International Review of Information Ethics* Vol.7 2007. URL: www.i-r-i-e.net/inhalt/007/01-capurro.pdf
Capurro 2008
Capurro, Rafael 'Intercultural Information Ethics' in Kenneth E. Himma and Herman T. Tavani (eds.) *The Handbook of Information and Computer Ethics* New Jersey: Wiley 2008 pp. 639-665. URL: www.capurro.de/iiebangkok.html
Capurro 2008a
Capurro, Rafael 'Interpreting the Digital Human' in Elizabeth Buchanan and Carolyn Hansen (eds.) *Thinking Critically: Alternative Methods and Perspectives in Library and Information Studies* Center for Information Policy Research,

School of Information Studies, University of Wisconsin-Milwaukee 2008 pp. 190-220. URL: www.capurro.de/wisconsin.html

Capurro 2009

Capurro, Rafael 'Etica intercultural de la información' in Henriette Ferreira Gomes, Aldinar Martins Bottentuit, Maria Odaisa Espinheiro de Olivera (eds.) *A ética na sociedade, na área da informação e da atuação profissional* Brasilia DF, Conselho Federal de Biblioteconomia 2009 pp. 43-64. URL: www.capurro.de/reforma.html

Capurro 2009a

Capurro, Rafael 'Ethik der Informationsgesellschaft. Ein interkultureller Versuch' *Jahrbuch Deutsch als Fremdsprache — Intercultural German Studies* Bd. 35 Munich: iudicium Verlag 2009 pp. 178-193. URL: www.capurro.de/parrhesia.html

Capurro 2010

Capurro, Rafael *Desafíos teóricos y prácticos de la ética intercultural de la información.* Keynote at the first Brazilian conference on Information Ethics, João Pessoa, Brazil 2010. URL: www.capurro.de/paraiba.html

Capurro 2010a

Capurro, Rafael *Information Ethics in Africa. Past, Present and Future Activities (2007-2010)* 2010. URL: www.capurro.de/wsis2010_africa_infoethics.html

Capurro 2010/2011

Capurro, Rafael *The Dao of the Information Society in China and the Task of Intercultural Information Ethics*. Beijing 2010 (Chinese translation by Julan Liang in *Social Sciences Abroad* 2011). URL: www.capurro.de/china_infoethics2010.html

Capurro 2011

Capurro, Rafael 'Never Enter Your Real Data' *International Review of Information Ethics* Vol. 16 2011 pp. 74-78. URL: www.capurro.de/realdata.html .

Capurro 2012

Capurro, Rafael *Ethical Issues of Online Social Networks in Africa* URL: www.capurro.de/OSNAfrica2012.html 2012

Capurro, Eldred & Nagel 2012

Capurro, Rafael, Michael Eldred & Daniel Nagel 'IT and Privacy from an Ethical Perspective — Digital Whoness: Identity, Privacy and Freedom in the Cyberworld' in Buchmann, Johannes (ed.) *Internet Privacy - Eine multidisziplinäre Bestandsaufnahme/A Multidisciplinary Analysis* Berlin: Springer 2012 pp. 63-141 (abridged version of the present book).

Capurro et al. 2007

Capurro, Rafael, Johannes Frühbauer & Thomas Hausmanninger (eds.) *Localizing the Internet. Ethical aspects in intercultural perspective* Munich: Fink 2007.

Capurro & Holgate 2011

Capurro, Rafael & John Holgate (eds.) *Messages and Messengers. Angeletics as an Approach to the Phenomenology of Communication* Munich: Fink 2011.

Capurro & Nakada 2009

Capurro, Rafael & Makoto Nakada 'The Public / Private Debate. A Contribution of Intercultural Information Ethics' in Rocci Luppicini und Rebecca Adell (eds.) *Handbook of Research in Technoethics* Hershey NY, Information Science Reference 2 Vols. 2009, Vol. 1 pp. 339-353. URL: www.capurro.de/iie_dialogue.html

Capurro & Pingel 2002

Capurro, Rafael & Christoph Pingel 'Ethical Issues of Online Communication Research' *Ethics and Information Technology* Vol 4 2002 pp. 189-194. URL: www.capurro.de/onres.html

Chalmers 2009

Chalmers, David J. 'Ontological Anti-Realism' in *Metametaphysics: New Essays on the Foundations of Ontology* Oxford: Clarendon Press 2009. http://consc.net/papers/ontology.pdf

***Chinese/English Four Books* 1992**

The Chinese/English Four Books translated by James Legge, revised and annotated by Liu Zhongde & Luo Zhiye, Changsha Hunan Press 1992.

Cicerchia 1998

Cicerchia, Ricardo *Historia de la vida privada en la Argentina* Buenos Aires: Troquel 1998.

Cooley 1888

Cooley, Thomas M. *Cooley On Torts* 29 (1st ed. 1888), quoted in http://cyber.law.harvard. edu/privacy/Gormley--100%20Years%20of%20Privacy--%20EXCERPTS.htm accessed August 2011.

Coy 2007

Coy, Wolfgang 'Sharing ideas and expressions in global communities' in R. Capurro et al. (eds.) *Localizing the Internet* Munich: Fink 2007 pp. 279-288.

Coyne 1995

Coyne, R. *Designing information technology in the postmodern age: From method to metaphor* Cambridge MA: MIT Press 1995.

Del Duca et al. 2008

Del Duca, Louis, Albert Kritzer & Daniel Nagel 'Achieving optimal use of harmonization techniques in an increasingly interrelated 21st century world — consumer sales: moving the EU harmonization process to a global plane' *UCCLJ* 2008 pp. 51-65.

Descartes 1996
Descartes, René *Regulae ad Directionem Ingenii* in *Philosophische Schriften* Meiner, Hamburg, 1996.
Devoto & Madero 1999
Devoto, Fernando & Marta Madero *Historia de la vida privada en la Argentina* Buenos Aires: Taurus 1999.
Dreyfus 2001
Dreyfus, Hubert L. *On the Internet* London: Routledge. 2001.
Dürmaier 2008
Dürmaier, Ana Thereza 'Ética Intercultural da Informação e Sustentabilidade' in *Revista de Filosofia* Vol. 5, 9 2008 pp. 107-127. URL: http://www.uece.br/kalagatos/dmdocuments/V5N9_etica_intercultural_sustentabilidade.pdf
Eboh 2004
Eboh, Simeon Onyewueke *African Communalism. The Way to Social Harmony and Peaceful Co-Existence* Vol. 3 Onuganotu Lectures, Frankfurt: IKO Verlag für interkulturelle Kommunikation 2004.
Eldred 1984/2010
Eldred, Michael *Critique of Competitive Freedom and the Bourgeois-Democratic State: Outline of a Form-Analytic Extension of Marx's Uncompleted System* Copenhagen: Kurasje 1984, e-book edition www.arte-fact.org 2010. With an extensive bibliography.
Eldred 1996/2002
Eldred, Michael 'As: A Critical Note on David Farrell Krell's *Daimon Life*' www.arte-fact.org 1996/2002.
Eldred 1997/2010
Eldred, Michael *Worldsharing and Encounter: Heidegger's Ontology and Lévinas' Ethics* www.arte-fact.org Ver. 1.0 1997, Ver. 3.0 2010.
Eldred 1999
Eldred, Michael *Phänomenologie der Männlichkeit* Dettelbach: Röll 1999.
Eldred 2000/2010
Eldred, Michael *Kapital und Technik: Marx und Heidegger* Dettelbach: Röll 2000; english version in *Left Curve* No. 24, May 2000; www.arte-fact.org Ver. 3.0 2010.
Eldred 2008/2011
Eldred, Michael *Social Ontology: Recasting Political Philosophy Through a Phenomenology of Whoness* Frankfurt: ontos 2008; 2nd emended, revised, extended e-book edition, www.arte-fact.org 2011. With an extensive bibliography.

Eldred 2009

Eldred, Michael 'Anglophone Justice Theory, the Gainful Game and the Political Power Play' www.arte-fact.org Ver. 1.0 2009; also in Eldred 2008/2011.

Eldred 2009a

Eldred, Michael 'Critiquing Feenberg on Heidegger's Aristotle and the Question Concerning Technology' www.arte-fact.org Ver. 1.0 2009.

Eldred 2009/2011

Eldred, Michael *The Digital Cast of Being: Metaphysics, Mathematics, Cartesianism, Cybernetics, Capitalism, Communication* ontos, Frankfurt 2009; emended, revised, extended e-book edition at www.arte-fact.org Ver. 3.0 2011. With an extensive bibliography.

Eldred 2010

Eldred, Michael 'Values, social and beyond' in *Indigo - Humanities Magazine for Young People* Vol. 3 Busan, South Korea 2010 pp. 34-45. URL: www.arte-fact.org

Eldred 2011a

Eldred, Michael *The Time of History: Hegel, Heidegger, Derrida, Marx* www.arte-fact.org Ver. 1.0 2011.

Eldred 2011b

Eldred, Michael 'Circulating Messages to Every Body and No Body' in *Messages and Messengers: Angeletics as an Approach to the Phenomenology of Communication* Rafael Capurro & John Holgate (eds.) Paderborn: Fink 2011 pp. 113-123.

Eldred 2012

Eldred, Michael *Out of your mind? Parmenides' message* www.arte-fact.org Ver. 1.0 2012.

Eldred 2012a

Eldred, Michael 'Turing's cyberworld of timelessly copulating bit-strings' www.arte-fact.org Ver. 1.0 2012

Ess 2005

Ess, Charles 'Lost in translation? Intercultural dialogues on privacy and information ethics. Introduction to special issue on Privacy and Data Privacy Protection in Asia' in *Ethics and Information Technology* Vol. 7 2005 pp. 1-6.

Ess 2006

Ess, Charles 'Ethical pluralism and global information Ethics' in *Ethics and Information Technology* Vol. 8 2006 pp. 215-226.

Ess 2008

Ess, Charles 'Culture and Global Networks. Hope for a Global Ethics?' in Jeroen van den Hoven and John Weckert (eds.) *Information Technology and Moral Philosophy* Cambridge U.P. 2008 pp. 195-225.

Ess 2009

Ess, Charles 'Floridi's Philosophy of Information and Information Ethics: Current Perspectives, Future Directions' in *The Information Society* Vol. 25 2009 pp. 159—168.

Ess 2010

Ess, Charles *Digital Media Ethics*. Malden MA: Polity Press 2010.

Ess 2012

Ess, Charles 'Digital Media Ethics and Philosophy in 21st Century Information Society' paper presented to *Critique, Democracy, and Philosophy in 21st Century Information Society* Uppsala University, 2-4 May 2012 (http://www.icts-and-society.net/wp-content/uploads/2011/12/abstracts.pdf accessed December 2011).

Feenberg 1999

Feenberg, Andrew 'Technology and Meaning' in *Questioning Technology* London and New York: Routledge 1999 pp. 183—199.

Fink 2010

Fink, Eugen *Spiel als Weltsymbol* Cathrin Nielsen & Hans Rainer Sepp (eds.) Freiburg/Munich: Alber Verlag 2010.

Floridi 1999

Floridi, Luciano *Philosophy and Computing: An Introduction* New York: Routledge 1999.

Floridi 2006

Floridi, Luciano 'Four challenges for a theory of informational privacy' in *Ethics and Information Technology* 8(3) 2006 pp. 109—119. Accessed August 2011 at http://www.philosophyofinformation.net/

Floridi 2006a

Floridi 'The ontological interpretation of informational privacy' *Ethics and Information Technology* 8(3) 2006 pp. 1—16. Accessed August 2011 at http://www.philosophyofinformation.net/Articles.html

Floridi 2008

Floridi, Luciano 'Information ethics: A reappraisal' in *Ethics and Information Technology* 10(2—3) 2008 pp. 189—204.

Floridi 2012

Floridi, Luciano 'The informational nature of personal identity' in *Minds & Machines* 2012. Accessed August 2011 at http://www.philosophyofinformation.net/Articles.html

Fortune 2012

Fortune Magazine 'Devices talking 24/7' 23 July 2012 http://money.cnn.com/galleries/2012/news/companies/1207/gallery.global-500-future.fortune/2.html

Foucault 1988
Foucault, Michel *Technologies of the Self. A Seminar with Michel Foucault.*L. H. Martin, H. Gutman, P. H. Hutton (ed.) University of Massachusetts Press 1988.
Freire 2010
Freire, Gustavo Henrique de Araujo (ed.) *Ética da informação. Conceitos — Abordagens — Aplicações* João Pessoa 2010. URL: http://ru.ffyl.unam.mx:8080/bitstream/10391/1328/1/teaching%20information%20ethics.pdf
Fuchs 2011
Fuchs, Christian. 'Towards an Alternative Concept of Privacy' in *Journal of Information, Communication and Ethics in Society* Vol. 9 (4), 2011 pp. 220—237.
Fuchs & Mosco 2012
Fuchs, Christian & Mosco, Vincent (eds.) *Marx is Back: The Importance of Marxist Theory and Research for Critical Communication Studies Today* in *tripleC* 10(2) 2012.
Fuchs 2009
Fuchs, Thomas *Das Gehirn — ein Beziehungsorgan. Eine phänomenologisch-ökologische Konzeption* 2nd ed. Stuttgart: Kohlhammer 2009.
Ganascia 2009
Ganascia, J.-G. 'The Great Catopticon' in *Proceedings of the 8th International Conference of Computer Ethics Philosophical Enquiry (CEPE)* 26-28 June 2009, Corfu, Greece.
Gavison 1980
Gavison, Ruth 'Privacy and the Limits of the Law' in *Yale Law Journal* No. 89 1980 pp. 421-471.
Giracca 2008
Giracca, Anabella 'El acceso a la información en países culturalmente diversos' in *Primera conferencia regional, latinoamericana y del Caribe sobre infoética en el ciberespacio* Santo Domingo, Ed. Funglode 2008 pp. 79-87. URL: http://www.redciberetica.org/documentos?func=startdown&id=%201
Gonzalbo 2004
Gonzalbo, Pilar (ed.) *Historia de la vida cotidiana en México* México: FCE-Colmex 2004ff.
Greenleaf 2012
Greenleaf, Graham 'The influence of European data privacy standards outside Europe: Implications for globalisation of Convention 108?' *Research Paper Series* No. 2012/12.

Grimm 1857
Grimm, Jacob & Wilhelm 'The Hare and the Hedgehog'/'Der Hase und der Igel' *Kinder- und Hausmärchen* (Children's and Household Tales – Grimms' Fairy-Tales) 7th ed. Berlin 1857) no. 187.

Habermas 1962/1990
Habermas, Jürgen *Strukturwandel der Öffentlichkeit* Frankfurt/M.: Suhrkamp 1962/1990).

Habermas 1995
Habermas, Jürgen 'Kants Idee des Ewigen Friedens. Aus dem historischen Abstand von 200 Jahren' in *Information Philosophie* 5, Dezember 1995 pp. 5-19. 1995.

Hauptman & Soffer 2011
Hauptman, Aharon Yair Sharan & Tal Soffer 'Privacy Perception in the ICT era and beyond' in von Schomberg 2011.

Hayek 1976
Hayek, Friedrich A. *Denationalisation of Money* London: Institute of Economic Affairs 1976.

Hegel RPh. 1970
Hegel, G.W.F. *Rechtsphilosophie* in *Werke* Bd. 7 Frankfurt/M.: Suhrkamp 1970.

Hegel VGPII 1971
Hegel, G.W.F. *Vorlesungen über die Geschichte der Philosophie* II *Werke* Band 19 Frankfurt/M.: Suhrkamp1971.

Heidegger SZ 1927
Heidegger, Martin *Sein und Zeit* Tübingen: Niemeyer 1927, 15th ed. 1984.

Heidegger GA24
Heidegger, Martin *Die Grundprobleme der Phänomenologie* Marburger Vorlesung SS 1927 *Gesamtausgabe* Band 24 (GA24) ed. F-W. v. Herrmann, Frankfurt/M.: Klostermann 1975 English translation: *The Basic Problems of Phenomenology* Indiana U.P. 1982.

Heim 1993
Heim, M. *The Metaphysics of Virtual Reality* New York/Oxford: Oxford U.P. 1993.

Hobbes 1651/1997
Hobbes, Thomas *Leviathan* (1651) eds. Richard E. Flathman and David Johnston, New York/London: Norton1997.

Höffe 1997
Höffe, Ottfried entry on Gerechtigkeit in *Lexikon der Ethik* Munich: Beck 1997.

Höffe 1989
Höffe, Ottfried 'Rechtsordnung als gerechter Tausch' in *Universitas* 1/1989 pp. 11-17.

Hongladarom 2007
Hongladarom, Soraj 'Analysis and Justification of Privacy from a Buddhist Perspective' in Hongladarom and Ess 2007 pp. 108-122.
Hongladarom & Ess 2007
Hongladarom, Soraj and Charles Ess (eds.) *Information Technology Ethics. Cultural Perspectives* Hershey PA, Idea Group Reference 2007.
Huizinga 1939/2004
Huizinga, Johan *Homo ludens. Versuch einer Bestimmung des Spielelements der Kultur Brave* Amsterdam 1939, Hamburg 2004 19th ed.
Huxley 1932
Huxley, Aldous *Brave New World* 1932, London: Folio Society edition 1971.
Ihde 2002
Ihde, Donald *Bodies in Technology* Minneapolis: University of Minnesota Press.2002.
Introna 1997
Introna, Lucas 'On Cyberspace and Being: Identity, Self and Hyperreality' *Philosophy in the Contemporary World* 1997 4(1&2) pp. 16—25.
Introna 2011
Introna, Lucas 'Phenomenological Approaches to Ethics and Information Technology' *The Stanford Encyclopedia of Philosophy* (Summer 2011 Edition) Edward N. Zalta (ed.), URL:
http://plato.stanford.edu/archives/sum2011/entries/ethics-it-phenomenology/
Introna & Nissenbaum 2000
Introna, Lucas & H. Nissenbaum 'The Internet as a Democratic Medium: Why the politics of search engines matters' *Information Society* 2000 16(3) pp. 169—185.
James 1890/1950
James, William *The Principles of Psychology* Vol. 1 1890 Mineola NY: Dover 1950 esp. Chapter X 'The Consciousness of Self'.
Jullien 1995
Jullien, François *Le détour et l'accès. Stratégies du sens en Chine, en Grèce* Paris: Presses Universitaires de France 1995.
Jullien 2008
Jullien, François *De l'universel, de l'uniforme, du commun et du dialogue entres les cultures*. Paris, Fayard 2008.
Kant 1781/1787
Kant *Kritik der reinen Vernunft* 1781/1787 *Werke* Bd. 2 Darmstadt: Wiss. Buchges. 1983.
Kant 1974
Kant, Immanuel 'Grundlegung zur Metaphysik der Sitten' in *Kritik der praktischen Vernunft* Frankfurt am Main: Suhrkamp 1974.

Kant 1974a
Kant, Immanuel *Kritik der praktischen Vernunft* Frankfurt/M.: Suhrkamp 1974a.
Kant 1975
Kant, Immanuel 'Beantwortung der Frage: Was ist Aufklärung?' in *Schriften zur Anthropologie, Geschichtsphilosophie, Politik und Pädagogik* Zweiter Teil, Darmstadt: Wiss. Buchges. 1975.
Kant 1975a
Kant, Immanuel 'Was heißt: sich im Denken orientieren?' in *Schriften zur Metaphysik und Logik* Darmstadt: Wiss. Buchges. 1975a.
Kant 1977
Kant, Immanuel *Die Metaphysik der Sitten: Metaphysische Anfangsgründe der Tugendlehre* Frankfurt/M.: Suhrkamp 1977.
Kimura 1972
Kimura, Bin *Hito to hito to no aida* Tokyo, 1972 (German transl. E. Weinmayr *Zwischen Mensch und Mensch. Strukturen japanischer Subjektivität* Darmstadt: Wiss. Buchges. 1995).
Kitiyadisai 2005
Kitiyadisai, Krisana 'Privacy rights and protection: foreign values in modern Thai context' in *Ethics and Information Technology* Vol. 7 2005 pp. 17-26.
Kleve & de Mulder 2008
Kleve, Pieter & Richard de Mulder 'Privacy protection and the right to information. In search of a new balance' in *Computer Law & Security Report* 24 (3) 2008 pp. 223—32.
Kranenburg 2008
Kranenburg, Rob van *The Internet of Things: A critique of ambient technology and the all-seeing network of RFID* Institute of Network Cultures, Amsterdam 2008. URL: http://www.networkcultures.org/networknotebooks accessed October 2011
Kusch 1962/1975
Kusch, Rodolfo *América profunda.* Buenos Aires: Hachette 1962, 2nd ed. 1975.
Kusch 1976/2010
Kusch, Rodolfo *Indigenous and Popular Thinking in América* Durham and London, Duke U.P: 2010 (orig. *Pensamiento indígena y pensamiento popular en América* 1976).
Laimer & Nagel 2012
Laimer, Simon & Daniel Nagel 'Rügeversäumnis und Beweislastverteilung im UN-Kaufrecht' *IHR* 2012 pp. 42-44.
Leibniz 1663/2003
Leibniz, Gottfried Wilhelm 'Das Leib-Seele-Pentagon und die moralische Sphäre des Verstandes' (1663) in *Frühe Schriften zum Naturrecht* Hubertus Busche (ed.) Hamburg: Meiner 2003.

Locke 1690
Locke, John *An Essay Concerning Human Understanding* various editions, original edition 1690.
Locke 1965
Locke, John *Two Treatises of Government* Peter Laslett (ed.) New York: Mentor 1965.
Löwith 1928/1981
Löwith, Karl *Das Individuum in der Rolle des Mitmenschen* (1928) reprinted in *Sämtliche Schriften* Bd. 1 K. Stichweh (ed.) Stuttgart: Metzler 1981.
Lü 2005
Lü, Yao-huai 'Privacy and data privacy in contemporary China' in *Ethics and Information Technology* Vol. 7 2005 pp. 7-15.
Lü 2007
Lü, Yao-huai 'Globalization and Information Ethics' in Capurro et al. 2007 pp. 69-73.
Mannuzza 2008
Mannuzza, Francisco 'Las culturas indígenas venezolanas en el ciberespacio: refléxiones éticas' in *Primera conferencia regional, latinoamericana y del Caribe sobre infoética en el ciberespacio* Santo Domingo, Ed. Funglode 2008 pp. 225-234. URL: http://www.redciberetica.org/documentos?func=startdown&id=%201
Marx 1974
Marx, Karl *Grundrisse der Kritik der Politischen Ökonomie* Ost-Berlin: Dietz 1974.
Marx 1962
Marx, Karl *Das Kapital* in *Marx Engels Werke* Bde. 23, 24, 25 Ost-Berlin: Dietz 1962 Abbreviated MEW.
McDougall & Hansson 2002
McDougall, Bonnie S. & Anders Hansson *Chinese Concepts of Privacy* Leiden: Brill 2002.
Michael & Michael 2010
Michael, G.M. & Katina Michael 'Toward a State of Überveillance?' *Technology & Society* Vol. 29 No. 2 2010 pp. 9-16.
MISTICA 2002
MISTICA Virtual Community *Working the Internet with a social vision* 2002. URL: http://www.funredes.org/mistica/english/cyberlibrary/thematic/eng_doc_olist2.html
Mizutani et al. 2004
Mizutani, Masashiko, James Dorsey & James A. Moor 'The Internet and Japanese conception of privacy' in *Ethics and Information Technology* Vol. 6 2004 pp. 121-128.

Moor 1997
Moor, James H. 'Towards a theory of privacy in the information age' in *Computers and Society* 27(3) 1997 pp. 27-32.
Nagel 1988
Nagel, Thomas 'Concealment and Exposure' *Philosophy and Public Affairs* 1988 No. 27. URL: http://www.nyu.edu/gsas/dept/philo/faculty/nagel/papers/exposure.html
Nagel 2011
Nagel, Daniel 'Beware of the Virtual Doll: ISPs and the Protection of Personal Data of Minors' *Philosophy & Technology* 2011 pp. 411-418 (DOI) 10.1007/s13347-011-0034-7.
Nagel & Weimann 2011
Nagel, Daniel & Thomas Weimann 'IPv 6 und Datenschutz: Personalisiertes Surfen mit Gefahren für die Privatsphäre' LTO Mar. 2011.
Nagel & Weimann 2011
Nagel, Daniel & Thomas Weimann 'EuGH zu IP-Adressen: Harte Zeiten für Datensammler' LTO Dec. 2011.
Nagenborg 2005
Nagenborg, Michael *Das Private unter den Rahmenbedingungen der IuK-Technologie. Ein Beitrag zur Informationsethik* Wiesbaden: VS Verlag 2005.
Nakada 2007
Nakada, Makoto 'The Internet within Seken as an old and indigenous world of meanings in Japan' in Capurro et al. 2007 pp. 177-203.
Nakada & Tamura 2005
Nakada, Makoto & Takanori Tamura 'Japanese conceptions of privacy: An intercultural perspective' in *Ethics and Information Technology* Vol. 7 2005 pp. 27-36.
Nissenbaum 1998
Nissenbaum, Helen 'Protecting Privacy in an Information Age: The Problem of Privacy in Public' *Law and Philosophy* No. 17 1998 pp. 559-596. URL: http://www.nyu.edu/projects/nissenbaum/papers/privacy.pdf accessed November 2011.
Nissenbaum 2004
Nissenbaum, Helen 'Privacy as contextual integrity' in *Washington Law Review* 79(1) 2004 pp. 119-157.
Nissenbaum 2010
Nissenbaum, Helen *Privacy in Context: Technology, Policy, and the Integrity of Social Life* Stanford U. P. 2010.

Novais & Schwarcz 1997

Novais, Fernando A. & Lilia Moritz Schwarcz *Historia da vida privada no Brasil* São Paulo: Companhia Das Letras 1997ff.

Olinger et al. 2005

Olinger, H.N., Johannes Britz & M.S. Olivier 'Western privacy and ubuntu: influences in the forthcoming data privacy bill' in Philip Brey, Frances Grodzinsky, Lucas Introna (eds) *Ethics and New Information Technology* Enschede, The Netherlands, CEPE 2005 pp. 291-306.

Orito et al. 2011

Orito, Yohko, Eunjin Kim, Yasunori Fukuta and Kiyoshi Murata 'Online Privacy and Culture: A Comparative Study between Japan and Korea' in *ETHICOMP* Sheffield Hallan University 2011. URL: http://www.ccsr.cse.dmu.ac.uk/conferences/ethicomp/ethicomp2011/abstracts/ethicomp2011_33.php

Penrose R. 1999

Penrose, Roger *The Emperor's New Mind: Concerning Computers, Minds and The Laws of Physics* 2nd ed. Oxford U.P.1999.

Pellegrini &Blumauer 2006

Pellegrini, Tassilo & Andreas Blumauer (eds.) *Semantic Web. Wege zur vernetzten Gesellschaft* Springer: Berlin 2006 .

Pfeiffer 2008

Pfeiffer, María Luisa 'Derecho a la privacidad. Protección de los datos sensibles' in *Revista Colombiana de Bioética* Vol. 3 No. 1 2008, pp. 11-36. URL: http://redalyc.uaemex.mx/src/inicio/ForazarDescargaArchivo.jsp?cvRev=1892&cvArt=189217248002&nombre=Derecho%20a%20la%20privacidad.%20Protecci%F3n%20de%20los%20datos%20sensibles

Pimienta 2007

Pimienta, Daniel 'At the Boundaries of Ethics and Cultures: Virtual Communities as an Open Ended Process Carrying the Will for Social Change (the MISTICA experience)' in Capurro et al. 2007 pp. 205-228.

Ramasota 2007

Ramasota, Pirongrong 'Information Privacy in a Surveillance State: A Perspective from Tahiland' in Hongladarom & Ess 2007 pp. 124-137.

Ramose 2002

Ramose, Mogobe B. 'Globalization and *ubuntu*' in Peter H. Coetzee & Abraham P. J. Roux (eds.) *Philosophy from Africa. A text with readings* Oxford U.P. 2nd ed. 2002 pp. 626-650.

Rawls 1971

Rawls, John *A Theory of Justice* The Belknap Press of Harvard U. P., first edition 1971.

Regan 1995
Regan, P.M. *Legislating Privacy: Technology, Social Values, and Public Policy* Chapel Hill NC: North Carolina U.P. 1995.
Ricardo 1821/1996
Ricardo, David *Principles of Political Economy and Taxation* (1821) New York: Prometheus Books 1996.
Rössler 2005
Rössler, Beate *The Value of Privacy* transl. R.D.V. Glasgow/Cambridge: Polity Press 2005.
Roth 2003
Roth, Gerhard *Aus Sicht des Gehirns* Frankfurt/M.: Suhrkamp 2003.
Sagredo & Gazmuri 2005
Sagredo, Rafael & Cristián Gazmuri (eds.) *Historia de la vida privada en Chile* Santiago: Taurus-Aguilar Chilena Ediciones 2005.
Scheule et al. 2004
Scheule, Rupert M., Rafael Capurro & Thomas Hausmanninger (eds.) *Vernetzt gespalten. Der Digital Divide in ethischer Perspektive* ICIE Schriftenreihe Bd. 3 Munich: Fink 2004.
Schomberg 2011
Schomberg, René von (ed.) *Towards Responsible Research and Innovation in the Information and Communication Technologies and Security Technologies Fields* A Report from the European Commission Services, Luxembourg Publications Office of the European Union 2011.
Sen & Kliksberg 2005
Sen, Amartya Kumar & Bernardo Kliksberg (eds.) *La agenda ética pendiente en América Latina* Buenos Aires, Fondo de cultura económica 2005.
Seneca 1974
Seneca *Ad Lucilium Epistulae Morales* Darmstadt: Wissenschaftliche Buchgesellschaft 1974.
Sevignani 2012
Sevignani, Sebastian 'The Problem of Privacy in Capitalism and the Alternative Social Networking Site Diaspora' in Fuchs & Mosco 2012 pp. 600-617.
Shannon 1948
Shannon, Claude E. 'A Mathematical Theory of Communication' in *The Bell System Technical Journal* Vol. 27, July, October, 1948 pp. 379—423, 623—656.
Shannon & Weaver 1949/1998
Shannon, Claude E. and Warren Weaver *The Mathematical Theory of Communication* Illinois U.P. 1949, 1998.

Singer 2004
Singer, W. 'Selbsterfahrung und neurobiologische Fremdbeschreibung' *Deutsche Zeitschrift für Philosophie* 2004, 4 pp. 175-190.
Smith 1759/2000
Smith, Adam *The Theory of Moral Sentiments* (1759) New York: Prometheus Books 2000.
Smith 1776/2000
Smith, Adam *The Wealth of Nations* (1776) edited with notes, marginal summary and enlarged index by Edwin Cannan, New York: The Modern Library 2000.
Swanson 1992
Swanson, Judith A. *The Public and the Private in Aristotle's Political Philosophy* Ithaca/London: Cornell U.P. 1992.
Tavani 2008
Tavani, Herman T. 'Informational Privacy: Concepts, Theories, and Controversies' in Kenneth E. Himma & Herman T. Tavani (eds.) *The Handbook of Information and Computer Ethics* Hoboken NJ: Wiley 2008 pp. 131-164.
Theunissen 1977
Theunissen, Michael *Der Andere: Studien zur Sozialontologie der Gegenwart* 2nd ed. Berlin/New York: W. de Gruyter 1977.
Turing 1936
Turing, Alan M. 'On Computable Numbers, with an Application to the Entscheidungsproblem' in *Proc. Lond. Math. Soc.* (2) 42 1936 pp. 230-265.
Van den Hoven 2001
Van den Hoven, Jeroen 'Privacy and the Varieties of Informtional Wrongdoing' in Richard A. Spinello and Herman T. Tavani (eds.) *Readings in CyberEthics* Jones and Bartlett, Sudbury MA 2001 pp. 230-242.
Von Barloewen 1992
Von Barloewen, Constantin *Kulturgeschichte und Modernität Lateinamerikas* Munich: Matthes & Seitz 1992.
Vedder 2004
Vedder, A.H. 'KDD, privacy, individuality, and fairness' in Spinello R.A. & Tavani H.T. (eds.) *Readings in CyberEthics* 2nd ed. Jones and Bartlett, Sudbury MA 2004 pp. 462-470.
Walzer 1983
Walzer, Michael *Spheres of Justice: A Defense of Pluralism and Equality* New York: Basic Books 1983.
Westin 1967/1970
Westin, Alan F. *Privacy and Freedom* New York: Atheneum,1967, London: The Bodley Head 1970.

Weyl 1918

Weyl, Hermann *Das Kontinuum* Leipzig: Veit & Co. 1918.

Wiener 1948/1961

Wiener, Norbert *Cybernetics, or Control and Communication in the Animal and the Machine* MIT Press 1948, 1961.

Winograd & Flores 1986

Winograd, Terry & Fernando Flores *Understanding Computers and Cognition. A new foundation for design* Norwood NJ: Ablex 1986.

Wohlfart 2002

Wohlfart, Günter 'Alte Geschichten zum *wuwei*' in Rolf Elberfeld & Günter Wohlfahrt (eds.) *Komparative Ethik. Das gute Leben zwischen den Kulturen* Cologne: Edition Chora 2002 pp. 97-106.

Woolf 1928/2007

Woolf, Virginia *Orlando: A Biography* 1928 *Selected Works* London: Wordsworth Editions 2007.

Woolf 1931/2007

Woolf, Virginia *The Waves* 1931 *Selected Works* London: Wordsworth Editions 2007.

Woolf 1938/2007

Woolf, Virginia *Three Guineas* 1938 *Selected Works* London: Wordsworth Editions 2007.

Zabala 2012

Zabala, Santiago 'I'm wired, therefore I exist. But has your existence started to belong to others?' *New Statesman* 29 July 2012, URL: http://www.newstatesman.com/sci-tech/sci-tech/2012/07/im-wired-therefore-i-exist

8 Name index

M

N

O

P

R

S

T

V

W

Bei Fragen zur Produktsicherheit wenden Sie sich bitte an:
If you have any questions regarding product safety,
please contact:

Walter de Gruyter GmbH
Genthiner Straße 13
10785 Berlin
productsafety@degruyterbrill.com

Bei Fragen zur Produktsicherheit wenden Sie sich bitte an:
If you have any questions regarding product safety,
please contact:

Walter de Gruyter GmbH
Genthiner Straße 13
10785 Berlin
productsafety@degruyterbrill.com